DELTA EPIPHANY

Robert Kennedy in Cleveland, Mississippi. April 11, 1967. Credit: Dan Guravich.

DELTA
EPIPHANY

Robert F. Kennedy in Mississippi

Ellen B. Meacham

University Press of Mississippi / Jackson

www.upress.state.ms.us

The University Press of Mississippi is a member
of the Association of American University Presses.

First printing 2018

∞

Library of Congress Cataloging-in-Publication Data

Names: Meacham, Ellen B., author.
Title: Delta epiphany : Robert F. Kennedy in Mississippi / Ellen B. Meacham.
Description: Jackson : University Press of Mississippi, [2018] | Includes bib-
liographical references and index. |
Identifiers: LCCN 2017049036 (print) | LCCN 2017051465 (ebook) | ISBN
9781496817464 (epub single) | ISBN 9781496817471 (epub institutional) |
ISBN 9781496817488 (pdf single) | ISBN 9781496817495 (pdf institutional) |
ISBN 9781496817457 | ISBN 9781496817457 (cloth : alk. paper)
Subjects: LCSH: Kennedy, Robert F., 1925–1968—Travel—Mississippi. |
Poverty—Mississippi—History—20th century. | African Americans—Mis-
sissippi—Economic conditions—20th century. | United States—Politics and
government—1963–1969.
Classification: LCC E840.8.K4 (ebook) | LCC E840.8.K4 M39 2018 (print) |
DDC 362.509762/0904—dc23
LC record available at https://lccn.loc.gov/2017049036

British Library Cataloging-in-Publication Data available

For Will

To understand the world, you have to understand a place like Mississippi.
—Attributed to William Faulkner

◆ ◆ ◆

Each time a man stands up for an ideal,
or acts to improve the lot of others,
or strikes out against injustice,
he sends forth a tiny ripple of hope,
and crossing each other
from a million different centers of energy and daring,
those ripples build a current which can sweep down
the mightiest walls of oppression and resistance.
—Robert F. Kennedy, Day of Affirmation Address, South Africa, June 6, 1966

CONTENTS

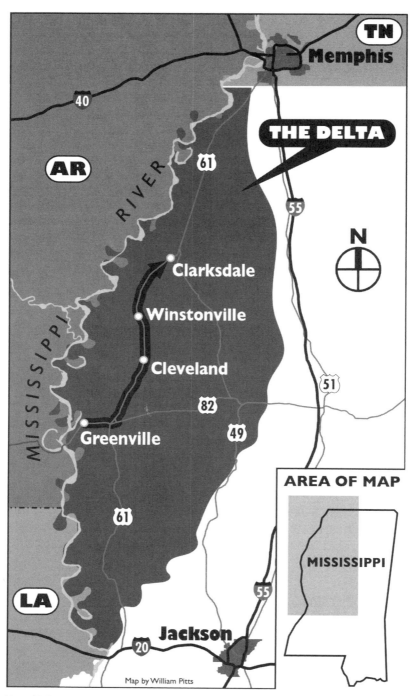

Map of Robert Kennedy's route through the Mississippi Delta.

PREFACE

Senator Robert F. Kennedy, a son of America's promise, power, and privilege, knelt in a crumbling shack in 1967 Mississippi, trying to coax a response from a child listless from hunger. After several minutes with little response, the senator, profoundly moved, walked out the back door to speak with reporters. He told them that America had to do better. What he was seeing, as he privately told an aide and a reporter, was worse than anything he had seen before in this country.

As he toured the Mississippi Delta, an impoverished cotton-producing region in the northwest corner of the state, that warm April day in 1967, Kennedy talked with mothers about how they fed their children. He looked in empty refrigerators and asked school children about their breakfast. The depths of deprivation he found in Mississippi stunned both Kennedy and, because of the press coverage that inevitably followed him, the nation.

During the forty-eight hours or so that Kennedy spent traveling through Mississippi, however, he did more than just encounter hungry children. He sparred with powerful members of the state's political elite, officials who resented money spent on early childhood education for poor black children. He toured job training programs and Head Start classrooms. He gave two impromptu speeches to wildly enthusiastic college students—one on a mostly white campus, and the other at an African American college. He dined with civil rights leaders, journalists, liberal business leaders, and educators at a lovely suburban home. In addition to all of that, he shared a drink by a hotel pool, talked New York politics and baseball with a local reporter, and even took a nap in the guest bedroom of a Jackson pediatrician.

Kennedy arrived in Mississippi at a pivotal point in American history. After the speeches, protests, legal showdowns, and violence of the 1950s and early 1960s, Congress had finally responded with sweeping changes. There were new civil rights laws, enhanced protections for voting rights, and a War on Poverty.

Furthermore, the war in Vietnam was going badly, and Americans were beginning to realize it, even if they were still deeply divided on what to do about it. Just a month before he arrived in Mississippi, Kennedy had stirred controversy by breaking with President Lyndon Johnson and offering a three-point plan to end the fighting in North Vietnam. Then, a week before Kennedy toured the Delta, Martin Luther King Jr. earned his own part of the controversy when he publicly criticized the war for killing the nation's young people and syphoning money away from programs that helped the poor. "A nation that continues year after year to spend more money on military defense than on programs of social uplift is approaching spiritual death," King told the congregation at Riverside Church in New York.

Kennedy's visit to Mississippi in 1967 provides a useful lens to examine the impact of these waves of change. His visit was a catalyst that drew out the extremes of Mississippi's culture at the time. In Jackson, members of the Ku Klux Klan met him at the airport, carrying signs castigating him for his position on Vietnam and distributing flyers predicting his death. They were only echoing the hatred of Kennedy that many white Mississippians harbored because of his role as attorney general in the integration of the University of Mississippi, and other conflicts over civil rights in the state.

However, both black and white civil rights advocates on the frontline in Mississippi were unimpressed with his record. Many of them had struggled through life-threatening violence with little or no help from the Kennedy administration's Department of Justice. They viewed Kennedy as a ruthless political dealmaker who put too much priority on placating powerful southern politicians in Congress.

In contrast, Kennedy and his brother were heroes to many of the ordinary African American residents of the state. In fact, just about forty-eight hours after Kennedy landed in the state to the belligerent shouts of the Ku Klux Klan, hundreds of African Americans in Clarksdale cheered him and, as one journalist who was traveling with him recalled, "reached up to him like they were trying to touch the robes of Jesus Christ" at his last stop in Mississippi.

Hints of other changes were in the Mississippi air as well. The day before Kennedy arrived, the daughter of Ronald Reagan, California's charismatic new conservative governor, was the guest of honor at a luncheon in Greenville designed to build support for Phyllis Schlafly as the conservative candidate for president of the National Federation of Republican Women. Clarke Reed, the Greenville businessman, who hosted Maureen Reagan Sills had little interest in Kennedy's visit. Instead, Reed had long been intent on building a strong, business-minded Republican Party in the state to offset the unmitigated power of the Democratic Party that had ruled the solid South for so long.

The day Kennedy left Jackson for the Mississippi Delta, Stokely Carmichael spoke in the same chapel at Tougaloo College where Kennedy had talked with students the evening before. Carmichael was a leading voice for a new breed of civil rights activist focused on black power. His passionate, uncompromising rhetoric was thrilling African American students and rattling the establishment across the South in the spring of 1967. He arrived in Jackson just days after a riot that broke out in Nashville following his speech at Vanderbilt University, and he left Jackson with a state lawmaker calling for charges of treason against him.

Perhaps the most powerful forces rolling through the Mississippi Delta as Kennedy arrived, however, were economic. From 1960 through 1967, changes in federal agricultural policies and new farming practices, like mechanization and the new herbicide chemicals on the market, had left tens of thousands of farm workers without jobs and homes.

Sharecroppers and plantation workers in the Delta had always been poor, but in 1967 they were especially desperate because well-meaning War on Poverty programs had worsened their plight instead of improving it. While at the public hearing in Jackson, Kennedy and the other senators had heard the impassioned pleas for help from advocates such as Marian Wright Edelman and a litany of statistical woes such as infant mortality and persistent childhood anemia, but nothing prepared Kennedy for the emotional impact of meeting and holding those babies.

On his return to Washington, Kennedy immediately began seeking ways to help the children he had met in Mississippi. However, institutional obstacles and powerful men who were indifferent to the suffering of poor, black children made getting aid to them much harder than he expected. Kennedy, who had yet to decide to run for president, spent only a few hours in the Delta, but he could not shake the memories of the children he had seen in Mississippi. He talked about it, even when it wasn't politic or popular, for the rest of his life.

Today, just as in 1967, the juxtaposition of Kennedy with the destitution in Mississippi makes for a compelling story. It is not, however, the whole story. Kennedy's visit to the Delta is often recounted in history books and biographies of Kennedy as a pivotal moment in his growth as a leader. For too long, however, the poor people—the hungry men, women, and children he encountered—have been faceless, and often nameless, little more than stock characters in a poverty backdrop for Kennedy, the main hero in a morality play.

Kennedy, however, certainly never represented himself as such. Today we are used to celebrities who travel to blighted places and use their fame to draw attention to the suffering of the people they encounter. Kennedy's trip was no "poverty tour," as we know it in contemporary terms. Instead, it was more akin to a fact-finding mission. He and the other senators with him wanted to know just how well War on Poverty programs were working. In fact, Daniel Schorr, the CBS newsman who covered Kennedy's Mississippi trip, likened the senator to an "inspector general," in his report that evening, a far cry from a celebrity using his fame for attention to an issue.

After he left the state, Mississippi remained on Kennedy's mind. He painted a grim picture of what he had seen for his children and urged them to action. Soon after, he told the wife of an aide in New York, "You don't know what I saw! I have done nothing with my life! Everything I have done was a waste! Everything I have done was worthless!" Kennedy maintained a fierce focus on the people he met in Mississippi, propelled by the urgency of their needs. The depth of those needs and the difficulties he met as he sought aid ultimately helped tilt him toward a 1968 run for president. Kennedy did indeed make a valiant effort to get help to the hungry families in the Delta, and it is important to examine his reaction and efforts. However, the experiences of these children and their parents are just as valid as his are, and, I would argue, just as heroic.

To this end, this work provides a wider focus on Kennedy's trip, going beyond its impact on him, which was significant, to include the stories and photographs of four children and their families who met Kennedy in 1967, following them through the decades after his visit. By sharing their stories along with his, I hope to bring the people he met into the light of history and bear witness to both their suffering and their perseverance.

In 1967 Kennedy pushed into places others would not go to see poverty for himself. What he found motivated him to work for change in ways that still reverberate today both in current food-aid policy and in the lives of those he encountered. This book tells the story of his visit, but it also offers much more, for when Robert Kennedy traveled deep into the Mississippi Delta, he took an essential step toward his and the nation's destiny.

PROLOGUE

Robert Kennedy stood waiting for the cheers to subside. It wasn't the first time the jubilant crowd had interrupted him. Despite the late hour—it was after midnight on June 5, 1968—and the heat of the crowded ballroom at the Ambassador Hotel in Los Angeles, his supporters had erupted in applause and shouts of approval as he spoke; they were in a celebratory mood.

The returns from the California primary were in, and Robert Kennedy (an unlikely candidate just months before) had, after a hard-fought campaign, won his fourth primary. After California, the campaign would shift to the state he represented in the Senate, New York, with its rich load of delegates. But there was still a long fight ahead before the August Democratic Convention in Chicago would determine the nomination. On that June night in Los Angeles, Kennedy, though weary, had been buoyed by the energy of the crowd.

He carefully thanked each element of the loose coalition that brought him the victory that night: young people, Latinos, working-class union members, and African Americans. But then his tone grew more serious as he transitioned to his agenda. "The country wants to move in a different direction. We want to deal with our own problems within our country, and we want peace in Vietnam," he said.

Then, as he stood waiting, the cheers died down. He and the country, Kennedy said, were ready to concentrate on solutions to the nation's problems, including "what we are going to do in the rural areas of this country," and, punctuating his words with a pointed finger tapping the podium, "what we are going to do for those who still suffer in the United States from hunger."

Kennedy placed a subtle emphasis on the word "suffer," and that was no accident, for he had seen the suffering firsthand. In fact, it was his stark

Robert Kennedy campaigns in California. Credit: Courtesy of JFK Presidential Library and Museum.

encounter with precisely this kind of suffering one spring afternoon in Mississippi that helped bring him to the primary and the podium in the Ambassador Hotel.

Fewer than five minutes later, an assassin's bullets tore into Kennedy, leaving him bleeding and paralyzed on the floor as a chaotic scene raged around him. As his wife, Ethel, knelt beside him, touching his face and chest, Kennedy whispered, "Is everybody else all right?" He died nearly twenty-six hours after those shots, and with him the hopes of voters and activists alike who wanted to see him in the White House.

The rising death toll and crushing cost of the war in Vietnam unquestionably dominated the international agenda of the 1968 campaign and weighed heavily in Kennedy's decision to run. However, presidential campaigns are typically not won with international issues alone but with concerns much closer to home. While ending the war in Vietnam was a crucial element of his decision to run, a key domestic concern that gave impetus to his ambitions began to crystallize in a dark, weather-beaten shack in rural Mississippi as he knelt to coax a reaction out of a listless, malnourished baby.

DELTA EPIPHANY

Robert Kennedy watches as former President John F. Kennedy's body is moved to its permanent memorial just hours before a hearing on poverty programs in March of 1967. Credit: Cecil Stoughton. John F. Kennedy Presidential Library and Museum, Boston.

Chapter 1

Now This Problem Has to Be Faced

A member of a military honor guard held an umbrella to shield Jacqueline Kennedy from the cold, driving rain at Arlington National Cemetery. On March 15, 1967, Robert Kennedy watched quietly as his sister-in-law, trim and elegant in a somber-hued dress, knelt and laid a small bouquet of lilies-of-the-valley on the black marble slab marking the grave of her husband and his brother. The eternal flame flickered and hissed in the cold spring rain, but it nevertheless continued to burn. Robert Kennedy stood silently at his brother's graveside, head bowed, stoically sharing another umbrella with President Lyndon B. Johnson. John F. Kennedy, the dashing, sometimes reckless, intellectual older brother Robert had admired as a child and, later, had served and protected for much of his adult life, had been dead for more than three years.

At the graveside, family friend Cardinal Richard Cushing led a simple private service just after dawn that consecrated President Kennedy's final resting place on the sloping Virginia hillside that overlooked the nation's capital. However, the night before that ceremony, Robert Kennedy and his brother Ted Kennedy had stood in the gathering shadows, watching as workers moved the remains of the slain president (as well as the bodies of his two children who had preceded him in death) to the just-completed permanent gravesite and the eternal flame memorial. Huge lights illuminated the tableau as if it were on stage in a dark theater. A force of 250 soldiers ringed the site, shutting out reporters. Much later, just an hour before midnight, the brothers returned again, staying for a few private moments.

"Be at peace, dear Jack," Cushing intoned at the service the next morning, "with your tiny infants by your side, until we meet again above this hill and beyond the stars."

News reports at the time noted that the two men's aides made a point of saying that Robert Kennedy and Lyndon Johnson had greeted each other and that their subsequent exchanges were not "marked by 'tension.'"

However, their relationship was indeed a tense one, even deeply hostile at times. Robert Kennedy had recently broken publicly with Johnson over the war in Vietnam, proposing his own three-point plan to end the hostilities. Johnson and Kennedy's mutual animosity would only deepen in the coming year. That morning in March, Robert Kennedy left the shelter of their shared umbrella for a congressional hearing, which highlighted some serious deficiencies in one of Johnson's signature domestic achievements, the War on Poverty. What he heard also helped to set Kennedy on an ill-fated course toward the office Johnson so jealously held. What neither man could know, of course, was that in little more than a year, Robert Kennedy would himself be laid to rest next to his brother on that hillside.

At 9:30 on the morning of March 15, Senator Joseph Clark of Pennsylvania called to order the second day of hearings by the Senate Subcommittee on Employment, Manpower, and Poverty, and both Kennedy brothers, Robert representing New York, and Edward, the senator from Massachusetts, had shaken off the chill of their brother's gravesite and were in their seats on the panel in the Senate Caucus Room, with its ornate black-veined marble walls. These hearings were the first round in a planned series examining the success of the War on Poverty two-and a-half years after its passage.

In 1964, Congress had passed this collection of programs and funding streams that came to be known unofficially as the War on Poverty, a title drawn from President Johnson's State of the Union address earlier that year. These ambitious initiatives took aim at the structural origins of poverty with programs that put economic development money and other types of aid into poor communities. In addition to the War on Poverty, Johnson's broader concept of the Great Society included educational opportunities, job training, housing assistance, and medical care for the elderly. The War on Poverty legislation, or the Economic Opportunity Act, set up early education programs such as Head Start and funded Community Health Centers, legal services, and more. In 1964, Johnson also signed legislation that made the food stamp program, which had only been operating in pilot programs, permanent and available nationwide. However, the 1964 legislation initially only covered 40 counties. By 1967, it had expanded to cover 2 million people, but was still not yet available in all parts of the nation.

For Johnson, the legislation, which eventually included the Economic Opportunity Act of 1964 (which was up for renewal in 1967), the Food Stamp Act of 1964, and the Social Security Act of 1965, marked a turning point to distinguish himself from his charismatic predecessor. It also gave him the chance to further the legacy of his own political hero, Franklin D. Roosevelt. Other presidents had asked for and implemented programs to address the problems of the nation's poorest residents, but it was Johnson alone who took the bold step of calling for a "War on Poverty."

Johnson's interest in poverty legislation had grown out of experiences both personal and political. His family was not wealthy like the Kennedys, and sometimes money was even scarce in the family's household. However, his father was a farmer and businessman who served in the state legislature, and the Johnsons came from respectable stock. In fact, Lyndon Johnson, who had a complicated and sometimes competitive relationship with the Kennedys, resented the often-unflattering comparisons between their urbanity and his coarseness. "Listen, goddammit," he once groused, "my ancestors were teachers and lawyers and college presidents and governors when the Kennedys in this country were still tending bar." Johnson could not escape his earliest impressions, however. He grew up in the Hill Country of Texas, an isolated, hardscrabble area that offered few modern amenities well into the twentieth century. As Johnson grew older, he accompanied his father on his political rounds, absorbing the hopes and struggles of the people of rural Texas, a place where nature could be harsh and those who tried to make a living from it often found the environment unpredictable and unforgiving.

After high school, Johnson set out for California, where he worked for a road construction crew and did other odd jobs. Once he returned to Texas, Johnson worked to help pay for his college at Southwest Texas State Teacher's College, pushing a janitor's broom and doing clerical work. However, the future president's first teaching job taught him the most searing lesson about the pain and grinding nature of extreme poverty. Like Robert Kennedy would soon discover on his trip to the Mississippi Delta, Johnson would find it nearly impossible to shake the memories of those children and the deprivations they faced.

Johnson had taken a position in a small school in the south Texas town of Cotulla in 1928. Decades later, he still remembered seeing his students go through the garbage, shaking coffee grinds off grapefruit rinds so they could suck the last drops of juice. "Thirty-eight years have passed but I still see the faces of the children who sat in my class. I still hear their eager voices speaking Spanish as I came in. I still see their excited eyes speaking friendship.

Right here I had my first lessons in poverty. I had my first lessons in the high price we pay for poverty and prejudice" he said in a 1966 speech in Cotulla.

Furthermore, Johnson had come of age politically during the Great Depression, where, as he saw it, government intervention lifted millions out of financial distress. He idolized Roosevelt and supported his policies, but he was also an instinctive politician who could not ignore the impact Roosevelt's approach had on the nation's only three-term president's electoral success. Johnson often told his aides, "If you do good, you will do well."

Johnson was committed intellectually to liberal economic theories as well. He once told one of his presidential speechwriters that he admired a book by a British economist called *The Rich Nations and the Poor Nations*. This book, he told her as he held up a worn copy, encapsulated his ideas about the role and purpose of government. "It's right here in one sentence-the mission of our times is to eradicate the three enemies of mankind-poverty, disease and ignorance," he said.

Within days of John F. Kennedy's death, aides briefed the new president on Kennedy's ongoing projects, including his final instructions to Walter Heller, who had been leading the exploration of possible antipoverty efforts. JFK's last directions to Heller were that they should move forward, "full-tilt" on the concept. Johnson clearly had a legitimate interest in addressing poverty, but he realized quickly that there were other benefits as well.

Seizing upon the poverty initiatives under discussion in the Kennedy administration gave Johnson a chance to, as the cliché says, have his cake and eat it too. Given the intensity of the civil rights movement in 1963, the pressures within the liberal wing of the Democratic Party, Johnson's desire to be seen as a president who transcended his southern background, and the sympathy for the slain president, Johnson felt bound to make JFK's civil rights proposals his top legislative priority. However, unlike civil rights, the public didn't know that JFK had been weighing new antipoverty programs going into the 1964 election, but the holdovers from the Kennedy administration that he desperately needed to impress did know what was in the works. Historian Carl Brauer argues that if Johnson embraced JFK's antipoverty impulses, he could co-opt the loyalty of his predecessor's aides but still get the public recognition that he so desperately craved for himself.

The day after JFK's death, Johnson told Walter Heller, who had prepared antipoverty recommendations for Kennedy, to spread the word to liberal supporters that he was no conservative looking to turn back the clock. "I'm no budget slasher," he said. "I understand that expenditures have to keep on rising to keep pace with the population and help the economy." However, as he talked, Johnson fell prey once again to his insecurities and could not resist a comparative dig at the late president, a personality trait that did not endear him to Kennedy's grieving aides and cabinet members, especially Robert Kennedy. "If you looked at my record," Johnson concluded, "you would know that I'm a Roosevelt New Dealer. As a matter of fact, to tell the truth, John F. Kennedy was a little too conservative to suit my taste."

Johnson gave an impassioned plea in his January 1964 State of the Union address. "This budget, and this year's legislative program, are designed to help each and every American citizen fulfill his basic hopes—his hopes for a fair chance to make good; his hopes for fair play from the law; his hopes for a full-time job on full-time pay; his hopes for a decent home for his family in a decent community; his hopes for a good school for his children with good teachers; and his hopes for security when faced with sickness or unemployment or old age."He knew he still needed to tread carefully around the slain president's memory, so he asked Kennedy's brother-in-law, Sargent Shriver (who was married to Eunice Kennedy and the head of JFK's Peace Corps), to explore the issue and help design a legislative package to attack poverty.

Johnson then gave a speech to the nation in March urging the passage of the proposed Economic Opportunity Act. Once the Economic Opportunity Act passed Congress in July of 1964, Shriver took over as head of the newly created Office of Economic Opportunity. Shriver had remained in Johnson's cabinet after the assassination, which rankled some of the Kennedys. However, he worked closely and energetically with Johnson and later became known as the "architect of the War on Poverty."

Johnson may have seen a chance to craft his own legacy with the War on Poverty, but Robert Kennedy was still raw from grief and as fiercely protective of his brother's legacy in death as he was of Jack in life. To him, poverty, like civil rights, more rightly belonged as part of his slain brother's legacy. Furthermore, though the public (and perhaps even Johnson) were unaware of their origins, many of Johnson's ideas about attacking the roots of poverty had come out of Robert Kennedy's own work as attorney general. Kennedy knew well that poverty relief had been part of his brother's plans, especially as JFK had begun to plot his 1964 reelection campaign. The poverty he had encountered in the Appalachians in West Virginia during the Democratic primary had prompted JFK to authorize a pilot food stamps program on his first day in office. And in the dark months following JFK's assassination in Dallas, Jacqueline Kennedy had given her brother-in-law the president's notes from his last cabinet meeting, in which he had written and circled "poverty" six times. Those notes now hung framed in Robert Kennedy's office.

Although JFK had just been turning his attention to poverty as he prepared to run for reelection, the intersection of poverty and justice had been on his brother's mind from his first days as attorney general. Early on, Robert Kennedy had proposed initiatives that examined access for poor defendants to legal aid. He then created a position to coordinate the Justice Department's efforts to counteract juvenile delinquency, a move that ultimately led to the creation of a cabinet-level commission on juvenile delinquency. Johnson eventually built much of his poverty legislation on proposals that were on the slain president's desk at the time of his assassination, and many of those proposals actually had their roots in the commission on juvenile delinquency.

Robert Kennedy's interest in the poor had grown during his tenure as attorney general, alongside his recognition of the nation's failure to secure civil rights for African Americans. Before he left the attorney general's position to campaign for New York's Senate seat in 1964, Kennedy was emerging from the pall of grief and shock that had almost shattered him after his brother's violent death. As he began to speak to audiences again, historian Edward Schmitt has pointed out, Kennedy's rhetoric shifted strikingly toward discussions of poverty. He urged a St. Patrick's Day audience of Irish descent to recognize that "walls of silent conspiracy blocked the progress of African Americans."

In testimony in the House of Representatives, Kennedy asserted that poverty was a national problem that urgently needed national solutions. A conservative Republican congressman from Nebraska took issue with Kennedy's position. Poverty didn't need a government solution, he said. Instead, poverty could only be solved through private assistance and individual initiative. Kennedy disagreed with the idea that the poor were only poor because of a lack of hard work. "Have you ever talked to the coal miners of West Virginia and told them what they needed was individual initiative?" he asked.

The conservative congressman went on to challenge Kennedy on the wisdom of seeking national solutions for local problems. Surely local communities knew best how to help their own neighbors, he argued. But Kennedy refused to let that idea pass unchallenged as well. The nation's problems with poverty were too big for many communities to solve on their own. The citizens of these poor communities were also US citizens. "This is fundamental," he said. "Those of us who are better off, who do not have that problem, have a responsibility to our fellow citizens who do."

During the spring and summer of 1964, Congress was considering three momentous pieces of legislation that were close to Kennedy's heart: the Civil Rights Act, the Economic Opportunity Act, and the Criminal Justice Act. Kennedy did what he could to support them, but at that point, he was still

reeling from his brother's death. He showed little evidence of a focused interest in poverty issues as the Economic Opportunity Act was under consideration, but parts of the bill were rooted in some of his enduring interests,
and his brother-in-law oversaw the national effort against poverty. Kennedy
cast about for a new direction, and, once he realized that Johnson would not
choose him as his running mate in the 1964 election, he settled on the Senate.

Kennedy had only been a senator a few months in 1965 when six days of
rioting, looting, and burning erupted in the Watts area of Los Angeles, illuminating deep racial divisions along with patterns of unemployment, discrimination, and accusations of police brutality. The riots, which began eleven
days after Lyndon Johnson had signed the Voting Rights Act, raised questions about similar issues in urban areas across the country. Historian Edward
Schmitt writes that both Kennedy and Johnson were deeply worried about the
riots' impact on the new War on Poverty programs. Johnson responded with
mixed messages: dishing out harsh criticism of lawbreakers along with $30
million on federal assistance to the area. In contrast, Kennedy responded in
ways more typical to his personality. His work as attorney general on juvenile
delinquency had taught him that the problems of poverty and race facing the
residents of America's cities were real, painful, and complex. During several
speaking engagements around that time, he urged audiences to understand
the reality of how many poor and minority residents of the nation's slums and
ghettos lived. He spoke sympathetically of their disappointment at the lack of
decent housing and schools, the limited opportunity for good jobs, and the
racism and frequent hostility they encountered.

Even though, or perhaps because, he had served as the nation's top law
enforcement officer, Kennedy had little patience for Johnson's reaction that
focused on rioters' respect for law and order. "There is no point in telling
Negroes to obey the law," he said. "To many Negroes the law is the enemy. In
Harlem, in Bedford-Stuyvesant, it has almost always been used against him,"
Kennedy said.

Kennedy and Johnson both realized that there was a connection between
inequality and the simmering cities. However, Kennedy differed from Johnson
in his approach to untangling such a complicated knot. New York's new senator was not convinced that government had all the answers for these problems
and was hesitant to embrace millions in unfocused aid. Instead, Kennedy, the
son of one of the nation's wealthiest businessmen, who had spent his entire
professional career in government service, believed that there was a role for
both the public and private sectors to play in alleviating urban poverty.

Troubled by the death and damage in Watts, Kennedy saw the potential
for more chaos in the cities, and as a new senator from the state with the

nation's largest, most diverse city, he felt duty-bound to address it if he could. That summer, he called his two aides, Peter Edelman and Adam Walinsky, out to his McLean, Virginia, home, Hickory Hill, to brainstorm solutions. By the fall of that year, they were drafting a series of speeches on the issue. Kennedy warmed to Walinsky's ideas that emphasized empowering communities and created public-private partnerships. He was particularly interested in programs that could move the poor into "full participation in the life of our communities," as he said in a speech a few months later.

Although welfare had been around since the 1930s, during the program's first three decades, until 1966, many states, cities, and towns seized upon a provision in law that required the money to only go to "suitable" homes. This meant that many fewer children actually received aid than were eligible. In one study done in 1960, only about 37 percent of children who should have received welfare support actually did. This interpretation made it especially easy to exclude children born outside of marriage and children of color. It also meant that case workers had tremendous power over their clients. They could and did investigate the families and cut off aid to anyone they deemed "unsuitable" for violations of a wide variety of regulations. In addition, many agricultural communities cut off aid during the harvest season to force poor mothers into the fields.

◆ ◆ ◆

In the months after the Watts riots, Kennedy gave three speeches that focused on conditions he saw ripe for improvement. In one, he proposed better racial and economic integration for cities and communities and pointed out the risks of concentrating those populations in public housing; in another, he proposed training and hiring poor people to rebuild and improve their own communities; and, in the third, he recommended that the nation create more jobs and educational programs targeted to help not just the poor, but also the working class.

However, Kennedy was interested in more than just ideas and speeches. He wanted an opportunity to demonstrate the validity of his ideas. He would be, of course, sensitive as well to the political benefit he might gain if he found a way to improve some of the worst parts of the largest city in the state he represented. After a tour of one of the most depressed areas of New York City, Bedford-Stuyvesant, Kennedy was troubled by the derelict buildings and idle residents. Local officials were worried about the potential for riots like in Watts. But Kennedy also could not shake off the angry accusation of a local activist. While he toured the area, the woman had challenged him: "You white politicians come out here and nothing changes." Kennedy biographer Evan Thomas recounts that her words gnawed at Kennedy as he contemplated the view from his well-appointed apartment in the UN Plaza. "I don't have to take that shit. I could be smoking a cigar in Palm Beach," he told an aide.

However, Kennedy did not let challenges, whether they be the complicated knot of inner-city poverty or the frank words of a frustrated inner-city resident, go by easily. Soon after, Kennedy directed his aides to find a way to put some of the ideas in his recent speeches into practice. A unique (at the time) approach to community development and revitalization emerged, and Kennedy worked closely on the details, even flying back to New York two or three times a week to bring the project alive, according to Edelman.

Working with New York's other senator, liberal Republican Jacob Javits, and New York City officials, Kennedy succeeded in enacting federal legislation which made it possible to designate the area of about four hundred thousand residents, most of whom were African American or Puerto Rican, as a Special Impact Program. The initial design of the program created a board of business leaders to partner with a board of residents to devise ways to improve the economic prospects of the area. It also aimed to draw in funding from charitable foundations. By March 1967, the project had suffered some infighting and disagreements over its direction and operation, but Kennedy could be confident that it had made real progress in attracting commitments from groups like the Ford Foundation and recruiting some high-profile business leaders to create jobs in the area.

Through his work on public-private initiatives in Bedford-Stuyvesant and what he had learned from his work as attorney general with the Commission on Juvenile Delinquency, Kennedy had gradually become convinced of two key concepts: the best solutions to poverty removed obstacles to opportunity rather than only transferring money, and the poor themselves should help design and administer the programs in their areas. He said as much at the dedication of the Bedford-Stuyvesant project's dedication ceremony. The initiative combined, Kennedy said, "the best of community action with the best of the private-enterprise system."

Attacking the root causes of poverty eventually became one of the organizing principles of the War on Poverty programs, and the second concept, community action, was at the heart of the War on Poverty, but it also became one of the most controversial aspects of the legislation. Kennedy believed that it was essential to allow poor people a voice in crafting and administering the programs designed to help them. One potential benefit that he saw was that it could minimize bureaucratic waste and shift control of federal money away from established and often unresponsive state leaders. This approach also empowered poor people, especially African Americans, who had for so long been shut out of the political process. However, this also meant that funds and other aid could bypass the entrenched local power brokers, and thus quickly the idea of community action triggered a backlash of complaints from both big city mayors and officials in rural states alike, including Senator John Stennis of Mississippi.

At the Senate subcommittee meeting on March 15, 1967, one of the witnesses in line to testify before Kennedy and the others that morning was no stranger to the resistance to efforts to help the state's poor of Mississippi. Marian Wright was a slender, twenty-seven-year-old African American lawyer with a Yale law degree and nearly three years of experience as an NAACP attorney in Mississippi. Wright knew firsthand about both the needs of the poor people that the new programs aimed to help and the attacks by state officials outraged at being bypassed by federal funds.

Seated beside his younger brother, Robert Kennedy—fidgeting, taking the occasional note, or asking a few questions—spent that morning listening to officials from Detroit and New Jersey talk about abstract ideas like administrative challenges, participation percentages, and funding opportunities.

As the witnesses droned on, Marian Wright waited her turn to speak. Dressed in a light, double-breasted wool suit, her hair smoothed back with a colorful headband, she looked impossibly young and deeply earnest. Wright's journey to testify in the ornately appointed Caucus Room of the US Senate had begun in a parsonage in Bennettsville, South Carolina, where she was born the youngest of a Baptist minister's five children. Unlike many of the poverty-stricken African Americans she represented in Mississippi, Wright's family was part of the tenuous black middle class in the cotton and mill town of about five thousand; her upbringing was rooted in faith, family, and community.

She later recalled the delicate balance her parents and other mentors had to achieve while raising their African American children in a racially segregated southern town. They had to help their children develop a sense of their own dignity and personal value, while at the same time teaching them the realities of the rigid, dehumanizing system, how to survive in it, and, hopefully, how to rise above it. They protected them as best they could, she wrote, from the "unfair assaults of Southern racial segregation and injustice by weaving a tight family and community fabric of love around us." Wright said, "All the external messages of the segregated South told me as a black child that I wasn't worth much." But her family's love and Christian faith provided an important counterbalance for that message: "One of the lessons of my childhood was that,

Marian Wright, a young attorney with the NAACP Legal Defense Fund first told a Senate subcommittee that people were hungry in Mississippi in March 1967.Credit: Associated Press/Henry Griffin.

'you're a child of God. You could look down on nobody, and nobody can look down on you.'"

The gap between this ideal and the reality of her childhood experiences was not lost on Wright. "I had lived with injustice all of my life, and I hated it. I was used to being excluded. I was used to being shunted aside. I was used to not being admitted to the library when I was a little girl, so I was always testing everything. There was never a time when I couldn't toddle or think that I didn't hate segregation."

Wright's parents emphasized education as another counterbalance to the rejections and prohibitions of the segregated society around them. They were attentive to and supportive of her schooling. In fact, as her father was dying, his last words to fourteen-year-old Marian were, "Don't let anything get in the way of your education." She took his words to heart, drawing strength from them for years to come.

From Bennettsville, Wright went on to Spelman College in Atlanta, which at the time was the premiere women's school for African Americans in the South. Wright was at first hesitant to attend Spelman, which had a reputation as "a tea-pouring, very strict school designed to turn black girls into refined ladies and teachers," but, despite her reservations, she thrived there. As a sophomore, she received a fellowship that allowed her to study at the Sorbonne in Paris for a year. Her travels in Europe deepened her self-confidence and expanded the scope of her ambition as she drew inspiration from the burgeoning civil rights movement back in America under Martin Luther King's leadership. Upon her return, she spoke to her fellow students in the Spelman chapel of her growing sense of moral responsibility: "I realize that I am not fighting just for myself, or my people in the South, when I fight for freedom and equality. I realize now that I fight for the moral and political health of America as a whole and for her position in the world at large."

Back in Atlanta, she soon put her newly found passion into action. She marched in the face of the Klan, participated in sit-ins, and helped organize the Student Nonviolent Coordinating Committee (SNCC). It was a heady time for Wright, who soon got to know leaders such as King and Lillian Smith, a white southerner who wrote about the corrupting influence of segregation on southern society. After hearing King speak for the first time, Wright wrote in her diary: "What people do with life—how much some do and others how little. Thank God for a glimpse of beauty, a taste of life's savor. I must go back for more and more. I want to live. To live well, high, humble, loving, completely."

By this time Wright knew she wanted to pursue a law degree, and, after her graduation from Spelman in 1960, she enrolled at Yale. But it was a spring break trip to Mississippi that shaped the direction of her life. While helping SNCC workers with a voter registration drive in Greenwood, she watched as police set police dogs on the young SNCC workers and the local citizens attempting to register and then arrested them, hustling them into an immediate trial without an attorney.

She tried twice to enter the courthouse but was shut out by police. "As I walked away through the milling, mostly white male crowd and past the police cruisers with police dogs, I knew I would get through law school, however dull, would come back to Mississippi, and would walk into that and other courthouses to provide counsel to those unjustly treated," she writes.

By the time she arrived to testify before Robert Kennedy and the committee in March 1967, she had been working as an attorney with the NAACP's Legal Defense Fund in Mississippi for almost three years. Wright was at the hearing at the request of Kennedy's senatorial counterpart from New York, Jacob Javits, a Republican who had invited her to the committee to highlight problems he saw with the poverty programs, problems Javits feared that the members of the subcommittee wouldn't hear about from the Johnson administration's witnesses.

Given a microphone and an audience of powerful men that morning, Marian Wright leaned in. She was there to talk about the Head Start program in Mississippi, but in a warm, rich voice tinged with traces of her native South Carolina, she spoke forthrightly about people. Decades later she wondered at her impromptu shift in emphasis. "I don't know what moved me to talk about hunger," she said. "I guess I stayed out on the field a lot, and was often visiting poor parents." What she told the committee was no calculated exaggeration, she said in later years. "People who had no income couldn't afford food stamps, and hunger, and even starvation, was increasing, and that's what came out of my mouth that day," she recalled.

During her testimony, Wright did not deal in bureaucratic concepts like poverty or programs but focused instead on suffering people who weren't just poor but actually hungry, people who were begging and worried about survival. The situation in the Delta, and elsewhere in Mississippi was untenable, and the current federal efforts were not enough, she said.

"After two civil rights bills and the third year of the poverty bill's operation, the situation of the Negro in Mississippi is that he's poorer than he was, he has less housing; he's as badly educated; he's almost in despair," she told the panel in her opening statement.

Wright's knowledge of the conditions in the state wasn't just academic. It was personal. Her work with the NAACP in one of the most violently recalcitrant states in the union meant she knew the names and stories of many of these poor families firsthand. She had been in their homes and their churches. She had held their hands in grief and spoken their truth to power, even when it put her life in danger.

Marian Wright's time on the frontlines of the battle for civil rights in Mississippi had not been easy. After almost three years there, she was long familiar with the stomach-clutching terror of listening for her car's engine to start rather than exploding. She knew the fear and outrage of having a white, married lawyer show up at her door one evening, implying a right to sexual favors from a young woman alone in a new town. She had learned to steel her nerve to stand with grieving parents as they viewed the bloody bodies of their young sons, beaten to death by police. She had heard bullets whizz past her head and strike the wall where she had been standing. She had persevered in the face of sheriffs who locked her out of public buildings, school boards deaf to the needs of black children, and fellow attorneys and judges who refused to shake her hand or acknowledge her as a colleague. As a member of the board of a pioneering Head Start program in the state, she also knew the intensity of attacks by the institutional resistance, including Mississippi's powerful elected leaders like Senator John Stennis, against community-led War on Poverty programs.

Wright operated out of an office in a drafty second-floor space above a pool hall at 538 1/2 Farish Street, in the heart of the African American business district in segregated Jackson, Mississippi. One reporter remembers climbing dusty stairs to find the young lawyer in a large room with few amenities.

She was one of only five black lawyers in the entire state of Mississippi and the only one dedicated full time to civil rights. In 1966, she told a Boston, Massachusetts, audience that she carried a caseload of about 130, which fell into two main categories: school-desegregation and defending civil rights advocates when charged in criminal cases relating to their civil rights work. Volunteer lawyers often visited and worked out of cubicles with space provided for that purpose in her office.

The Mississippi State Sovereignty Commission, the state-funded agency set up in 1956 to spy on anyone involved in civil rights, kept tabs on her movements and her work. The commission sent memos to officials warning about the pamphlets she authored and of her inquiries about school desegregation. The main reason for the state's spy agency's attention and concern? Wright was telling poor Mississippians what the law said about how to appeal if the state denied a welfare application.

With the support of the NAACP, she had come to Mississippi to help the state's people exercise their civil rights, but, as she writes later, she quickly realized that many local people were already risking their lives and making deep sacrifices to secure their rights and had been for decades. "Never have I felt the company of such a great cloud of witnesses for divine and human justice willing to risk life and limb and shelter so that their children could be free and educated."

These experiences lent an urgency to Wright's testimony that distinguished her from the witnesses—bureaucrats and local officials—who had testified ahead of her that day. With a confidence belying her years, she told Kennedy, Javits, and the rest of the panel that they must act quickly and that their focus should be on people, not just programs.

"Now, what are we going to do with these people? Frankly, I don't know," she said. "Here you have a number of people who have never had any skills, who are basically illiterate in a large part, who have little housing, absolutely no place to go, no jobs, and no hopes of getting any." She went on to say, "Now this problem has to be faced. The single largest problem facing all of us in Mississippi right now is how can people eat during the winter. . . . This is an urgent situation which much be looked into and met."

Welfare programs in Mississippi were woefully inadequate, and federal programs were not meeting people's needs, she told the panel. "For most people, the poverty program held out the largest hope, I think it has also held out the largest disappointment in many ways," she said. The community action piece of the War on Poverty legislation was not functioning as envisioned in Mississippi. Wright supported the idea of community action, but the money in many of the programs was going "through the very same power structures that created or helped create the poverty program in the first place."

Furthermore, racial harassment and violence still plagued the state. Senator Jacob Javits pressed Wright to discuss this further, asking if outside interference would be resented by local leaders.

"Mississippi is [a] mighty dangerous place, though it is one of the fifty states. Can it be done despite the resentment or, are we still at the point where a person's life is in danger if there is resentment?" he asked.

"Life is still in danger, Senator, but that is one of the risks that many people are willing to take," Wright responded.

Senator Joseph Clark jumped in, asking if she ever felt under threat: "What happens to a girl like you from Yale law school who goes down to Mississippi and tries to take on this?" Wright at first demurred, saying that what she had faced was nothing like the experiences of local people, but Clark pressed her.

"On the whole, Mississippi has not been a very pleasant place," she answered. "But I went to Mississippi knowing certain problems, and I got there, and this, this is a real, everyday thing in my life. You do it. You take certain risks, and that is that. There is violence, but your expectations, I guess are there, so that it does not shock you terribly much," she said.

The immense need for her services as an attorney in the state kept her going, she said. As one of but five black lawyers in the entire state of Mississippi and the only one dedicated full time to civil rights, Wright told the committee that despite the Voting Rights Act of 1965, which removed most official obstacles to political participation, African American voter registration lagged in many parts of the state.

Here, Chairman Senator Joseph Clark interrupted her, incredulous.

"There are only five Negro lawyers . . . ?" he asked.

"There are only five Negro lawyers in the State," Wright repeated.

Astonished, Clark said, "In the state?"

"In the entire state, and two of those never went to law school," she said. Mississippi was failing its people, she told them, so the federal government must meet the urgent basic needs of the people in the Mississippi Delta. Mississippi's policies, she went on, seemed calculated to drive thousands of poor blacks out of the state. Their migration could only exacerbate problems in the nation's urban areas still simmering after race riots in 1965 and 1966. She went on to argue that the simmering problems in northern slums were directly tied to the deficiencies of the southern states' policies. She said:

> Focusing on what we can do about the urban ghetto and there is nothing more than the failure of Mississippi, Alabama and other Southern states to do their jobs 15, 20, 30 years ago. . . . Most of these people do not have enough education to read the signs on the employment office even if they go there.
>
> I cannot think of a northern ghetto that has enough room for 20,000 people or 15,000 people, even 10,000 people. And these people are attached to Mississippi. And unfortunately, one sees evidence of a state policy which is intended to make things so bad that people will have to leave.

Wright's mention of the riots was a shrewd calculation. She could not be at all sure that these senators cared about what was happening in Mississippi, but it was a pretty sure bet that they cared about their own states. In fact, it was the riots in the Watts section of Los Angeles in the summer of 1965 that sparked Kennedy to seek solutions that ultimately grew into his Bedford-Stuyvesant project. Five of the nine members of the subcommittee, including the chair, represented states with large cities. Chairman Joseph Clark represented Pennsylvania; Senator George Murphy served for California; Robert Kennedy and Jacob Javits represented New York; Edward Kennedy was there for Massachusetts; and Gaylord Nelson was from Wisconsin. Furthermore, many large cities, such as Philadelphia, Pittsburg, New York, Los Angeles, and Milwaukee, were common destinations for African Americans seeking better opportunities over the oppression and destitution many of them faced in the South.

Wright went on. Mississippi's poor, especially in the Delta, were facing a crisis, one made worse by some of the policies designed to help them. The forces of mechanization and the increase in the farm worker's minimum wage had squeezed many families out of jobs and their homes. Many counties in the region had recently switched from the federal commodity system, which distributed free food, to food stamps, which families had to purchase.

Under the new regulations, a family of six had to buy twelve dollars' worth of food stamps. Those stamps would in turn allow the family to buy seventy-two dollars' worth of food. Without their jobs in the fields, however, even twelve dollars was hard to come by. Someone, Wright said pointedly to the senators, must do something about it.

As she concluded her testimony, Marian Wright focused her forthright gaze expectantly on the powerful men arrayed at the table before her. No one there could have known that one year and one day from that moment, Robert Kennedy would launch his campaign for the presidency in that very room. And Wright had no idea that his candidacy, although clearly driven by the urgency of the unfolding catastrophe in Vietnam and the sudden vulnerability of the incumbent Johnson, would also be a continuation of his efforts to do exactly what she was asking of him that morning—to help the nation's hungry children.

Marian Wright knew that she could show these senators how Mississippi's children were suffering, if only they would leave Washington. What she didn't know was that back in Kennedy's senatorial office was an industrious young aide who would soon win her heart and offer her a lifetime of love and support. Nor did she know that the upcoming trip to Mississippi would pave the way for her to spend the next four-and-a-half decades in the corridors of the capitol, advocating for the nation's children.

But on that March morning in 1967, it was Wright's forthright testimony that energized the committee and prompted them to settle on Mississippi for the site of their next hearing. Within days, Kennedy's journey to Mississippi and into the Delta—where children ached with hunger in the heart of one of the most fertile spots on earth—began to take shape.

Bobby Kennedy, first from left, was the seventh of nine children, and often in the shadow of his older siblings. Credit: Courtesy of JFK Presidential Library and Museum.

We Were to Try Harder
than Anyone Else

I t was almost time for dinner, and the Kennedy family was gathering, that is, all except for one. Four-year-old Bobby, the family's seventh child (the "runt" of the family, as his father had once called him), was still on his way. Overly anxious to meet expectations, he knew his father, Joseph P. Kennedy, had strict rules about punctuality. Bobby was in a hurry, but he didn't quite make it. With a crash, the freckle-faced boy ran into a glass door, breaking it and cutting his head in the process.

In contrast to the children Marian Wright had described to the Senate Subcommittee on Employment, Manpower, and Poverty in March 1967, there was always plenty to eat in Robert Kennedy's childhood home, even as the darkest days of the Great Depression settled over the nation. Instead, the boy the family called Bobby hungered instead for his parents' attention and approval.

Robert Francis Kennedy was born in 1925 in Brookline, Massachusetts, a suburb of Boston, and grew up in Riverdale, then Bronxville, New York, and, for a time, even in London, England, until he went to a series of boarding schools in the Northeast. He spent much of his childhood in the shadow of his six older brothers and sisters, and there was little indication in his early years that he would find himself in a US senator's seat, much less on a podium as crowds cheered him toward the presidency.

His father, a wealthy and ambitious businessman, had made his fortune in banking, on Wall Street, in real estate, in shipping, and in a wide range of other pursuits, including a shrewd recognition of the moneymaking potential of movies in the early days of Hollywood. But for the senior Kennedy, making money was mainly a means to an end, an activity he did not discuss with his children. His real passion was ensuring that his family was successful, both as individuals and as a united force in twentieth-century American public life and government.

Robert Kennedy's mother, Rose Kennedy, was the eldest daughter of a political family. Her father, John F. Fitzgerald, a man so charming he was known as "Honey Fitz," served six years in Congress, was mayor of Boston twice, and served in the Massachusetts state. Rose Kennedy maintained an active social life, spoke French effortlessly, and loved the arts, music, and travel.

During Bobby Kennedy's early life, Joe Kennedy was away from home frequently, but when he was there, he focused most of his attention on his two eldest sons, Joe Jr. and John (whom the family called Jack), and his second daughter, Kathleen. He aimed to shape them to be leaders, grilling them on current affairs and writing them long letters about public affairs. His eldest daughter, Rosemary, also drew time and attention, especially from Rose, because of her mental disabilities.

In the busy, peripatetic Kennedy household, the nine children of Rose and Joseph Kennedy competed fiercely in sports and games and, most intensely, for their parents' attention and approval. Bobby, who was small for his age, shy, and had little natural athletic ability, struggled to keep up, often taking reckless chances to impress. Once, heedless to the fact that he could not yet swim, he jumped headlong off a boat into Nantucket Sound, requiring Joe Jr., who was ten years his senior, to rescue him. "It showed either a lot of guts, or no sense at all, depending on how you looked at it," his brother Jack later observed.

Bobby Kennedy was not a strong student. Because of his father's work and later his official duties, such as Joseph Kennedy's appointment in 1937 as the US ambassador to Britain, the boy changed schools frequently. This often left him feeling awkward and left out. "What I remember most vividly about growing up was going to a lot of different schools, always having to make new friends, and that I was very awkward. I dropped things and fell down all the time. I had to go to the hospital a few times for stitches in my head and my leg. And I was pretty quiet most of the time. And I didn't mind being alone," he later told a writer about his childhood. He was clearly conscious of his status within the family hierarchy. "I was the seventh of nine children, and when you come from that far down, you have to struggle to survive," he once observed.

With the family's center of gravity tilted toward Joe Kennedy's growing ambitions for his oldest three children, Bobby grew close to his mother. His former nanny, calling him "the most thoughtful and considerate of the Kennedy children," recalled for one biographer how attentive and loving Bobby was as a young boy to Rose. Because he was closest to her, Rose's own deeply religious nature influenced Bobby. He enthusiastically served as an altar boy, prayed regularly, and went to Mass even more than was required while at Catholic boarding school.

While it almost certainly must have been painful for Robert Kennedy as a child to be outside of his charismatic father's primary focus of influence (which could also be demanding and oppressive), one of his biographers, Evan Thomas, has argued that this very exclusion preserved in Bobby a certain sweetness and sensitivity that his older siblings lacked. It was also this sensitivity that later made him prickly at times, but sympathetic to those on the margins. These personality traits helped him to connect instinctively with people who were suffering, especially children, Thomas concluded. Psychiatrist Robert Coles, who came to know Kennedy in the 1960s because of the doctor's work with poor children, believes Kennedy (unlike his brothers and older sister) was not pressured by his father to grow up too soon and therefore never lost a certain element of childlike wonder and enthusiasm and could therefore access his emotions more easily.

In contrast to Evan Thomas's more psychological analysis of impact that the senior Kennedy may have had on his children's psyche, another historian, Arthur Schlesinger, who wrote biographies of both John and Robert Kennedy, looked more kindly on Joseph Kennedy's role as a father. He argued that the Kennedy patriarch found a balance, one rarely achieved in wealthy households of that era, between motivating his children through love and attention and setting high standards and expectations for them. Whatever the impact of Bobby Kennedy's childhood, one of his sisters observed that in his early years, "nothing came easy for him. Perhaps that gave him sympathy later in life for those who were less fortunate. He, in some peculiar way, understood their soul."

Family meals in Joe and Rose's household included impromptu current events quizzes, discussion, and lively debate on the issues of the day, with their father often taking opposite sides of an issue to sharpen the children's critical-thinking skills. The young Kennedys were groomed to take what their parents saw as their rightful place as leaders of action on the world's stage. "We were to try harder than anyone else," Robert Kennedy wrote for a tribute volume to his father.

As a child of the Great Depression, Bobby could not have escaped an awareness of the suffering that played out on the pages of the news and in popular culture as the national crisis deepened. His family weathered the Depression quite well, but they understood that the rest of the nation was not as fortunate. Robert Kennedy recalled his parents telling him regularly that "there were a lot of people that were less fortunate, and a lot of people that were hungry."

However, while Kennedy's family maintained an attitude of aloof compassion and generosity toward those less fortunate, his father's embrace of capitalism and his antipathy toward socialism hardly encouraged a close identification with the individual struggles of America's poorest populations, as historian James Hilty has noted.

In an oral history in 1964, Robert Kennedy reflected on what shaped his sensibilities on class and race. His upbringing did not focus on the inequities and indignities that African Americans suffered in twentieth-century America. "What we did grow up with," he recalled, "was the idea that there were a lot of people who were less fortunate and a lot of people who were hungry—this was during the 1930s—people who had a difficult time. White people and Negroes were all put in that same category. One had a social responsibility to do something about it." The Kennedys also knew what it was like to be excluded and looked down upon for being Irish in Boston's society, he believed.

◆ ◆ ◆

The Kennedys reared their children with a sense of intense family loyalty. It was this commitment to family responsibility that motivated Robert Kennedy to answer the call, albeit reluctantly the first time, to manage his brother's Senate campaign in 1952 and his 1960 presidential campaign. After the family's oldest son, Joe Kennedy Jr., had died in a risky volunteer mission during World War II, their father's ambitions had shifted to John F. Kennedy. Bobby, who was at Harvard for much of the time and never saw action during the war, remained in the shadow of Jack, who had earned medals and renown for rescuing the crew of his boat after a Japanese attack in the Pacific.

Although Bobby had taken a job he liked in the Justice Department when he graduated from the University of Virginia's School of Law, he was soon back in Boston and involved in politics. He was there at the request of his old football buddy Kenneth O'Donnell, to join in Jack's campaign for the Senate in 1952. O'Donnell needed someone to serve as intermediary between the young candidate and Joseph Kennedy. The father and son didn't see eye-to-eye on much beyond their mutual ambition for a Kennedy to seize one of Massachusetts' seats in the US Senate from the incumbent Republican.

Perhaps it was sublimated frustration at having to abandon work he liked for the family's needs, the stress of trying to placate both his father and brother, or the demands of a close-fought campaign, but, a new side of his personality emerged. Biographer Arthur Schlesinger has argued that it was the 1952 Senate campaign where Kennedy's later reputation as "ruthless" was born.

John Kennedy was in a tight race, and the dictates of the family culture meant that Kennedys could not fail, so Bobby took the reins decisively. He focused on money and crafting strategies that would yield votes, not necessarily friends. He cut out free sandwiches, for example, and expected people at the headquarters to work. He had no compunction about showing them the door if they didn't pitch in or if they just bothered him. He could be terse and prickly. At twenty-six years old, Kennedy worked harder than anyone else, so much so that he lost sleep and weight.

Once the returns were in, Kennedy was satisfied with the victory, but not yet enamored with politics. However, he had earned his older brother's respect and finally caught his father's attention. "Bobby's the tough one," Joseph Kennedy would be telling a journalist within just a few years. "He'll keep the Kennedys together, you bet."

Robert Kennedy also came out of his brother's campaign with a new set of political skills, even if he was still conspicuously lacking in political graces. He had learned to mute his gentler side and do what had to be done in service to his family's ambitions. He had learned to balance the two outsized and, often, conflicting personalities and viewpoints of his father and his older brother. Importantly, he learned the difference between courting friends and counting votes.

As John F. Kennedy took his seat in the Senate and spent the 1950s making a name for himself in national politics, Robert Kennedy sought his own path—to a point. He had a young family to provide for and still relied on his well-connected father's help to land a job. The job his father soon found for his son put Kennedy right at the heart of Cold War politics and fueled liberal doubts about him until his death. It also gave him a deep understanding of how the Senate worked, especially the potential impact of public hearings. Joseph McCarthy, the Republican senator from Wisconsin and a hard-drinking Irish Catholic, was a family friend. He rose to national prominence in 1950 after he told a Republican women's group in Wheeling, West Virginia, that he had a list of dozens of Communists who worked in the State Department. In the Cold War atmosphere of the 1950s, his claims went off like a bombshell, and the concept that Democrats were "soft" on Communism put the party on the defensive and reverberated through American politics and policy for years to come.

Kennedy was a staff member on McCarthy's committee, which held protracted televised hearings. McCarthy, a demagogic, passionate figure, produced little evidence against any of his targets, but his aggressive and dramatic questioning of witnesses, a performance laden with innuendo and outrage, still ruined reputations and careers. To many of his fervent supporters at the time, he was a patriot protecting American institutions and values. But other leaders in both parties, including the new Republican president, Dwight Eisenhower, were appalled at his grandstanding and tactics. Consequently, in later years, Kennedy and his supporters tried to downplay his connection with the Communist-hunting senator. However, as Kennedy's biographer Larry Tye found, when Kennedy took the position with McCarthy, he brought a sincere admiration for the Wisconsin senator.

"Like his father, Bobby was drawn to qualities in McCarthy that echoed his own: his roughneck spirit, his unapologetic embrace of religion, and his willingness to take on and, if need be, shame the political establishment," Tye says. Both McCarthy and Kennedy had "the instincts of alley fighters."

However, as criticism of McCarthy and his chief counsel, the abrasive Roy Cohn, mounted, Kennedy soon distanced himself. After six months, he quit. Years later, after McCarthy's downfall and his censure by the Senate, Kennedy responded to a critic who questioned why he had ever worked for such a man. At the time he took the job, Kennedy responded, he had sincerely believed that here was a "serious internal security threat" to the nation and that McCarthy was the only one addressing the problem. "I was wrong," he said, yet when McCarthy died, Robert Kennedy quietly attended his funeral.

◆ ◆ ◆

During his late twenties and his thirties, observers often described Kennedy as having been rigid, judgmental, angry, rude, arrogant, and occasionally belligerent. He got into fistfights. He was testy and touchy, even with friends. After resigning from McCarthy's committee and working elsewhere on Capitol Hill in another job arranged for him by his father, Kennedy returned to work for the investigations subcommittee, but this time for the Democrats as minority counsel.

Kennedy's fortunes changed in 1955 when the Democrats won a majority in the Senate and were now in charge. After the election, they named him as chief counsel of the investigations subcommittee. As such, he could shape its focus. Kennedy had moralist tendencies, and he soon set his sights on corruption, exploring the connections between organized crime and labor unions. Following up on tips, he concentrated on the Teamsters, a union with 1.5 million members that represented truckers, warehouse workers, and others in the shipping and freight business.

As one of the largest and most powerful unions in the country, the organization had a fat pension fund and loose internal oversight, making it a lucrative target for Mafia infiltration. Working with information provided by the Bureau of Narcotics investigators and newspaper reporters who were tracking and writing about organized crime and labor, Kennedy became convinced that racketeering was a serious issue that Congress needed to investigate.

Perhaps Kennedy saw the chance to make a name for himself independent of his famous family, or perhaps he saw himself as a righteous standard bearer in a fight between good and evil. Perhaps it was mix of both, but whatever his motivation, his decision was not without risks both personal and political. His decision put him in direct conflict with John's presidential ambitions. Union members were a key constituency in the Democratic Party, and angering a large union like the Teamsters might make it much more difficult to elect John Kennedy president. On top of that, the Mafia was not a Sunday School. By the time he decided to launch his investigation, Kennedy was well aware of the potential for violent retaliation against him and his growing young family.

Kennedy pushed forward on the investigation, even though his sudden assertion of independence resulted in a fight with his father that his sister Jean called "the worst ever." He convinced the chairman of the investigations subcommittee, Senator John McClellan of Arkansas, to create the Select Committee on Improper Activities in the Labor or Management Fields in 1957, which quickly became known as the Rackets Committee, to look further into Kennedy's initial findings of violence and corruption.

From 1957 until 1959, Kennedy threw himself into the investigations with the Rackets Committee, ultimately supervising a staff of more than one hundred investigators in what became "one of the deepest and broadest congressional inquiries ever." The media attention, including national broadcasts of the hearings, put his drive and determination as an interrogator on display, for better or for worse, in the nation's living rooms. As chief counsel, he focused much of his attention on Jimmy Hoffa, a shrewd and tough Teamster boss from Detroit with, Kennedy believed, significant ties to organized crime.

Kennedy was not inclined to nuance, and, in Hoffa, he had found an adversary he thought worth the risks of the investigation. He later wrote in his book, *The Enemy Within*, that "there were times when his face seemed completely transfixed with this stare of absolute evilness. It might last for five minutes—as if he thought by staring long enough and hard enough he could destroy me." During this time, anonymous callers threatened Kennedy and his family with death, yet Kennedy appeared unfazed. The only time he accepted a change in routine was when a caller threatened to throw acid in the faces of his children. As a result, they had to wait at school in the principal's office until their mother, Ethel, picked them up.

It was during his hard-nosed pursuit of Hoffa that Kennedy met John Seigenthaler, who later became his aide and friend. However, the first meeting between the two men did not go well. Seigenthaler, a news reporter for a Nashville, Tennessee, paper, had done a series of investigative pieces about a corrupt Chattanooga judge who had received checks from Hoffa. Kennedy wanted to know more. Fastidious about punctuality, Kennedy thought Seigenthaler was late for their meeting and had his hat and coat on ready to leave; Seigenthaler was convinced that he was actually ten minutes early. The two men argued, and Kennedy was arrogant and dismissive. He acted the same way during a second encounter, but in the third conversation, Kennedy redeemed himself.

"About six weeks later, I was at home, and he called. It was about an hour [conversation] and he knew every single salient fact. At the end of the conversation, he said he was sending two investigators to Tennessee," Seigenthaler recalled. Kennedy pledged to look into the corruption. "We are going to see what else is there," he told the young reporter. "That was enough to change your attitude," Seigenthaler said.

Later, the two laughed about their first meeting. "Many times when we would be in meetings with people, and they would sort of gush, 'Mr. Attorney General, you are so upright, and we love you.' Sometimes he would say, 'This is the first time we have met—John, tell them about the first time *we* met.' And I would tell them about how it was a bad first meeting and how I thought he was a rude, rich prick.... The point would be made, and everyone would have a nervous chuckle, and they would move on to the business at hand."

The years Kennedy spent with the investigations subcommittee and as the lead counsel of the Rackets Committee taught him lessons that would serve him well later as both attorney general in his brother's administration and once he himself was elected to the Senate. As he observed Senator Joseph McCarthy's surging popularity, subsequent overreach, and downfall and then later sparred with Jimmy Hoffa, he learned both the power and the limitations of public hearings. He came to understand the importance of well-prepared and reliable witnesses, and he had seen the impact of public hearings on public opinion. And, importantly for his later career in that legislative body, he learned about the inner workings and conflicting personalities of the Senate.

◆ ◆ ◆

By the end of the 1950s, Robert and his wife, Ethel—a spirited, loving young woman he had married in 1950—had a still-growing family of seven children. They moved to a large brick home, Hickory Hill, in the Washington,

Bobby Kennedy and his wife, Ethel, with eight of their nine children on the lawn of their home at McLean, Virginia, in October 1966. The couple would eventually have a total of eleven children, including one born after his death. From right: Kathleen, Joseph, Robert Jr., David, Mary Courtney, Michael, Kerry, and Christopher. Credit: AP Photo.

DC suburb of McLean, Virginia. Kennedy was a devoted, affectionate father. Colleagues remember him making an effort to be home for dinner at least three nights a week and on the weekends, often convening meetings with witnesses or aides beside the swimming pool. If he worked late, then he invited the children to his office for lunch or supper. At 7:00 a.m. every morning, any child who wanted to join him could play touch ball with him outside before he went to work.

Ethel's support and encouragement were unfailing, giving him the stable home base full of love that he had always longed for. During this time their house, a rollicking place full of pets and children, was a refuge of sorts from the pressures of the hearings. Kennedy reveled in playing with his children.

The lively Kennedy home was also suffused with a Catholic sensibility, one that was overseen primarily by Ethel, but supported by her husband. Daughter Kerry Kennedy called Catholicism "central to her upbringing" in an interview. She described a childhood punctuated by prayer, church attendance, and spirituality. According to Kathleen Kennedy Townsend, the family's oldest child, Ethel and Robert Kennedy emphasized a pair of Bible verses to their children repeatedly: Luke 12:48, "To whom much is given, much is expected" and the portion of Mathew 25 that says, "As you did it to one of the least of these my brethren, you did it to me."

Like his children, Kennedy was steeped the teachings and attitudes of the twentieth-century American Catholic Church from an early age. He remained faithful to it, although at times questioning, throughout his life. It almost certainly shaped his view of the world and his role in it. As historian Edward Schmitt points out in *President of the Other America*, Kennedy's adult life coincided with a time of ferment and change in the Catholic Church. Catholic activists like Dorothy Day were articulating a view of the church as a force for social change. Pope John XXIII convened the Second Vatican Council in 1962 to examine the church and its role in the modern world. As a result, Mass was no longer always said in Latin, and the church reaffirmed its commitment to scripture and took a more ecumenical stance toward other Christians.

Kathleen Kennedy Townsend also writes that in the early 1960s, Robert Kennedy began reading from the Bible each night during the family's evening prayers. Robert Kennedy Jr. remembered going to church with his parents and that his father always brought a Bible with him. "When the priest started talking about right-wing stuff, he would pointedly read the Bible or he would read the Catholic newspapers at the back of the church," he said.

◆ ◆ ◆

Once the 1960 campaign for the presidency began in earnest, Robert Kennedy was once again at the helm of his brother's campaign and remained intensely focused on victory. As he worked to chart a winning course through the Democratic primaries and then in a national presidential campaign that fall, he gained a deeper understanding of the nation's complex racial landscape.

However, it was not long before both John and Robert Kennedy learned that African Americans had waited long enough to take their rightful place in the nation's civic arena. Their quest for equal treatment and civil rights had to be recognized in the campaign, and it would propel the fledgling administration into a political minefield. Events soon demanded that the Kennedy brothers pick a side and enter the fray.

As attorney general, Robert Kennedy was soon on the front lines of the battle to enforce federal court orders regarding integration and other civil rights issues. Kennedy had not volunteered to serve as the nation's top law enforcement official; publicly, he made it appear that he was practically drafted by his family.

But he could not have been surprised by the idea. The suggestion that Robert would serve as his brother's attorney general had been mentioned as early as 1956 in a magazine article quoting Joseph Kennedy's predictions about his two sons.

Robert Kennedy knew his selection would be seen as bald-faced nepotism. Furthermore, as he said in an oral history after his brother's death, he had spent three years "chasing bad men" and didn't want to do that for the rest of his life. Ethel later claimed that her husband was set against the idea and that it would eventually take "every ounce" of his brother's considerable charm to change his mind. Robert knew the political outcry would be sharp and loud. Indeed, critics charged that he was inexperienced, too young, and had never even tried a case.

Joseph Kennedy, however, had made his wish—no, his command—clear. In his mind, John Kennedy had a cabinet full of powerful, accomplished men, but he knew none of them well. The new president, Joe argued, needed someone in the room he could trust beyond a shadow of doubt. Joe was impatient with John's hesitancy. "I don't know what's wrong with him. Jack needs all the good men he can get around him down there."

In mid-December, John Kennedy made his case to his younger brother, saying, "Look, I have a cabinet of people I don't know. . . . There are times, Bobby, when I have got to rely on somebody who is going to tell me what is in my best interest, and you are the only one I can count on to do that."

◆ ◆ ◆

The next afternoon, as reporters gathered on a cold day in front of the president-elect's Georgetown house under the glare of a bright winter sun, John looked confident with his younger brother smiling by his side. He announced that he had sought the most qualified men for his cabinet, "men of ability, determination and a desire to serve their country. I have applied that same test in this case."

At thirty-five, Robert Kennedy was the third youngest US attorney general, but he quickly showed some of his first real resistance to the demands of his father and brother. He had a growing sense of his own independence, and he wasn't about to be the kind of attorney general that pundits predicted and his sister Eunice had joked about in 1959 when she said, "Bobby we'll make Attorney General so he can throw all the people Dad doesn't like into jail."

However, the critics (and there were many) of his nomination were correct in at least one respect. He was inexperienced in race relations and civil rights. He was also ill-informed when it came to the pain, deprivation, and frustrations of the experience of African Americans in mid-twentieth-century America—especially in the segregated South. Robert Kennedy himself later said that civil rights had not always been a paramount concern: "I won't say I stayed awake nights worrying about civil rights before I became Attorney General."

In 1963, speaking on CBS television's *Washington Report,* Robert Kennedy acknowledged that, early on, he had a surprising lack of awareness on the issue, despite earning his law degree in segregated Virginia. He said, "I think if there was anything that shocked me when I became Attorney General, it was the fact that there are large numbers of our population, hundreds of thousands of individuals, who cannot vote because of the fact that they are Negroes."

Neither Robert Kennedy nor the president was prepared for the fierce conflicts that were about to erupt in the former Confederacy. It was not until his tenure as his brother's attorney general that Robert Kennedy grew to understand that the conflict over race in America was not just a complex and intractable political problem. Instead, it went to the very heart of the American ideal. And, with Mississippi and many of its leaders serving as rancorous tutors, he soon learned that the struggle over that American ideal could turn poisonous and deadly.

Chapter 3

It's to Hell with Bobby K

U S marshals and plainclothes policemen paced the wide, low concourse of the Jackson Municipal Airport. The April 9, 1967 flight carrying Senator Robert Kennedy and three other members of the Senate subcommittee to Mississippi's capital was due to land shortly, and the waiting officers cast wary glances outside the airport's entrance. About twenty men, women, and children walked in a single line in the spring sunshine, carrying Confederate flags and signs. One sign read, "Race Mixers Go Home." Other signs spoke to Kennedy's speech in the Senate a month earlier calling for an end to US involvement in Vietnam: "American Soldiers' Blood on Bobby's Hands," "LBJ—Send Bobby to Hanoi, not Mississippi," they said. As Kennedy passed, some of the picketers shouted at him: "Communist!" "Nigger lover!" Although the group's spokesman told reporters that these picketers were only concerned individuals demonstrating "on behalf of America, free speech and victory over Communism," law enforcement officials bluntly identified them to reporters as members of the South's leading homegrown terrorist organization, the Ku Klux Klan.

While the protestors looked peaceful enough, the marshals' careful security measures were hardly an overreaction. In 1967, Mississippi was dangerous territory for even moderate supporters of civil rights for African Americans. With a deadly riot during the integration of the University of Mississippi in 1962, the assassination of NAACP field secretary Medgar Evers in Jackson in 1963, and the murder of three young men working to register voters during

Anti-Kennedy sentiment ran deep with many white Mississippians. Here someone slapped protest
bumper stickers on a US Army truck sent to quell the riot over integration at Ole Miss in 1962.
Credit: The Ed Meek/Meek School of Journalism and New Media Collection, Department of
Archives & Special Collections, University of Mississippi.

1964's Freedom Summer, white supremacists in Mississippi had proven they
could and would kill for their cause.

The arrival of four senators to discuss poverty in a state as conservative
and reactionary as Mississippi certainly carried some security risks, but it was
Bobby Kennedy's presence more than any other that accounted for such height-
ened safety concerns. Just the year before, when his brother Senator Edward
Kennedy arrived in the city for a speech to Dr. Martin Luther King's Southern
Christian Leadership Conference, someone had poured ten pounds of carpet
tacks along the route from the airport, disabling two police cars in his escort.

Long before Bobby Kennedy's airplane even touched down in Jackson, he
had a complicated history with the state. As his brother's US attorney general
from 1961 through 1964, Kennedy had played a pivotal role in some of the most
significant events in Mississippi's turbulent journey through the civil rights era.
Kennedy's involvement in events such as helping Medgar Evers's family after
his assassination, the Freedom Riders, and, perhaps most significantly, the integration of Ole Miss, loomed large in the minds and memories of Mississippians
both white and black.

In those two populations, the Kennedy brothers, and especially Robert
Kennedy, produced almost polar-opposite emotions. By 1967, conservative

white Mississippians bore the Kennedys considerable antipathy for their part (both actual and perceived) in the wrenching changes the state had undergone, some of them even celebrating at John Kennedy's assassination. In contrast, many average black Mississippians revered the Kennedys for their role in the civil rights struggle, and the slaying of President Kennedy had only intensified their admiration of his brother. Photos of John Kennedy, and even at times Robert Kennedy, often decorated the walls of spare and crumbling shacks across the state. This deep admiration by average African Americans in Mississippi contrasted, however, with the skepticism and disappointment of many civil rights activists like Marian Wright, who were well aware of the canny calculation with which he and his brother had pursued civil rights goals.

The Kennedys' relationship with Mississippi was not always so fraught with intensity, however. It had once been one of wary comity. Robert Kennedy's initial connection with the state was an indirect one that grew out of his older brother's political activities. Before the dramatic events of the 1960s, which transformed the Kennedy brothers into the bête noire of southern segregationists, the political realities of the "solid South" meant that the region played an outsized role in the presidential nominating process of the Democratic Party. Thus, any path to the White House that John Kennedy took would have to twist toward the South at some point.

John Kennedy represented a small number of black voters as a congressman from Massachusetts and had quietly supported a few civil rights measures while in the House and then later in the Senate during the 1940s and 1950s. But he also hedged his bets in ways such as supporting an amendment to 1957 civil rights legislation that southern senators like James O. Eastland of Mississippi wanted, which required a jury trial to convict someone of contempt for failing a civil rights court order. The amendment significantly weakened the bill, civil rights groups believed, because in the South they would be all-white, all-male juries.

John Kennedy was generally inclined toward progressive civil rights policies, but he was an ambitious politician, not an activist. Biographer Robert Dallek describes John Kennedy in the 1950s this way: "He could not empathize, and only faintly sympathize with the pains felt by African Americans. He did not even consider an aggressive challenge to the deeply ingrained southern racial attitudes, and he was far from alone." During his congressional and Senate career thus far, he had managed to remain cagey enough about his position on the issue to garner significant southern support in 1956 for his unsuccessful run for the vice-presidential slot at the Democratic Convention.

At the 1956 Democratic Convention, John Kennedy's main rival for Adlai Stevenson's running mate was Tennessee senator Estes Kefauver, a controversial figure among his fellow southerners. It was a time of fevered, hardline reactions to the slightest crack in the South's massive resistance to civil rights progress, and southern conservative Democrats feared Kefauver was insufficiently committed to segregation. Kefauver was by no means a civil rights activist, but he generally favored liberal issues. However, his main offense was that he had, along with only two other senators (Al Gore Sr., also of Tennessee, and Lyndon B. Johnson of Texas) refused to sign the Southern Manifesto, a declaration from 101 southern federal lawmakers opposing integration and civil rights written in the months after the US Supreme Court's desegregation ruling in *Brown v. Board of Education.*

The burgeoning civil rights movement brought long-simmering tensions in the Democratic Party for years into the open at the 1956 convention. The decision in *Brown* had stripped the legal cover from white supremacy masquerading as "separate but equal." Furthermore, Martin Luther King's eloquent leadership of the ongoing bus boycott in Montgomery had given a new, urgent voice to the hopes of black Americans who had suffered the injustices of southern society for decades. And the firebombing of King's house a few months before the convention had demonstrated the dark, murderous forces that swirled beneath the surface of official segregation.

For the Democrats, however, the competing forces held the potential to destroy party unity and cost them the election. Southern Democrats represented states with almost all-white electorates because of discriminatory voting laws and practices like the poll tax and literacy tests. They could deliver a crucial number of electoral votes in an election against popular incumbent and war hero Dwight D. Eisenhower that was already going to be difficult. Their support was anything but certain because many of them had already shown they would walk away from the party over civil rights when they bolted to form the short-lived States Rights, or Dixiecrat, Party in 1948 in outrage over President Harry Truman's desegregation of the military and creation of a commission on civil rights.

However, millions of African Americans had surged into the cities of the North, Midwest, and West during the Great Migration of the first half of the twentieth century. According to historian James N. Gregory, from the beginning of World War II through the Vietnam era, as many as 5 million people left the South, and millions more moved from rural areas to the South's cities. "In doing so, they reshaped their own lives and much more."

Gregory writes that "within one generation, a people who had been mostly rural became mostly urban. A people mostly southern spread to all regions of the United States. A people mostly accustomed to poverty and equipped with farm skills now pushed their way into the core of the American economy.

And other changes followed. A people who had lacked access to political rights and political influence now gained both."

Both committed liberals who were genuinely moved by the injustice of racial discrimination and savvy politicians looking for new voting blocs were united in their desire for the Democratic Party to embrace progressive civil rights principles. Eventually, the party found a compromise and adopted its 1956 platform, calling *Brown* the "law of the land" but remaining silent on how and when desegregation should take place.

With his eye on these fault lines in the months leading up to the convention, John Kennedy began to temper what had been, until then, his consistent but quiet support for civil rights during his time in Washington. He started using more cautious statements about the limitations of federal congressional authority in civil rights matters, and he advocated a gradual approach to desegregation. This softening was enough for some southern delegations to set aside their doubts about his northeastern pedigree and Roman Catholicism and consider casting their votes for the charismatic war hero as their vice president.

In the last-minute scramble to get his brother on the ticket, Robert Kennedy, with Johnson's help, openly courted southern delegates and, in that role, almost certainly had to reassure them of his brother's moderate approach to desegregation. Journalist Bill Minor, who covered Mississippi for the *New Orleans Times-Picayune*, spent time in the Kennedy suite in Chicago with Bobby Kennedy as they waited to see Jack with Minor's friend, Mississippi congressman Frank Smith. Smith was a rare racial moderate from Mississippi and had become close friends with Jack Kennedy when they served in Congress together. Minor recalled no direct conversation with either Kennedy brother about desegregation at the 1956 convention. "In those days, if you came head on about segregation, they wouldn't talk to you. They'd talk around the perimeter," he said. However, somehow the Kennedys let the Mississippi delegation know that "they were going to tone it down," Minor said.

Delegate William Winter, the state's tax collector in 1956, recalled a frantic night of campaigning after Stevenson threw the vice-presidential selection to the convention. Bobby Kennedy visited with Winter and several other representatives of the Mississippi delegation to make his brother's case. "He was young and just full of energy. He was into the idea of getting Jack the nomination," Winter said. Bobby wanted to know if there was really a chance that Mississippi would support his brother. According to Winter, even though the entire delegation, including himself, were segregationists at the time, there was a split between those who favored a moderate, progressive approach to the issue, and rabid, combative conservatives. "They were the old 'states righters.' There were those who just really didn't want to do anything related to the national Democratic Party," he said.

However, during his visit, Bobby Kennedy made no explicit promises that John Kennedy would change his position on civil rights. Instead, Winter said Frank Smith served as an intermediate for Kennedy. "He'd say, 'you know Kennedy's for civil rights. He's not going to back up on that, but he understands the sensitive political nature of the issue,'" Winter recalled. Kefauver was considered a crusader on civil rights and a traitor to the South by much of the Mississippi delegation. "As much as anything, it was who had the best chance to stop Kefauver."

However, the state's delegation was not immune to the young Senator's famous appeal. Winter agreed that Kennedy's charisma and charm were a part of what won over some of the state's delegation. "Fresh faced, young, a veteran of World War II. He seemed to have a lot of idealism in what he was proposing for the country. I liked his approach. Here was a man from whose leadership the Democratic Party could benefit," Winter said.

The Kennedy brothers did promise the state's delegation that if it voted for him, then Jack Kennedy would come to Mississippi to speak, Minor said. Winter doesn't remember any direct promises being made, but says many of the Mississippians were impressed with Kennedy. "There was a strong feeling among several of us that, you know, we need to get this guy to Jackson," he said.

After Bobby's busy night of wheeling and dealing, Mississippi and most of the southern states lined up in John Kennedy's column. In fact, some of Mississippi's delegation even let loose Rebel yells as they cast their votes for Kennedy. "There was still a defiance there," Winter said, noting that the Mississippi delegation saw its vote as much as a rebellion against Kefauver and the party's position on civil rights as it was genuine enthusiasm for Kennedy's personality. After Mississippi voted, Johnson's Texas delegation, against a backdrop of Confederate flags, joined them. Other southern states, including South Carolina, Louisiana, Alabama, Arkansas, Georgia, North Carolina, and Virginia also fell into line behind Kennedy.

Governor J. P. Coleman had led the state delegation and overruled anyone who opposed Kennedy, according to Winter. Coleman later wrote to Kennedy that the delegation was proud to have supported him. "We would be happy to have the opportunity to do so much again," he wrote. (In 1963, however, Coleman paid a steep political price for his welcoming attitude toward Kennedy. His opponent in the Democratic primary run-off blasted him for being close to the Kennedys, a devastating allegation in a state that was still seething over the integration of Ole Miss. Coleman lost the race.)

John Kennedy kept his promise to visit Mississippi. As he set his sights on the 1960 Democratic nomination for president, he sought to soothe southern nerves, and with this goal, he came to Jackson to give a speech to Mississippi's Young Democrats in October 1957. However, he soon realized that the visit would require more than a smooth speech and some backslapping. Just ahead of Kennedy's speech, the state's GOP chairman, Wirt Yerger Jr., called on Kennedy to clarify his position on the federal government's role in the integration of Little Rock's Central High School. In the context of Mississippi politics, this was tantamount to a slap of the glove, challenging Kennedy to a duel. Mississippi's political class knew the charged question had no easy answer.

Kennedy risked losing the respect of key supporters in the state if he failed to take up the provocation. However, even though he was a gradualist, Kennedy did support civil rights. He had said so publicly in the past, even if he had tried to remain vague about the pace and timing of progress on the issue. Reiterating that support could cost him the South. Equivocating on the issue would make him look dishonest. To make matters worse, *Time* magazine, which was firmly in the Republican camp, sent a reporter and photographer to Mississippi to watch Kennedy squirm. His supporters in Jackson, such as William Winter, recognized the trap set for the young senator and waited.

At the time of Kennedy's visit to Jackson, Mississippi, leaders in the statehouse and the press were bristling with offense. Just three weeks earlier, President Eisenhower had federalized Arkansas' National Guard and sent troops to oversee the federal court-ordered desegregation of Central High School. White southern leaders were horrified at this turn of events and on guard for any sign of support for federal intervention in what they saw as a "states' rights" issue. But Kennedy found a way to deftly maneuver himself out of the trap the Republican state leader had set for him.

Once in Jackson, the young senator made a point of associating himself with the state's segregationist power structure. He spent time with the state's two US senators—avowed segregationists James O. Eastland and John Stennis—and stayed at the governor's mansion. Kennedy even spent the night in the Theodore Bilbo bedroom, a key detail reported across the state. The symbolic link to Bilbo, a virulent and outspoken racist, was not lost on Mississippians. Bilbo, though dead for a decade, still loomed large in the state's memory. He had served the state twice as governor and in the US Senate before his death in 1947. For Kennedy to sleep in Bilbo's bed was an honor, at least in many white Mississippian's eyes, as one historian put it, "akin to sleeping in the Lincoln Bedroom in the White House."

As he opened his speech to a packed room hosted by Jackson's Young Democrats, Kennedy managed to finesse the question of Little Rock and school desegregation. Southern Democrats had warned him to steer clear of civil rights and integration, and Kennedy had a careful speech prepared. But, on the flight to Jackson, he had scrawled an addendum to his prepared remarks on a few sheets of paper from a yellow legal pad. The original copy of the speech is marked up, with scratched out words and phrases and tempering clauses added here and there. The young senator from Massachusetts was clearly wrestling with what to say to his southern audience.

The current times were "times of tensions and bitterness—times that favor extremists, not voices of calm reason, not voices of conciliation," Kennedy told the audience. He acknowledged that there would always be dissent within the Democratic Party. "But," he said, "the common bonds of our party—a common tradition, a common spirit, a common cause and an inseparable destiny—holds us within the Party we honor and serve."

Then Kennedy stood his ground and took the GOP chairman's dare. "I have no hesitancy in telling him the same thing I have said in my own city of Boston, that I have accepted the Supreme Court's decision on segregation as the law of the land. I know that we do not agree on that issue. I think most of us do agree on the necessity to uphold law and order in every part of the land."

Kennedy quickly pivoted to offence, delighting the audience by issuing a challenge of his own: "I now invite Chairman Yerger to tell us *his* views on President Eisenhower and Mr. Nixon," Kennedy said. Kennedy went on to say that he was not in Jackson to argue over desegregation, but to call them to work together for a common ideal.

"What unites us is greater than what divides us—and, in that spirit, we meet tonight as Democrats—not as Northern or Southern Democrats, Massachusetts or Mississippi Democrats—but as just plain unashamed, unyielding and unbeaten Democrats," he said.

Although mollifying southern Democrats on the issue of race was no easy task, Kennedy made headway toward his goal while in Jackson. The group, made up of many of the state's top business and governmental leaders, him a standing ovation. Winter still marveled at his achievement almost sixty years later: "He said it in a way that he got the applause of that crowd, even some of those old Mississippi Democrats." Even the state capitol's morning newspaper, the *Clarion-Ledger*, arguably the most racist, inflammatory, truculent mainstream newspaper in any American city at the time, praised the senator's charm and humor. However, the young war hero may have been more nervous than he let on. At dinner, he reached for cream to pour into the cup of his Mississippi friend in Congress, Frank Smith, and, instead, topped off the cup with "a generous serving of salad dressing."

The editorial writers for the *Clarion Ledger*, aggrieved and upset with Eisenhower and the GOP over Little Rock, were inclined to give Kennedy the benefit of the doubt. One wrote, with a dose of both projection and wishful thinking, that "like many other good Democrats in the north, he wishes it [the *Brown* decision] had never been rendered."

Not everyone in Jackson was on board with Kennedy's campaign, however. Gene Wirth, a columnist for the *Clarion Ledger*, was mostly unimpressed with the young senator, although he did concede that Kennedy handled the integration question "masterfully." Wirth called Kennedy "bushy-haired" and "fidgety" and judged that the senator missed an opportunity to make heavy gains in the state. "Unless he sharpens up his approach appreciably, it will be no fault of his if he finds himself in the White House some day."

By 1960 John Kennedy was indeed firmly on the path to the White House. As the Democratic nominee, he had lent his support to the surprisingly strong new civil rights plank in the Democratic Party's platform and was actively seeking African American votes. At the same time, though, the candidate was still sending backdoor signals to southerners that he would approach the issue with due deliberation and caution. Meanwhile, Robert Kennedy had once again signed on to manage his brother's campaign and pursued that goal with his characteristically single-minded purpose.

Although supportive of civil rights in theory, he was perfectly willing to make political accommodation for the party's segregationist wing to put his brother in the White House. During the campaign, he aimed to tamp down southern objections to the party's civil rights platform by quietly stressing the hope that the region's voters could find some ground for unity and would continue to support a ticket that had purposely included Texas senator Lyndon Johnson (against Bobby's wishes) to help allay fears in the South.

In the end, however, the strategy failed to win over Mississippi's political class, which was troubled by Kennedy's youth, his Catholicism, and his embrace of the civil rights planks in the party's platform. Consequently, the Mississippi delegation supported Johnson for the top of the ticket at the convention and even nominated Governor Ross Barnett, who by this time was in full command of the delegation on the second ballot.

The civil rights movement had continued to gain momentum in the years leading up to the 1960 campaign. From December 1955 to December 1956, Martin Luther King Jr. prevailed as a leader in the Montgomery bus boycott. College students in Greensboro, North Carolina, began to use nonviolent sit-ins at segregated lunch counters in February 1960. And in April 1960, the SNCC organized. The nation's African American press, voters, and leaders began pressing for more legal and political remedies. Television's popularity burgeoned, and the young medium's news broadcasts brought the painful, often violent, realities of the segregated South into Americans' living rooms. American public opinion was slowly losing its tolerance for the South's version of legalized racial oppression, even if many Americans in the North and West were in denial about the racial inequities in their regions.

This put Mississippi's white political leaders and segregationist voters on the horns of a dilemma. Both the Democratic and Republican Parties had made civil rights a significant part of their platforms that summer. It was clear that national sentiment was turning against the positions they held so dear.

Pathologically unable to admit, at least publicly, that they were on the losing side of national opinion and likely to be marginalized politically, they imagined scenarios where a close election would give the state a key role in choosing the leader of the free world. They embraced a scheme devised by leaders of the White Citizens Council, a network of white-supremacist groups heavily promoted by the Magnolia State's Governor Ross Barnett.

The plan allowed Mississippi voters who were uncomfortable with either Kennedy or Nixon to choose a third option on the November 8 ballot. Mississippi, Louisiana, and Alabama voters could vote for a slate of fifteen unpledged electors. Under the scheme, if neither Kennedy nor Nixon garnered a majority of the votes in the electoral college, these southern states could pressure the candidates to bargain away their civil rights commitment in exchange for the unpledged electors and victory either in the electoral college or by using southern clout if the election was thrown into the House of Representatives.

From his governor's perch, Barnett had warned that a vote for either of the top two presidential candidates would bring about immediate school integration, which meant that African Americans would "mingle socially with our white sons and daughters." On election day, he urged Mississippi voters to support the slate of unpledged electors to "save the children."

Once the votes were counted, most Mississippi voters, 92 percent of which were white, could not bring themselves to support either Kennedy or Nixon in the general election and took Barnett's advice. The GOP picked up three counties, and, although Kennedy carried twenty-four mostly northeastern Mississippi counties, fifty-four other counties and the unpledged Democratic electors won seventy-nine-hundred votes more than any other candidate on the presidential ticket. All eight of the state's electoral-college votes ultimately went to staunch segregationist US Senator Harry Byrd, but Kennedy defeated Republican Richard Nixon for the White House in one of the closest presidential races in history.

Despite the hopes of many black Americans and the fears of the South's segregationists, once in office, the nascent Kennedy administration moved slowly on civil rights. John Kennedy had promised an administration that would end federal housing segregation "by a stroke of the president's pen," and "oppose any foe to ensure the survival and success of liberty," but he and his brother remained focused on Cold War struggles. Charles Evers writes that Robert Kennedy's privileged background meant that he had always had "the best doctors, the best of everything and grew up assuming America was the land of the free and the home of the brave. I knew it was no damn such thing."

Robert Kennedy later admitted: "I won't say I stayed awake nights worrying about civil rights before I became Attorney General." He tended to clumsily equate segregation with the discrimination that the Irish had faced in Boston in the previous century. Arthur Schlesinger, a Kennedy biographer, pointed out that for the young attorney general in 1961, advocating for civil rights was undeniably the moral position, but it was "filled with operational difficulties." At this point in his life, "he did not see racial injustice as *the* urgent American problem, as the contradiction, now at last intolerable, between the theory and the practice of the republic," Schlesinger wrote.

However, domestic events almost immediately swept the young attorney general into the fray and Mississippi into the spotlight. In May 1961, just a few months after the inauguration, civil rights activists, inspired by the lunch-counter sit-ins that had occurred across the South, planned Freedom Rides to test past and recent court rulings by integrating interstate bus travel and segregated waiting rooms across the South.

The protestors, a mix of middle-aged activists and young college students from the Congress of Racial Equality (CORE) and SNCC, were taking aim at one of the most visible and humiliating manifestations of the South's Jim Crow laws. Under these state laws, blacks were relegated to segregated waiting rooms, restrooms, and lunch counters at bus and train terminals throughout the eleven states of the former Confederacy. However, the more personally humiliating manifestation of these laws forced African Americans who crossed into these states to give up their seats to white riders and to sit in the rear of the bus, often leaving them to stand or sit in crowded conditions while seats reserved for whites sat empty. The Freedom Riders' plan called for a series of mixed race groups to buy tickets from Washington, DC, on Trailways and Greyhound buses to New Orleans, Louisiana, and peacefully refuse to comply with local segregation laws.

When they arrived at the first stop in Anniston, Alabama, an angry crowd of Ku Klux Klan members, encouraged and recruited by local and state law enforcement officials, attacked the bus, slashing its tires and firebombing it. The Freedom Riders barely escaped incineration. In Birmingham, the Klan, encouraged by the city's racist police chief, Bull Conner, attacked the Riders with baseball bats and pipes. On a later ride, in Montgomery, Kennedy's friend and aide John Seigenthaler, whom he had sent down to help defuse the situation, tried to intervene as a group of men beat a young African American woman. Her attackers turned on him, fracturing his skull with a pipe.

Throughout the crisis, Robert Kennedy had wrestled with possible solutions, looking for a way that would have kept his brother's administration out of direct, public confrontation with the South over segregation. Although all indications are that Kennedy thought segregation was unjust, his Justice Department did not make any press statements in support of the riders or condemning the violence. Although he sent FBI observers, Justice Department negotiators and Seigenthaler, Kennedy refused to provide federal protection for the riders, instead pressuring local and state officials, including Alabama's governor, to take action to keep them safe.

Kennedy also pressured bus company officials to get drivers, ordered federal marshals to leave for Montgomery and sought alternative ways to take legal action against hate groups interfering with interstate travel.

In the Kennedys' view, the conflict building in the South over segregation could not have come at a worse time. The administration was wrangling with the aftermath of the Bay of Pigs fiasco and planning a European trip for a summit with the Soviets. Kennedy officials were caught off guard by the Freedom Riders, so much so that after reading an early *New York Times* account of the beatings in Birmingham, John Kennedy had snapped at his civil rights adviser, Harris Wofford, "Tell them to call it off! Stop them. Get your friends off those buses," he said and left it for his brother to find a solution. Nicholas Katzenbach, an assistant attorney general, later said that JFK seemed to think the whole conflict was a "pain in the ass."

Although he was shocked by the ferocity of the Birmingham attack and especially the attack on John Seigenthaler in Montgomery, Robert Kennedy was still more focused on eliminating the propaganda opportunity it gave the Soviets than furthering the Riders' cause. After the rescue of Martin Luther King from a mob-besieged church in Montgomery by federal marshals and the Alabama National Guard in May of 1961, Kennedy still desperately hoped the crisis would subside as the riders moved into Mississippi and worked political back channels to defuse the issue.

Mississippi was as volatile as Alabama or more so, and Robert Kennedy was looking to avoid the violence that had erupted in Alabama. He quickly concluded that Senator Eastland was the only person powerful enough to have even a chance of reining in Mississippi's violent reactionaries and their state-sanctioned enablers. This realization was made all the more sensitive given Eastland's position as chairman of the Senate Judiciary Committee, gatekeeper to the federal judiciary. Robert Kennedy knew that any of his brother's appointments to lower federal judgeships or even the Supreme Court would have to go through Eastland. However, even though Eastland wielded plenty of power in Washington, it paled in comparison to the length and breadth of political sway that he held in 1960s Mississippi.

Eastland was born a son of the Mississippi Delta on a five-thousand-acre plantation in Sunflower County but grew up in an area of the state populated by poor, struggling farmers. He rose to power after forging a populist alliance with then-governor Theodore Bilbo while serving in the state House of Representatives. Named to the US Senate in 1941 to fulfill the term of one of the state's senators who died in office and then elected to the Senate in 1943, Eastland was an outspoken opponent of civil rights and virulently anti-Communist, dangers that he saw as inextricably linked. As Arthur Schlesinger notes, Lyndon Johnson once said of Eastland, "Jim Eastland could be standing right in the middle of the worst Mississippi flood ever known, and he'd say the niggers caused it, helped out by the Communists—but, he'd say, we gotta have help from Washington."

Over the years, with his history as champion of the poor white farmer in the legislature and his Delta connections, he developed and fine-tuned a behind-the-scenes political network with influence throughout the state at every level, from local beat supervisors to county sheriffs to judges and legislators. By the 1960s, perhaps more than any other southern senator, he was a dominating presence in his state's political arena, with an outsized impact on the public policy that emerged from it.

Back in Washington, Eastland, now Mississippi's senior senator, had consolidated his power at the national level just as the civil rights movement gathered momentum, taking over as chairman of the Judiciary Committee two years after the US Supreme Court struck down school segregation in *Brown v. Board of Education*. Eastland, who was on record with his belief that blacks were "an inferior race" and spoke more than once in the Senate and in Mississippi about what he considered the dangers of the "mongrelization" of the races, made it a personal mission to bury dozens of civil rights bills that arrived in his committee, even telling his constituents back home that he had a "special pocket sewn in his trousers so he could carry civil rights bills around with him to make sure no one called them up for consideration in his absence."

However, despite their different backgrounds, Kennedy and Eastland had a surprisingly cordial relationship, one that had begun as Kennedy made the rounds of the Senate to shore up support for his nomination as attorney general in 1960. Eastland, with his round face, Mississippi drawl, cigars, and daily scotch-and-waters, practically embodied the satirical ideal of a southern politician. Eastland and Kennedy had dramatically different backgrounds and personalities, but the two apparently got along well. Eastland and various members of his family even visited Kennedy's home, Hickory Hill, from time to time. There were political risks for both of them, but especially Eastland, if the connection had come to light.

Why did Kennedy like Eastland? Maybe they were cordial because the two had similar feelings about the dangers of Communism. Eastland was almost as vociferous on the subject as he was on equality of the races, partly because of his fear of the ideology's potential impact on the African American workers in his home state. Also, Eastland and the other senator from Mississippi, John Stennis, were fiercely antiunion, and, as such, they approved of Robert Kennedy's aggressive pursuit of Jimmy Hoffa and the Teamsters.

Or, maybe, as Arthur Schlesinger speculated, it was because of Kennedy's "Irish weakness for rogues." When Edward Kennedy had arrived in the Senate in 1962 and visited Eastland one morning, the senator from Mississippi had plied the youngest Kennedy brother with so much Scotch that he was practically knee-walking drunk (despite trying to surreptitiously pour some of it into potted plants) by the time he left. However, Eastland sent the freshman senator staggering away with committee assignments—immigration, civil rights, and the Constitution—that were exceptionally valuable for Ted Kennedy's political ambitions.

Robert Kennedy also knew that despite Eastland's outsized public opposition to civil rights, even northern liberals considered him a straight shooter who was careful and fair when it came to handling judicial nominations and other issues. In a 1964 interview with Anthony Lewis, Kennedy also described how in one of their first meetings, Eastland subtly telegraphed his opinion of Eisenhower's attorney general's work on civil rights. Bill Rogers' Department of Justice did not take a single civil rights case in Mississippi, Eastland told Robert Kennedy. Then Eastland, himself a lawyer who certainly knew about racial injustices in Mississippi better than most, winked at Kennedy.

"The whole thrust of his statement was just the fact that Bill Rogers hadn't met his responsibility and done his duty on Mississippi. And Jim Eastland felt a certain amount of contempt for him," Kennedy recalled. He went on to say Eastland never tried to impede any of the Kennedy administration's work in Mississippi or held legislation hostage because of RFK's work on civil rights in his state.

"And he always kept his word, and he was always available, and he always told me exactly where he stood—what he could do and what he couldn't do. And he told me who I could trust and who I shouldn't trust in the state of Mississippi.... I found it much more pleasant to deal with him than many of the so-called liberals in the House Judiciary Committee or in other parts of Congress and the Senate," Kennedy told Lewis in 1964.

However, Eastland was not above sending Kennedy a not-so-subtle reminder of his position and power. One former Mississippi city official remembers calling on his senator early in 1962 (months before the conflict at Ole Miss) as part of a local delegation in the capitol to seek a national bank charter. As he met with the group from Cleveland, Mississippi, Eastland left Kennedy, who had arrived at about the same time, waiting in his office's ante-room while he met with the group for at least forty minutes.

"We kept telling the senator 'you've got the attorney general sitting out there; let us go,' but he wouldn't. He'd say, 'Oh, let the little so-and-so sit and cool his heels,'" said Nevin Sledge, part of the Cleveland delegation. Sledge remembers Kennedy as "cool and modest, extremely modest" when Eastland finally introduced them. Kennedy may have been quietly frustrated by the wait, but, as the grandson of a consummate local wheeler-dealer like "Honey Fitz" Fitzgerald, he was probably well aware of the political necessities of talking to home folk first.

As for Kennedy, even if he liked him personally, he was under no illusions about Eastland regarding civil rights. John Seigenthaler, one of his aides, recalled a Kennedy comment about Martin Luther King's efforts to help African Americans gain the vote in Deep South states. More black voters there would mean that "men like Jim Eastland would not be so fresh" with their racist rhetoric, he remembered Kennedy saying. Years later, Kennedy inscribed a copy of his 1967 book, *To Seek a Newer World*, for Eastland, with "Jim, it's not too late—Read this—repent and we'll take you into our fold—Bobby."

After his efforts to get the Alabama governor to keep the peace during the Freedom Rides ended in violence, Kennedy showed a pragmatic understanding of the state's political landscape and reached out to Eastland, rather than dealing with Mississippi governor Ross Barnett.

Barnett, the son of a Confederate Civil War veteran, had worked his way through college and then law school. He was a successful, folksy trial lawyer who was known more for his way with a jury and colorful stump speeches than his intelligence. After losing two gubernatorial elections, he had come into office in 1959, after two more moderate candidates split the vote. Barnett coasted to victory on a wave of support from the White Citizen's Council when he pledged to "never" allow integration.

However, he had nothing like the political network that Eastland maintained in the state. As the protestors made plans to continue their rides, Kennedy worked the phones, making more than sixty phone calls to Eastland, eventually negotiating a deal. Ultimately, they came to agree that Eastland would guarantee the safety of the riders, but only if the Justice Department would not object when the local police arrested the protestors as they arrived.

Subsequently, when more Freedom Riders took up the journey, a frustrated Robert Kennedy publicly criticized in an official statement the "curiosity seekers and publicity seekers who are seeking to serve their own causes" and then angered civil rights leaders by calling for a "cooling off" period. Kennedy's statement, however, delighted many southern leaders like Mississippi's Barnett.

In Jackson, the Freedom Riders (eventually more than three hundred) who were arrested were sentenced to sixty days in jail. Most of them chose to serve out their sentences and suffered mistreatment in Mississippi's brutal prison system that hot summer. After all his backdoor deal making, Kennedy was stunned when Martin Luther King told him that the riders would serve their sentences rather than be quietly released; Kennedy's Justice Department remained silent.

Robert Kennedy acquiesced to Mississippi's blatant violation of the riders' civil rights, made ambivalent public statements, and conducted back-channel negotiations with segregationists during the Freedom Riders crisis. According to historian Nick Bryant in his book *The Bystander*, these accommodations encouraged Barnett and others to think that they could continue to flout federal civil rights laws as long as they kept the peace, a belief that would set the tone for Barnett's negotiations with the Kennedy administration over James Meredith's entry into Ole Miss.

While the Freedom Riders faced the gauntlet of southern resistance and tested the commitment of the Kennedys to their own civil rights rhetoric, an African American air force veteran named James Meredith was battling this same intransigence through the courts in his quest to attend the University of Mississippi. After listening to John Kennedy's inaugural address, Meredith had applied in 1961 to attend the University of Mississippi, the state's oldest institution of higher learning. An enigmatic, single-minded man, Meredith, who firmly believed he was on a mission from God, was deeply committed to taking his rightful place as a full citizen of Mississippi at the state's best school. The university, located in Oxford, about seventy-five miles south of Memphis, commonly goes by the nickname "Ole Miss," a reference to the name slaves and family members had often called the matriarch on southern plantations.

Although he respected the civil rights leader, Meredith wrote in 2012 that he fundamentally disagreed with Martin Luther King Jr.'s tactic of nonviolence.

"I had been a soldier all of my adult life," Meredith wrote. "Soldiers are the keepers and users of organized violence, legally applied." This belief shaped his strategy. It is often reported that Meredith was inspired by the new president's address, but in his 2012 memoir, Meredith argued that he was under no delusions about John F. Kennedy. "I knew that so far in his career JFK had done virtually nothing to help the cause of black Americans. Like the vast majority of Americans, he was a segregationist collaborator, and a millionaire power politician who I knew had to be forced to do the right thing," Cold War politics also meant that the United States' treatment of black citizens began to be damaging to the nation's image abroad, especially in countries where the United States and the Soviet Union were competing for the allegiance of nations made up of people of color. Furthermore, as Meredith calculated, John Kennedy had just squeaked to victory in a tight race, in part because of the support of black voters. To Meredith, this meant that the president was "on the spot and would be forced to act if put under pressure."

After more than a year of legal battles, the final word came down. Justice Hugo Black of the US Supreme Court ruled that Meredith must be admitted to Ole Miss for the 1962 fall term.

"The ruling was supported by the Justice Department," Nick Bryant writes in his book *The Bystander*, "which had joined the case as a friend of the court . . . primarily so it could serve as an interlocutor between the courts and state authorities and exercise a certain measure of control over unfolding events." However, pragmatic politicians that they were, neither the president nor his brother were interested in picking a fight with an unpredictable, entrenched southern governor such as Barnett. Kennedy certainly spoke with Eastland behind the scenes about the issue, but this time, Barnett, with the full backing of the White Citizen's Council, was vocal about taking the lead.

As Meredith's case made its way through the courts, Kennedy's Department of Justice kept an eye on it. Victory looked tantalizingly close when the US Court of Appeals for the Fifth Circuit ruled that the university must admit Meredith. However, one member of the Fifth Circuit, Judge Benjamin Cameron, a Mississippi native who opposed desegregation and believed strongly that the Constitution left the power to decide most issues to the states, issued several stays of the court's decision in favor of Meredith.

At that point, the Department of Justice joined Meredith, arguing that Cameron's stays were "lawless." The Justice Department's support of Meredith enraged state officials, and, as historian Charles Eagles notes in *The Price of Defiance*, they began to focus their ire on the Kennedys personally. State attorney general Joseph T. Patterson told the Jackson newspaper that "Robert Kennedy criticizing a judge of Judge Cameron's stature is like a jackass looking up into the sky and braying at the great American eagle as it soars above" and complained that "the House of Kennedy" was being manipulated by pressure from the NAACP and other civil rights groups.

Despite the fiery rhetoric coming out of Mississippi, Robert Kennedy hoped that Meredith's entrance to Ole Miss could be handled diplomatically and smoothly. Kennedy negotiated with Barnett in a series of secret telephone calls (which were recorded) over the next two weeks in an effort to defuse the situation, but Barnett continued to equivocate.

Kennedy and the president alternated between communicating a firm position that the executive branch would enforce the court's ruling and searching for ways to accommodate Barnett's political considerations. At one point during the back-and-forth calls with Barnett, Kennedy observed to Arthur Schlesinger that he "regarded Gov. Barnett as 'a genuine loony.'"

Barnett and Kennedy were at fundamentally cross-purposes, as Kennedy later acknowledged in an oral history after his brother's death. The Kennedys wanted to uphold the court's order without sending in federal troops. Barnett, he said, wanted to avoid integration, but if he couldn't avoid it, he only wanted to submit at the end of a bayonet, so to speak. However, in his conversations with Barnett, Kennedy made it increasingly clear that he believed that the federal courts had long established their supremacy over state law.

Robert Kennedy emphasized that he needed Barnett's cooperation to avoid violence and keep Meredith safe. Kennedy repeatedly tried to persuade a vacillating Barnett to compromise and find a way to save face, even considering for a moment the governor's cartoonish suggestion that all of the federal marshals draw their guns and aim at his head before he would stand aside and allow Meredith to enroll, even though Kennedy thought it was foolish and dangerous. Aide John Seigenthaler recalled, "He laughed about Barnett at that time. He had thought from the outset that the whole thing was ludicrous—that whole concept of putting on a show." But with the example of the violent resistance to the Freedom Riders still in recent memory, Kennedy also knew Barnett's idea was dangerous and held firm against it.

After several aborted plans to enroll Meredith, Kennedy and Barnett finally agreed to have federal marshals move Meredith onto the campus on a Sunday evening in preparation for enrollment the next morning. But Kennedy miscalculated. The atmosphere in the state was highly combustible. Local radio stations played "Dixie" again and again, and newspapers urged readers to take a stand against federal intervention. Barnett himself had stood before a crowd of fifty thousand howling, maniacal Confederate-flag-waving supporters at an Ole Miss football game the night before in Jackson. He pledged his love for Mississippi, her people, and their "customs" and was bathed in wave after wave of approbation. At the tops of their voices, tens of thousands of his constituents sang a song especially written for the occasion: "Never, never, never, never," went the first line. A later line singled out Kennedy: "Ross is standing like Gibralter, he shall never falter. Ask us what we say, it's to hell with Bobby K."

But not all Mississippians were ready to fight the second round of the Civil War. Mississippi native and journalist Curtis Wilkie was a senior at Ole Miss in the fall of 1962 and in the football stands that night, as was Barnett. Wilkie told a journalist soon after that it was "like a big Nazi rally. . . . It was just the way Nuremberg must have been."

Wilke later recalled the unforgettable scene that night in his memoir:

As the thousands howled, Barnett lifted his arms in triumph. It was an incredible instant. Even as a dubious spectator, I could feel flesh curdling on my arms. I harbored strong misgivings about the governor; I thought he was an idiot. I did not wave a flag and I did not cheer. But I would not have traded my seat for a million dollars. I knew I was witnessing the final convulsions of the Civil War. All the crowd lacked were pitchforks and rifles. That would come the next night.

With talk of insurrection in the air throughout the state, Wilkie's mother wrote to him from south Mississippi: "Son: Your great-grandfather Gilmer set out to fight the federals from Ole Miss with the University Greys, called the Lamar Rifles, nearly a hundred years ago. He didn't accomplish a thing. See that you don't get involved!!!!"

On Sunday, September 30, 1962, four hundred helmeted federal marshals and a team from the Department of Justice brought Meredith to campus and set up a perimeter around the Lyceum, the school's administration building. The Lyceum was a slave-built red brick building with white columns at the symbolic heart of the campus, and the whipped-up segregationists immediately perceived this move to be a provocation. As night began to fall, contrary to Barnett's deal with the Kennedys, the state's highway patrol left their posts and hundreds of men, many of them armed, flooded to the campus, joining the students who had been heckling the marshals all afternoon.

About twenty-four hours after Barnett's performance in the stadium in Jackson, President Kennedy announced on a national television broadcast that Meredith had peacefully enrolled. However, as he spoke of peace, rocks, Molotov cocktails, and bullets rained down on the marshals guarding the campus administration building in Oxford. John Kennedy first federalized the local national guard unit. Then thousands of army troops arrived at the tiny Oxford airport to restore order on campus and ensure Meredith could safely attend classes. However, there was a delay of about five hours in which the marshals were under siege in the Lyceum while the Kennedys fretted in the White House before the army arrived. As the riot intensified, two people were killed, and dozens were injured.

◆ ◆ ◆

Robert Kennedy later acknowledged that much of the ultimate responsibility for the operation's mistakes ending in deadly violence rested with him, though he also faulted the army for its inept delays. However, Kennedy voiced his dismay with characteristically dark humor. As the administration faced the Cuban Missile Crisis about two weeks later, when he heard that the Russians had missiles in Cuba, he deadpanned, "Can they hit Oxford, Mississippi?" He knew, however, the mistakes at Ole Miss put his brother in a difficult position as well, "torn between an Attorney General who had botched things up and the fact that the Attorney General was his brother," Kennedy later said. At this point, few Mississippians knew about Barnett's secret negotiations with the brothers. After a seven-month investigation, a state legislative committee placed almost all of the blame on the Kennedys, portraying them as power-hungry provocateurs, and presented Barnett and other state officials as essentially blameless.

To Barnett and his supporters, integrating Ole Miss meant much more than just allowing a black citizen to attend a state university. It struck at the very heart of an elaborately constructed delusion. Most white Mississippians believed they could continue to build a society that excluded and oppressed a large portion of their fellow citizens, while America, as it had for decades since it gave up on Reconstruction, would look the other way. Meredith understood this as well. Historian Charles Eagles writes that Meredith was determined to challenge white supremacy and was convinced that "only by breaking 'the monopoly on rights and privileges held' by whites could he and other blacks achieve their potential. To challenge the control of powerful Mississippi whites, he could have selected no better initial, *tactical* target than the university in Oxford."

In scathing editorials, newspapers across the state singled out Robert Kennedy and the president as the scapegoats for the debacle. One of the state's congressmen, John Bell Williams, compared the Kennedy brothers' actions at Ole Miss to "the dastardly acts of Adolph Hitler and his infamous Gestapo" and singled out the attorney general, saying, "The bestiality, cruelty, and savagery of Justice Department employees under the direction of Robert Kennedy . . . were acts beyond the comprehension of normal minds."

Although civil rights leaders had criticized him for doing too little too slowly, Robert Kennedy's direction of the operation that finally registered Meredith meant that Kennedy bore much of the public criticism and approbation in Mississippi too. In fact, many white Mississippians believed that Kennedy and the president had put Meredith up to applying for admission. When Barnett and his supporters floated the idea of closing the university rather than integrate, a former lieutenant governor argued that closing the university would "mean a triumphant victory for the NAACP and the Kennedy boys." State newspapers singled out the Kennedys, even more so than the judges in the case, as they cast blame. State legislators railed against them; bumper stickers that read "From Occupied Mississippi," and slogans like "We're Backing Ross—Beat Lil' Brother—The South Will Rise Again," flanked by Confederate flags, attacked them. Disliked before, the Kennedy brothers had quickly become anathema to Mississippi's white establishment.

Robert Kennedy himself recognized that he had not been able to insulate his brother from the anger felt by segregationists over his work as attorney general. He later said that part of his hesitation to take the attorney general's position had been based on its potential to damage his brother's political prospects, especially if he took a tough stance on civil rights issues. "I don't know if we foresaw or anticipated the great number of problems, but that was a factor we had discussed, which I felt very strongly about," he said. Kennedy knew he was going to be immersed in the Justice Department's civil rights work.

"So much needed to be done that it could only create tremendous political difficulties and problems for him—not only in the '64 election but in attempting to obtain the passage of legislation in other fields," he said in his oral history with journalist Anthony Lewis after JFK's death. "By '63, in my judgment, the fact that I was Attorney General caused him many more problems than if I hadn't been his brother." This was especially true in the South. "Yes, in fact, as we said, instead of talking about Robert Kennedy, they started talking about the "Kennedy brothers"—which he used to point out to me frequently."

The animosity in Mississippi and other parts of the South continued through the assassinations of both men. However, it was one of the first assassinations of the civil rights era that brought Robert Kennedy face to face with the devastating personal consequences of Mississippi's intransigence on issues of race. In June 1963, President Kennedy spoke in passionate moral terms to the nation with a televised address about his proposed civil rights bills. Later that night, a fertilizer salesman from Greenwood, Mississippi, shot the NAACP field secretary for Mississippi, Medgar Evers, in the back a few steps from his front door.

The shooting of Evers, whom Robert Kennedy had come to know during the Ole Miss crisis, was a dark day in the Kennedy home. Robert Kennedy Jr.

said, "I remember the day that Medgar Evers was killed and how it affected my mother and father at home. It was almost as if a member of our own family had been killed."

Horrified by the brutality of the shooting, Robert Kennedy helped arrange for Evers to be buried in Arlington National Cemetery and escorted Evers's widow and young children to the White House. He also gave Evers's brother, Charles, his personal telephone number, urging him to call day or night. The two men grew close. It was "that shared tragedy, that shared sense of darkness and hope," Robert Kennedy Jr. said, that created a bond that lasted the rest of his father's life. Two years after Medgar Evers's death, Charles Evers's impassioned support won Robert Kennedy an endorsement from the NAACP at a crucial moment in his campaign for the Senate in New York.

By November 1963, it was Robert Kennedy's turn to mourn his brother's assassination. In the shattering aftermath of John Kennedy's death, Robert Kennedy turned introspective, a time that John Seigenthaler called his "black period." Kennedy mourned in private, but any onlooker could see his brother's loss had taken a devastating toll. Friends and family reported that he seemed lost, falling silent and losing focus during meetings. He dropped weight and looked haggard. He wore his slain brother's jacket, which dwarfed him. Though he comforted his family and drew comfort from his dearly held Catholic traditions, John's shocking death shook Robert Kennedy's faith. His elegant, well-read companion in grief, Jacqueline Kennedy, shared poems and literature from the ancient Greeks, Shakespeare, and the Old Testament that reflected the exquisite darkness and light of the universal human experience.

Robert's daughter Kathleen remembered him during this time as withdrawn, reading in his room. But it was this time of grief that helped him connect with the suffering of others, according to Townsend. "I think he tried to really feel the pain. He said, 'I'm going to dwell in the pain, and I'm going to understand that something terrible has happened.' . . . Oftentimes, people in the public life don't go deep into pain, and he was willing to do it," she said.

Although Kennedy's grief burned intensely, it did not consume him. He had lost his brother and, in the process, much of the power he had wielded. Another loss pressed in on him during this time. Not long before Jack died, their father had suffered a devastating, silencing stroke. He could no longer try to dictate the direction of his son's life. Slowly Robert Kennedy emerged out of the shadow of his grief, and eventually found, in the process, his way out of his brother's shadow and his father's influence.

◆ ◆ ◆

In Mississippi, the assassination of John Kennedy had prompted cheers and open celebration in some quarters. In contrast, many of the state's African Americans grieved in private and quietly hung the slain president's portrait next to those of Jesus and Martin Luther King on their walls. Yes, as civil rights activists across the nation knew, John Kennedy and his brother had been slow to act on civil rights, had yielded too often to political calculations, and preferred gradual progress to the fundamental change that was so badly needed. However, in the eyes of many of Mississippi's black residents, John Kennedy had used the full force of the US Army to make sure one black man could enroll at the state's flagship university.

The Kennedys believed in civil rights, at least in the abstract, even if they were disappointingly cautious. Mae Bertha Carter, a woman from Sunflower County in the Delta whom Marian Wright represented in a desegregation lawsuit, writes to civil rights activist and author Constance Curry of her admiration of John Kennedy after his death: "I knew when he was campaigning to be president, that he was concerned about white people and black people and all races of people. . . . So I always thought he was the best president for the country and the best one I ever lived under." Mississippi's African American population also knew that some of the same people who cursed them and called them "nigger" when they tried to register to vote had rejoiced when the bullets ripped through Kennedy's skull. And that was enough for them to feel his murder as a grievous loss.

In the months between the riots at Ole Miss and the president's death, Robert Kennedy had grown bolder in his pursuit of civil rights issues. His Justice Department had initiated voting rights suits in Mississippi and other southern states, including one in Eastland's home county of Sunflower. Robert Kennedy had also begun pushing his brother for voting rights legislation.

However, by the end of the year, John Kennedy was dead, and Robert Kennedy had agreed reluctantly to stay on as attorney general in the fledgling Johnson administration, despite his visceral dislike for Lyndon Johnson. Kennedy, protective of his brother's legacy to the last, had remained, in part, to support ongoing efforts to pass his brother's civil rights legislation.

In July 1964, Johnson succeeded where the Kennedys had not and signed the bill into law as Robert Kennedy sat watching, glum and distracted. Supporters in the Senate had finally found a way to bypass Eastland's Judiciary Committee through some shrewd political maneuvering. Segregationist lawmakers, however, did not go down without a fight. Eighteen senators filibustered the bill for fifty-four days. The nation had a new civil rights law that prohibited discrimination in employment, education, and public facilities based on race, color, religion, sex, or national origin, but attempts to secure those rights still came with a deadly price in Mississippi, as Kennedy soon learned.

In the spring and early summer of 1964, while Johnson was doing the hard work of twisting arms in the Senate as Robert Kennedy lent his support, Martin Luther King Jr. and other civil rights leaders kept the nation's attention focused on the injustice and oppression that were still the way of life in the South. Several key civil rights groups began to prepare volunteers—many of them college students, both white and black—for the "Mississippi Summer Project."

The plan was to dispatch hundreds of the young civil rights workers and volunteers to the state to teach civics and black history to children and adults in "Freedom Schools" and, more critically, to register African Americans to vote. White Mississippians recoiled at the idea that "outside agitators" were invading their state and reacted violently. During the hot days of that Mississippi summer, the workers were under constant threat. But near the end of June, that threat became an ominous reality. Three civil rights workers—James Chaney, Andrew Goodman, and Mickey Schwerner—disappeared in Neshoba County, near Merdian, Mississippi. Fellow volunteers, their leaders, and their families grew more worried and made frantic, futile calls to the FBI offices in the region. But, as had happened before, their appeals for help to federal officials in Robert Kennedy's Justice Department went unheeded.

As pressure mounted throughout the day after their disappearance, Robert Kennedy directed the FBI to investigate, eventually ordering more than 150 federal marshals to the area. In the days following, Kennedy met with parents of two of the workers and continued to monitor the situation, but remained largely out of the public eye on the case. According to Schlesinger, he did make one crucial decision to recommend to President Johnson that the FBI use infiltration techniques perfected in its investigations of Communism. Johnson agreed and ordered FBI director J. Edgar Hoover, who was no supporter of civil rights and often looked for ways to undermine the movement, to transfer investigations of the Ku Klux Klan to a program that went beyond investigating such organizations to disrupting and destroying them.

The three civil rights workers' disappearance caused a national outcry, which only built as Johnson pressed forward for the passage of the 1964 Civil Rights Act. Congress finally approved it on July 2. Mississippi officials, however, reacted to the disappearances with staunch denial and claimed that the disappearance of the men was a stunt designed to make the state look bad. However, acting on a tip from a paid informant, federal law enforcement officials searched a rural earthen dam. After days of searching with navy divers, they ultimately found the bodies of Chaney, Goodman, and Schwerner on

August 4. During the search, divers also found the bodies of two other men with no connection to the civil rights workers.

Despite the denial of Mississippi officials, followed by the legitimately shocked and horrified reaction of many white Mississippians, the murders of the three civil rights workers were, at their heart, crimes of the establishment. They were the logical extension of the inflammatory, dehumanizing, fear-mongering rhetoric and policies that had permeated the state's political discourse for decades. Urged on by leaders of the Ku Klux Klan, at least twenty-one men conspired to murder Schwerner, Goodman, and Chaney, including the Neshoba County sheriff, deputies, and local police officers. The night of the murders, as the bleeding bodies of the young men cooled under the Mississippi mud, one of those deputies, Cecil Price, praised his fellow killers for their work.

He said, "Well, boys, you've done a good job. You've struck a blow for the white man. Mississippi can be proud of you. You've let those agitating outsiders know where this state stands. Go home now and forget it. But before you go, I'm looking each one of you in the eye and telling you this: 'The first man who talks is dead!'"

There was every reason for these men to believe not only that they would get away with murder, but also that friends, family, and neighbors would commend them for their effort. The other bodies found in the search for the three men missing in 1964 bore witness to a tragic truth: this had happened before in Mississippi, hundreds of times, in fact. Between 1882 and 1964, 581 people had died at the hands of their fellow citizens in the Magnolia State. All but 42 of the victims were African Americans.

The 1964 killings in Neshoba County happened under cover of night, but many of the lynchings (defined as extrajudicial killings regardless of method) in Mississippi's history had been public affairs. The brutality of the victims' deaths often went beyond hanging to include the kind of mutilation, torment, burning at the stake, and public display that would be instantly familiar to any medieval executioner or inquisitor. However, rarely did the state of Mississippi or even the United States government hold anyone accountable in these murders.

The pursuit of justice in the deaths of Goodman, Schwerner, and Chaney met with the usual obstacles at the state level and one surprising stumbling block, a direct result of the political deal Robert Kennedy and his brother had made with Eastland during their first days in the White House. Although the FBI initially identified and arrested twenty-one men involved with the crime, local prosecutors declined to prosecute them for murder under state law. The Justice Department charged eighteen of them, including the sheriff and Cecil Price, with conspiring to violate the civil rights of the three victims, a federal crime.

The federal judge in the case, however, was W. Harold Cox, the first judiciary appointment John F. Kennedy ever made, and a prime example of the kind of deals the Kennedys were willing to make during the early days of JFK's administration, actions that deeply disappointed civil rights leaders such as Martin Luther King. Cox had proven himself a staunch segregationist in the years since that appointment, a worldview Robert Kennedy said he did not reveal during a private interview between the two men before his appointment.

Cox was born in Indianola, a town deep in the Delta. Although a few years older, he had known another Sunflower County native, Mississippi senator James Eastland, since they were children. In fact, the two had even roomed together in law school at Ole Miss. Eastland had been campaigning for years to get his friend an appointment to the federal bench, but the Eisenhower administration had significant reservations about Cox's views on race. However, the fledgling Kennedy administration had more than seventy judgeships to fill, and Eastland, as chairman of the Judiciary Committee, manned the gateway to Senate approval for Kennedy's other appointees.

The Kennedys knew that Eastland expected the traditional senatorial courtesy of approving the appointees for his state. Moreover, Cox was one of the few judges in Mississippi who had not joined the Citizen's Council and had an excellent rating by the American Bar Association. Robert Kennedy still had doubts, but he allowed Cox to assuage them when they met in Kennedy's office in Washington. In 1961, the young attorney general was sure that Cox had been honest with him. However, as he looked back at that conversation years later, Kennedy was blunt in his assessment of Cox's honesty. "He wasn't," he said.

Cox quickly became an embarrassment to the Kennedys. He called African Americans appearing before him in court "chimpanzees" and went on to decide for segregationists in a string of cases, just to have them all reversed on appeal.

In the 1964 slayings in Philadelphia, Cox at first dismissed all but three of the indictments. However, the US Supreme Court subsequently overturned his ruling. Cox went on to allow the defense to strike all potential African American jurors, but he denied a challenge to a white juror who admitted to having once been a member of the Ku Klux Klan. Eventually the jury convicted only seven of the men, and none of them served more than six years in prison. When one of the jurors balked at convicting a pastor, the reputed mastermind of the plot, Klan leader Edgar Ray Killen, walked free until finally convicted in 2005.

The end of the summer of 1964 brought a change for Robert Kennedy. With the civil rights bill finally through Congress and the bodies of the civil rights workers recovered, Kennedy resigned as attorney general to begin his run for the Senate in New York against Republican incumbent senator Kenneth Keating. However, his victory was by no means certain, and it was a Mississippian whose intervention at a crucial moment in the campaign helped swing the election his way.

Charles Evers and Kennedy had grown close over the years. The day after the assassination of Medgar Evers in June 1963, Robert Kennedy had called Charles. "Bobby said he and the president felt terrible about Medgar's murder, and he would personally run the murder investigation," Evers writes. Robert Kennedy pushed for Medgar Evers, an army veteran who fought in the Battle of Normandy, to be buried in Arlington National Cemetery, "where America buries its biggest soldiers and heroes." At the graveside service, Robert Kennedy represented the president, who chose not to attend, but instead met with the Evers family at the White House.

"All through the service, Bobby Kennedy stayed right with me," Charles Evers recalled in his memoir. "I'll never forget how hard he tried to console me. I needed every bit of Bobby's help to keep from going crazy with the pain. He could have just come to the funeral, given his sympathies to Myrlie [Medgar Evers's widow] and left. Men less important than Bobby would have done just that. But Bobby wasn't built like that."

After meeting with President Kennedy at the White House, Evers wrote that he concluded that the president "had been raised to think the Southern white man was a rascal on race but had Negro welfare at heart. Now Kennedy was seeing the other side of the white Southerner—the cold killer. And it shook him up." As the Evers family left the White House, John Kennedy observed to them, "[Y]ou know, they'd kill me, too, if they could."

Robert Kennedy continued to reach out to Evers. "Bobby Kennedy not only urged me to call, day or night—*he called me.* That was the difference between Bobby Kennedy and John: John told me to call when I needed him; Bobby didn't wait," Evers recalled. According to Evers, Robert Kennedy called him at least once a week for months after Medgar Evers's death and would take his call at any time, "sunrise or deep in the night, whenever I had the need," he says.

Five months later, Evers would rush to Washington to be near Robert Kennedy when the president was assassinated. "Our strongest link" he wrote, "was having our favorite brother gunned down by the haters. . . . Losing our brothers to murder, the same year, for the same reason brought us so close. Both of us thought a lot about death."

When Kennedy decided to run for the Senate seat in New York, in the fall of 1964, he faced criticism on several fronts. His opponent, first-term incumbent senator Kenneth Keating was a moderate Republican who had a good relationship with the state NAACP. The race was close.

Charles Evers took time off from his work with the Mississippi NAACP to campaign for Kennedy in New York. In his memoir, Evers later wrote that the national NAACP's executive director, Roy Wilkins, told him to support Keating, but Evers responded, "I don't give a damn what Keating's' done. Bobby's my man." As the race tightened, Evers wrote a column supporting Kennedy in the *New York Post* and spoke on his behalf at the state meeting in Buffalo, New York, even though it angered NAACP officials.

"You're lucky to have a man of Bobby Kennedy's caliber running for senator. Bobby's one of the few whites in power who cares about you, and if we in Mississippi were lucky enough to have Bob Kennedy running for *dogcatcher*, he'd get out every Negro vote in the state," Evers reports telling the crowd. He went on, "Bobby Kennedy means more to us in Mississippi than any other white man I know. I want every Negro who believes in me to vote Bobby Kennedy for Senator." After Evers's speech, the NAACP did not vote to endorse Keating, and after a close race but a successful campaign, Kennedy took his place in the Senate.

Robert Kennedy appealed to young people across the nation. In 1965, the new senator received an unexpected invitation from law school students at Ole Miss. Kennedy made plans to travel to Oxford in March 1966, but not without much hesitation and deliberation. Even though he was now the senator from New York and no longer attorney general, there was still plenty of animosity toward him in Mississippi. He talked with Seigenthaler and requested a report from the FBI about safety.

After Robert Kennedy's death, his aide Peter Edelman recalled in an oral history the deliberations about accepting the invitation. Kennedy asked Edelman to talk with H. M. Ray, who was the US attorney for the northern district of Mississippi, which included Oxford. Edelman also had several conversations with Joshua Morse, who was the dean of the Law School at the University of Mississippi. Kennedy's aide talked to others who knew the state well, such as Aaron Henry and John Kennedy's old friend Frank E. Smith, a former congressman from Mississippi.

"It was like many things; we went back and forth over what seemed like an excruciatingly long time, having the same conversation and not finishing it," Edelman recalled. He said that Kennedy would want to know what people in the state said about him: "Am I just going to be booed? Is there anything I can say? Is there anything that we'd be able to . . . Will there be any common

Robert Kennedy was surprised at the warmth of his reception in Oxford in 1966. Credit: The Ed Meek/Meek School of Journalism and New Media Collection, Department of Archives & Special Collections, University of Mississippi.

ground at all?" Edelman could only say, "I think it's okay, they think it's okay, but obviously no one can give assurances."

But Kennedy was still skeptical. "He would profess some disbelief about that, profess some uncertainty because no one could promise that the whole thing would go off well," Edelman said. Kennedy also asked for an FBI report on safety.

Still undecided, Kennedy turned to his closest southern friend, John Seigenthaler, who was by then the editor of the *Nashville Tennessean*. Kennedy, Seigenthaler said, was trying to "lay the groundwork for what he thought might have been a hostile environment." The students had assured Kennedy that they really wanted him, but Kennedy told Seigenthaler, "[W]ell, you know, they are not going to like what I say."

Once he accepted the invitation, Kennedy and his aides, including Adam Walinsky, wrestled with the speech, but Kennedy still wasn't satisfied. So, on a trip to New York, Kennedy and Edelman took the draft to the Fifth Avenue Hotel Pierre to meet with Kennedy's friend Richard Goodwin, who had written speeches and worked in John Kennedy's and Lyndon Johnson's administrations. Goodwin and another friend and occasional speechwriter, Arthur Schlesinger, were having lunch with Jacqueline Kennedy. Over the meal, they all went over the draft of the speech, with several of them contributing ideas.

If the proposed speech caused Kennedy to fret, in Mississippi, the idea triggered an uproar. The Ku Klux Klan threatened to march in protest, university alumni wrote scathing letters, and newspaper editorials railed about the visit. Younger white Mississippians may have been open to hearing from Kennedy, but their elders, who still controlled the state's levers of power, clearly were not.

The university's chancellor and the state's board of trustees of the Institution of Higher Learning pressured Morse, a young, Yale-educated Mississippi native, to withdraw the invitation. Morse refused because, as he said, the invitation had come from the law students themselves. "I said, now, you've got the power to withdraw it if you want to withdraw it, so you go ahead," he recalled. The trustees let the invitation stand.

The invitation scandalized many Mississippians and university alumni. One legislator said Kennedy's visit was like "a murderer returning to the scene of his crime." Objections poured into Chancellor J. D. Williams's and Morse's offices. Some writers worried about the effect the invitation would have on delicate negotiations over appropriations in the legislature.

Other correspondents got right to the point. "Who invited this Carpetbagger de luxe?" asked a woman from Bolivar, Tennessee, in a letter to the chancellor. "How can you call yourself a true Mississippian and Southerner and still let this happen?" wrote another. A couple from Baton Rouge worried that this invitation would give Kennedy a "sense of acceptance in the state which he surely does not have."

Others sought to defend the students' minds from Kennedy's rhetoric. "As a 72-year-old World War I veteran and grandson of a civil war veteran of Shiloh, Missionary Ridge, and Atlanta, I insist you do everything possible to keep Robert Kennedy and his kind away from the young people of our beloved Southland."

If law students were truly responsible for inviting him, "They could not possibly understand the anguish of a mother of a 'coed' at the University during the invasion of Oxford," wrote Mrs. Vera W. Pierce of Vicksburg. Southerners weren't the only ones upset. A conservative woman from California put it simply. "What is wrong with you people down there?" she asked.

In a more ominous development, the *Klan Ledger*, which billed itself as an official publication of the White Knights of the Ku Klux Klan of Mississippi, took note of Kennedy's scheduled appearance, calling him "an apostle of the evil science of Bolshevism" and "a monster." It went on to say that "every individual or group who recognizes him and permits themselves to give him respectful audience will be paying tribute to the institution of lies, deceit, treachery and dictatorship which he represents. In short, they will be worshipping the institutions of Satan." Another flyer asked students to wear some item of red in silent protest of his visit. A white supremacist group threatened a "ride in," which was later canceled.

In the spring of 1966, Kennedy and his wife, Ethel, flew to Mississippi for a speech at the invitation of University of Mississippi law students. With an eye to the potential for violence, school officials had planned the Kennedys' arrival and movements with great care, according to Dean Joshua Morse. Morse was to ride with the Kennedys from the airport. "We drove our cars right up under the wing of the airplane where we could load people—we were afraid somebody was going to shoot at them," he said.

The arrival was going as planned until, as Robert and Ethel Kennedy were stepping into the car, the crowd of hundreds that had gathered near the runway began to applaud. "And Kennedy says, 'Come on, let's go!'" Morse recalled. "And they headed right out in the middle of that crowd . . . right where we had been trying to keep them away from, right in the middle, just grabbing hands. They had a big time for about 30 minutes."

The crowds were so large, the university had to move his speech from the campus chapel to the new basketball coliseum. Morse and other officials had planned for the car to drive into a loading area where they could disembark in safety. When the Kennedys finally broke away from the crowd at the airport and started to drive down the ramp toward the coliseum, Kennedy objected, the dean recalled in 2007.

"Whoa! Whoa! What, what is this? Dean, what's this! Where are we?' Kennedy said to Morse.

"We're going under here to unload," Morse said he told Kennedy.

"No, no we're not. We're getting out right here," Kennedy responded.

As Robert and Ethel Kennedy walked into the coliseum, the crowd spotted them. "That's when the, the big applause, *thunderous* applause broke out," according to Morse.

◆ ◆ ◆

Acknowledging the circumstances of his visit in his opening remarks, Kennedy amused the crowd of about six thousand by saying that although some people had likened his visit to "putting a fox in the chicken house. Some of my friends feel it is more like putting a chicken in a fox house." In his speech, Kennedy also commented on the many changes in the South over the decades since the 1930s and emphasized to the Ole Miss students the importance of national unity and shared burdens. "You have no problem the nation does not bear. You share no hope that is not shared by your fellow students and young people across this country. You carry no burden that they too do not carry," he said. He then challenged the students to look toward the future and work to solve local, national, and global problems. "This is the reality of the new South. . . . Your generation is the first with the chance not only to remedy the mistakes which all of us have made in the past, but to transcend them."

He went on: "Your generation—this generation—cannot afford to waste its substance and its hope in the struggles of the past, when beyond these walls is a world to be helped, and improved, and made safe for the welfare of mankind." he said. When he was done, the students gave him a sustained standing ovation.

Although his speech was well received, his comments during the question-and-answer period that followed became the big news. Responding to a question in the crowd about a few national news reports regarding behind-the-scenes negotiations with by-then-former governor Ross Barnett during the Meredith crisis, Kennedy had the crowd cheering. With wry candor, he described Barnett's wavering and cartoonish suggestions, and the crowd laughed uproariously.

However, there was at least one person who was not amused by Kennedy's revelations about the behind-the-scenes negotiations regarding the integration of the university in 1962. Kennedy's remarks horrified Barnett, who planned on running again for governor in 1967. He immediately and vehemently denied making any deals with the Kennedys and tried once again to blame them for the disaster at Ole Miss.

Kennedy was surprised and gratified by the cordial reception the students and faculty in Oxford gave him in 1966. "An interesting state," he told Mississippi native Willie Morris, the young editor of *Harper's Magazine*, as he recounted his visit with a chuckle upon their meeting in New York. At the time, Morris was surprised by Kennedy's shy manner and struck by the senator's "private half-disguised vulnerability." Morris also noted Kennedy's sly humor. Around the same time, when James Meredith, who was now in graduate school at Columbia University, arrived at a party Morris and Kennedy were attending, Kennedy stood up to shake Meredith's hand and said, "[I]ntegrated any schools lately, Jim?"

In any event, Kennedy returned to the capitol from Oxford, his biographer Schlesinger writes, convinced that the next battle for racial justice lay in the northern cities. Voting rights and integrating public accommodations in the South were "an easy job compared to what we face in the North," he recounts Kennedy as saying.

◆ ◆ ◆

Through Robert Kennedy's involvement with Mississippians, both white and black, during these conflicts, he had grown from a campaign manager inclined toward political calculation to a leader whose great personal loss had left him with a deepening commitment to civil rights and social justice. Each of these events taught Kennedy a great deal about the painful realities and injustices of the South's Jim Crow laws and the courage and dignity of the many black and a few white Mississippians struggling for civil rights.

The threats, shootings, and riot had shown him that the "southern way of life" was much more than just an objectionable regional custom and tangled political knot. Instead, as Kennedy had come to realize, a radical violence lay at the heart of the South's philosophy of white supremacy. In the coming days, he would see that the policies that sprang from this philosophy also had a much quieter but no less devastating impact on poor families and children.

Once his plane landed in Jackson for the subcommittee's hearing in Jackson on April 9, Kennedy shook a few hands as he made his way through the airport, past a sign that said, "Welcome to Jackson: Crossroads of the South" and, to the relief of law enforcement and his entourage, passed by the Klan picketers without incident or comment. At the hearing the next morning, he would face a familiar Mississippi leader who, though he approached the issue in a more civilized fashion than the Klan, was no less committed to the maintenance of the white-dominated political and social order as the protestors at the airport.

Marion Wright rebutted criticism of War on Poverty programs and pleaded with the senators to help the people of the Delta at the hearing in Jackson. Credit: Jim Lucas Estate.

Chapter 4

They Are Starving

S enator John Stennis of Mississippi was not happy. As the opening witness in the hearings before the Senate Subcommittee on Employment, Manpower, and Poverty at Jackson's Hotel Heidelberg, he had crafted a carefully planned attack. By offering proof that one of the central War on Poverty programs at work in Mississippi—Head Start—was wasteful and mismanaged, he would discredit the testimony of the community advocates on the witness list later in the day, framing them as money-hungry and radical.

But Robert Kennedy had a plan and some proof of his own, and, when he produced it, he caught Stennis off guard and left him casting about for a way to save face. After Kennedy's public refutation, Stennis' attack, instead of undermining the advocates for Mississippi's poor on the witness list, served as a stark demonstration of Mississippi officials' desire to hold onto power and underlined their cold indifference to the suffering of the state's poorest residents.

The stakes for Stennis were high. Although many of the nearly one thousand people in the audience were African Americans, there was still a portion of the crowd in the Olympic Ballroom who had come to see him discredit the federal poverty programs and their supporters. National television reporters were there, and a local television station, which reached thousands of his constituents, filmed the hearing. It was also live on radio in the barbershops, kitchens, and automobiles of voters across central Mississippi.

In the days leading up to the hearing, Jackson's two newspapers—perennially staunch opponents of civil rights "interference" by the federal government and almost any social program—had run front-page stories highlighting

Stennis's planned attack on the parent agency of Head Start in Mississippi. However, when they arrived in Jackson, Kennedy and the subcommittee's chairman, Senator Joseph Clark of Pennsylvania, had announced that they considered the Head Start funding controversy a closed issue and would not devote time to rehashing it. In response, Stennis promptly leaked his prepared statement for the committee. The *Clarion Ledger* ran it the next morning at the top of the front page under the headline "Stennis Renews Attack on Activities of CDGM."

Stennis and other Mississippi officials had been sharply critical of Head Start, and especially its operating agency, the Child Development Group of Mississippi (CDGM), since it had opened its doors in 1965. A key element of the War on Poverty programs, the creation of Project Head Start was prompted by emerging research on the vital importance of early childhood education. It aimed to help poor children overcome the disadvantages in their environment and prepare them to start school by offering an enriching environment, medical treatment, education, and training for their parents. In keeping with the War on Poverty's goal of offering the poor a say in the programs meant to help them, Head Start was funded with grants to community groups, a method that bypassed the traditional path of federal money through state and local authorities.

And this is exactly what upset Stennis and his allies in Mississippi the most. When the program was announced, Mississippi's governor had staunchly rejected the idea that his state would seek funds to educate its low-income preschoolers, even though at the time Mississippi had no publicly funded kindergartens or preschools for any children. Southern power brokers were not alone in their distrust of new federal programs and money that could bypass local officials. And even some groups working in grassroots organizing for civil rights were suspicious of the control and political limitations that might come with federal money. Many northern mayors and congressmen also found the idea of community empowerment objectionable. But in Mississippi, the concept was more than just cause for concern, it was a radical, frightening threat to the established social order.

With the $1.4 million grant in 1965 from the Office of Economic Opportunity (an agency overseen by Kennedy's brother-in-law Sargent Shriver) the Child Development Group of Mississippi had immediately opened Head Start centers in fourteen Mississippi counties. Most of the six thousand five-year-olds who walked through their doors that summer were used to being hungry. Too many of them had never held a book, played with a toy, or seen a doctor or dentist.

For their parents, the centers were a revelation as well. Head Start hired many of them to care for their own children for between fifty and seventy-five dollars a week, a vast increase from the ten to fifteen dollars a week they could make as farm workers or maids. Program directors sought their opinions about what their children needed to learn. In addition to more money, these jobs came with a kind of political freedom that was rare for blacks in Mississippi. Working for CDGM meant their white employers couldn't pressure or fire them for seeking the right to vote, school desegregation, or better treatment.

◆ ◆ ◆

The centers had been open only eight days before Stennis, who sat on the Senate's Appropriations and Armed Services Committees, and state officials began their scrutiny of the program. "They wanted receipts. But the only people whom we could deal with were the small black merchants who wrote their receipts on the back of a paper bag," the group's first director, Tom Levin, later recalled. Stennis and other Mississippi officials objected to the Head Start staff, some of whom they claimed were civil rights agitators from "out of state." They charged that money was being mismanaged. They also said the children were being brainwashed with "black power" signs in the classroom.

There was also violence and intimidation. Some Head Start workers awoke to crosses burning in their yards, and buildings were burned down. In some towns, police followed Head Start workers and issued frequent tickets, often for non-existent offenses. Someone shot into more than one of the Head Start classrooms.

The federal dollars coming into Mississippi posed an unprecedented threat to the status quo, according to Hodding Carter III, a Princeton-educated son of the Delta, whose family operated the moderate *Delta Democrat-Times* in Greenville.

"What was really a threat," Carter said in a 1994 interview for a documentary on the War on Poverty, "was these independent, independently financed power centers, which did not require the "OK" of the governor and the legislature and the like, except in the most indirect way. So, you know, there were suddenly two reactions: we either gotta kill 'em or we gotta control 'em, and there was an effort made on both fronts."

Violence, however, as Carter saw it, was not the first choice of Mississippi's white power structure. It wasn't like "a spigot, turned on by someone in the power group." Instead, what occurred was more spontaneous. "Whenever the possibility or probability of real change emerged, violence and opposition would intensify. It was an organism's reaction to a threat, and the organism was white supremacy, and the threat could be almost anything—a voting campaign, or, it could be a poverty program."

"What the whole resistance, after the Supreme Court desegregation decision of 1954 was supposed to be built on, was a very carefully controlled set of graduated responses, from pressure, to economic pressure, to political isolation . . . [A]lmost to the last person, the white leadership wanted to avoid violence, because violence was the one thing the rest of the country could focus on and react to. Violence, almost always, was sort of the "twitching of the snake's tail," when problems had happened to the command and control center at the top. When the leadership didn't seem to be able to stop something from happening, violence emerged," Carter said.

By the time Kennedy and the other senators arrived in Mississippi for the hearings, CDGM was embattled but still standing. A Stennis-backed investigation that was widely publicized had flagged some irregularities, and Shriver and OEO had responded by removing Levin as director. Shriver made plans to fund an alternative biracial group made up of local black and white moderate leaders. Many of CDGM's supporters castigated the members of the new group as tools of the governor's racist administration and felt betrayed by some of the members of the new group, including civil rights supporters like Hodding Carter III and activist Aaron Henry of Clarksdale. (Carter would later say that he agreed to serve because he was told that there would be no other way to preserve Head Start in the state.) However, as historian Crystal Sanders has pointed out, Carter dreamed of a biracial Democratic Party in Mississippi and could have seen "a new, biracial statewide Head Start program as laying the foundation" to accomplish that goal. Furthermore, Sanders quotes author John Dittmer's point that "Carter and Henry must have been aware that controlling millions of dollars of Head Start funds would give them political patronage and power, enhancing their position as a credible alternative to the Freedom Democratic Party." But in the end, pressure, protest, and national publicity from civil rights groups organized by Marian Wright and the National Council of Churches eventually persuaded Shriver to refund CDGM alongside the new group in 1966, and by 1967, there were 125 Head Start centers in twenty-eight counties reaching nine thousand children.

Stennis, however, wasn't giving up. When the subcommittee announced it would hold hearings in Mississippi, Stennis asked to testify, and, because it was his home state, the unwritten rules of Senate courtesy meant the panel would agree. Therefore, as Senator Joseph Clark of Pennsylvania called the meeting to order, Stennis took his seat before the panel in the Olympic Ballroom.

Giant interlocking rings of the Olympic emblem decorated the wall near Kennedy and the others seated at one end of the ballroom at the Hotel Heidelberg. The three-hundred-room art deco building from the 1930s loomed large in Jackson's skyline and in the city's social scene.

Local television stations were broadcasting the hearings live, and the technology of the day demanded huge black-rimmed television lights that beamed down on the senators, illuminating them like players on a stage. The big lights generated such a glare that Senator George Murphy, a deeply conservative Republican from California, wore his sunglasses during the hearing, a move that struck some observers as humorous because of Murphy's previous career as a movie star.

Prior to entering politics, Murphy had sung and danced his way through more than forty movies, including popular films like *Broadway Melody of 1938* and *For Me and My Gal*. However, after serving two terms as president of the Screen Actors Guild, he had retired from show business in 1950 and entered politics. He won his Senate seat the same year as Kennedy by defeating Pierre Salinger, a Kennedy family friend who had served as presidential press secretary to John Kennedy.

Kennedy, looking very tan, even perhaps a little sunburned, was more used to the heat and light of the television cameras than his counterparts from the Senate. Dressed in a light gray suit with a crisp white handkerchief in his pocket, Kennedy sat at the end of the table, which was convenient when he slipped out several times during the hearing to take telephone calls. He wore his thick, auburn hair longer than many men of the time, especially in the South, a choice that was fodder for a local opinion columnist, who mockingly wondered in print whether Kennedy would have time to get a haircut while in Mississippi. After the group's press conference the night before, the *New York Times* reported that several political science students gathered around Kennedy. One student wanted to know if it were true that Kennedy didn't have for a haircut and had called President Johnson an "S.O.B." Grinning, Kennedy responded, "I don't even know what those initials mean."

Clark and Senator Jacob Javits of New York joined Kennedy at the elevated front table, with a row of aides, including Peter Edelman, sitting right behind them. A row of reporters with their notebooks and cameras sat at a table off to the committee's left. A witness table with a microphone sat between the senators and the audience. Outside the glare of the hot television lights, an overflow crowd filled rows and rows of seats and made the warm room even stuffier. Initially, the hearing had been set for a room that would only hold three hundred, but after such intense publicity in the local media, the committee had moved it to the ballroom to accommodate the crowd of more than one thousand. A few federal marshals in plainclothes blended in with the audience, while uniformed city police stood outside.

Scanning the crowd, twenty-three-year-old William Dunlap was astonished. As a drummer in the popular local band Tommy Whitsett's Imperial Show Band, he had seen the ballroom full of drunken revelers many times. However, he had never seen an audience like this in Mississippi, one packed with poor people, with African Americans and white people sitting together, side by side in the same room. Just about everyone smoked in those days, and as they smoked, a haze settled over the room, giving the setting an otherworldly atmosphere.

"It was as though I had been given a glimpse into the future," Dunlap recalled. "The affair had about it something of a revival. There was a great concentration of the spirit, and it was easy to feel transported, even optimistically so."

Dunlap had cut his Bible class that day at Mississippi College, a Baptist school in nearby Clinton, to see Kennedy. Already an accomplished artist, Dunlap talked his way onto the front row by pointing to his sketchbook, and saying, "I'm here to draw." Dunlap had always regretted not seeing John Kennedy when he spoke to Jackson's Young Democrats ten years earlier, so he was determined not to miss Robert Kennedy's visit to Mississippi.

Unlike many of his fellow white Mississippians, he didn't hate the Kennedys. Instead, he admired them. They liked art, music, and poetry, just like him. But he well knew there was still plenty of ill-will toward Kennedy in the state. Dunlap, a cousin of former Mississippi governor J. P. Coleman, vividly remembered how Ross Barnett had used Coleman's 1957 invitation to John Kennedy to defeat him, accusing Coleman of letting Kennedy "defile" the bedroom of the virulently racist former governor and senator, Theodore Bilbo.

As he opened the meeting, Chairman Joseph Clark welcomed Mississippi's current senator, one who was by no means as vicious as Bilbo, but, like him, believed in white supremacy and segregation nonetheless. Clark went on to stress that at the hearing that day, the committee planned "neither a witch hunt or a whitewash. We are here to find out the basic facts," he said.

Despite his courtly manner, the junior Mississippi senator was a resolute segregationist. John Stennis—a balding, jowly man with severe-framed glasses—was generally well respected by his Senate colleagues, even those who did not agree with him on racial matters. Known as "the conscience of the Senate," his peers had made him the first chair of the newly created bipartisan Senate Ethics Committee in 1966. He was known as a steadfast supporter of the military and for his careful scrutiny (one of his colleagues called him "a plodder") of spending bills in his position on the powerful

Robert Kennedy (at right) questions a witness as the other senators on the Subcommittee on Employment, Manpower, and Poverty—Senator George Murphy of California, (from left) Senator Jacob Javits of New York and Senator Joseph Clark of Pennsylvania—look on. Credit: Jim Lucas Estate.

Unita Blackwell and Fannie Lou Hamer, civil rights advocates from the Delta, praised poverty programs and spoke of widespread hunger. Credit: Jim Lucas Estate.

Appropriations Committee. This also meant he knew how to deliver for his constituents, bringing high-dollar projects home to Mississippi.

However, unlike his counterpart, Senator James O. Eastland, Stennis was temperate in his habits and language. A Presbyterian of Scottish stock, he didn't drink, chose not to swear, and rarely used racial epithets, despite his support of segregation. In college, he was inducted into Phi Beta Kappa, and like Robert Kennedy, he was a graduate of the University of Virginia's Law

School. When he spoke on the Senate floor, he commanded immediate and complete attention, starting with an echoing snap of his fingers for a glass of water that instantly quieted his colleagues.

Stennis didn't snap his fingers for silence as the hearing in Jackson began, but Clark immediately chided the flock of television and radio reporters for their noise, noting that he knew "what a stickler for order, you are yourself." Invited to proceed, Stennis acknowledged in his opening statement that there were indeed poor people in Mississippi. But, he complained, the new programs designed to help them were costing more money than Congress had been led to expect. He was only there to see that the taxpayers were protected.

Furthermore, Stennis argued that the federal government had passed over "responsible, honest, and capable local leadership" in the development of the Head Start program. Instead, people from New York and Massachusetts managed Head Start in Mississippi, and the headquarters was a "stake hold of beatniks and immorality." Then, echoing the "states' rights" philosophy that had threaded through every conflict with the federal government since the time of slavery, he called for the program to be changed to give the governor veto power over "any project he determines not in the public interest."

The Mississippi senator especially focused on a figure of $500,000 and an additional $650,000 that he said could not be accounted for by CDGM in the government's audit. Calling it a "scandalous situation," he said the poor would suffer because they didn't receive money that has been mismanaged or misspent, and it won't be on "the hands and conscience of concerned Mississippians." Instead, Stennis claimed, the blame would rest on irresponsible bureaucrats who fail to recognize or ignore "irrefutable facts such as I have presented here today."

As Stennis concluded his testimony, Clark dryly thanked him for his "forthright and controversial statement" and opened the floor to the other senators on the panel. Javits reminded the audience that Stennis's charges had not been proven. He then pointed to a more recent audit that differed greatly from Stennis's report.

Robert Kennedy took over from there. "I have before me the report of Ernst and Ernst, which made an audit of this organization [CDGM] and came out with some figures that are quite different," he said. The room grew silent. He read a portion of the report that called any disallowed expenditures "relatively minor."

Stennis was taken aback. "You say it's the opinion of whom?" he said.

The auditor with the New York–based accounting firm had submitted its report in March to the board of directors at the community college that hosted CDGM, Kennedy said. "They go into this whole question of the $500,000 and the $650,000, and basically they don't find any substance in the charges—to the allegations."

Scrambling with news cameras rolling, Stennis complained that the audit had not been sent to the Appropriations Committee. Then he asserted that "the original facts are still correct."

Kennedy picked up the report and opened it. "The whole report is right here," he said.

Stennis countered that he had heard that the auditors could excuse certain accounts or expenditures. "Under that method, you can balance any books," he said.

Kennedy shot back: "I don't think that's what the situation is here."

Stennis huffed in response, "It's a mighty late date, if this bears out what you say, to let those know about it, including the Senate Appropriations Committee, and I am a member of it. It's another illustration of the mysterious way in which this independent agency operates." With that, Stennis thanked the committee and left.

If he had stayed, Stennis would have heard a litany of Mississippi's woes and the desperate needs of Mississippians he was elected to serve. As the morning progressed, a series of witnesses offered first-hand testimony about the state's poorest residents. The statistics were stunning. The infant mortality rate was high overall, and it was twice as high in the black population, one of the state's few black doctors told them. Furthermore, the death rate of African American babies from preventable illnesses such as diarrhea and pneumonia in the first twelve months of life was five times that of white babies. Older children, who had been examined in the Head Start program, had high rates of anemia and other deficiencies, the witnesses said.

Their parents were also struggling. Agricultural jobs had disappeared, and those workers had few portable skills, had little access to job training or transportation, and often faced discrimination for the jobs that were available. Perhaps the biggest obstacle of all, according to local business executive Robert Ezelle, who was a former president of the Jackson Chamber of Commerce and a board member on job-training and Head Start programs, was the grave inadequacy of the state's educational system. Out of the state's more than 2 million residents, 200,000 adults over twenty-five had only a fourth-grade education or less, and 40,000 of them had had no schooling at all, Ezelle said. Within the state's nonwhite population, which was about 42 percent, or 985,000 residents, of the overall population, 7 out of 10 had not completed elementary school.

One of the state's very few African American physicians, A. B. Britton painted a bleak picture of life's prospects for typical displaced black farm workers in Mississippi: "What are their choices? They are limited." He went on to say, "Take, for example, an able-bodied 37-year-old male, who has been told that he no longer can remain on this plantation and chop cotton for $3 a day. He lives with his wife and has four children. He resides in a shack on the plantation where he may have electricity and well water, and so forth. But it is made clear to him that he must get rid of any livestock that he may have and that he will not be able to have a garden. He can no longer get credit at the local grocery store, so where does he turn for assistance? With no income, if the county where he lives has switched from free commodities to food stamps, he can't buy them because his income is gone."

Britton went on to describe how, in his example, the man would find no other farm work nearby. For generations, the state, which had no compulsory attendance laws, had proven unwilling to provide schooling for its African American citizens. There, the only other job he was prepared to do was jani-torial, but there were no jobs like that open. He could participate in a federal War on Poverty literacy or job-training program, but in Mississippi, employers were still unlikely to hire him because of his race once he completed it, Britton said. The man in his example couldn't qualify for welfare in Missis-sippi (which was capped at 31 percent of a family's need and could not exceed ninety dollars, as Marian Wright had told the committee in Washington in March) because he was not aged or disabled. His family could only receive it if he left the household. If he migrated up North and found work, they would lose the welfare if he was caught sending money home.

"It is a tragic day when a man must leave his family in order for them to get this type of service," Britton concluded.

As the hearing progressed, Ken Dean, executive director of the Mississippi Council on Human Relations, told the panel that although the poverty programs were helpful, to be most effective, they would have to deal with the racial realities of Mississippi.

Dean's organization viewed poverty as a form of alienation from society, he said. "That is the problem . . . the matter of alienation of people because of the color of their skin. I think the poverty program, if it is going to be effective, will have to deal with this issue of race, and not just the matter of economics."

Dean's praise of the War on Poverty programs' policy of community action, which involved local people in finding solutions to their problems, caught Kennedy's attention.

"I think this is the real genius of the poverty program, and I think it is the real hope for the State of Mississippi. It not only gives these people better services, but it gives them an experience in a program which causes them to grow both emotionally, as well as intellectually," Dean told the panel.

Kennedy followed up by asking, "To be successful and effective it therefore requires the active participation of those who are recipients of the program?

"Yes sir, it does," Dean replied.

After a few more questions, Kennedy asked Dean, "So it is really a question of whether we want it to go with the philosophy of handouts either by the Federal Government or by the Federal Government through the State, or whether we want to have a philosophy of the people themselves developing the programs and making them effective themselves and participating in them in an active degree at all levels?"

Dean responded that he thought that, as it was written, the poverty program could "very well deal with the root cause of poverty."

Kennedy, like a prosecuting attorney making his final cross-examination, went on:

"Would you say that the key to really any success we might have in the future. . . . is really the active participation of those who are the recipients of the poverty program, the subjects of the poverty program?"

"Yes sir," Dean said.

◆ ◆ ◆

Throughout the morning's testimony, the subcommittee had heard a recitation of statistics—infant mortality, unemployment, and high levels of anemia, just to name a few—concrete measurements of the plight of thousands of the state's poorest residents. However, it was a panel of community leaders that spoke from painful personal experience and brought the statistics to life. One witness, Fannie Lou Hamer from the Mississippi Delta town of Ruleville, had been active in the civil rights movement in Mississippi for several years. Furthermore, in 1964, Hamer had electrified the nation when she spoke movingly on national television as a member of a biracial group of delegates asking to be seated at the Democratic National Convention. The group argued that the all-white regular delegation was illegitimate because it did not represent the voting population of the state.

As Hamer testified before the committee in Jackson, she argued that local governance and parental participation were essential to the success of Head Start and other poverty programs. "Not only does it give the children a head start, but it will give the adults a head start," she told Kennedy and the other senators. Hamer was skeptical about Stennis's insistence on channeling federal

Artist William Dunlap, a student at Mississippi College at the time, talked his way onto the front row of the Jackson hearings to sketch Robert Kennedy. Credit: Courtesy of William Dunlap.

poverty money through the established local leadership. "I am not convinced at this time that the landowners that's on the board, the people who have caused us to be in poverty, is going to get us out of it," she said.

The next witness, Unita Blackwell from Issaquena County, also in the Delta, said the area was the "ruralest of the rural." The county had no hospital, no health service, and a plantation economy, she told the committee. CDGM had been operating a Head Start program in Issaquena County since 1965 and had the support of the community. "It's the only program that ever reached down to where the poverty-poverty-poverty-stricken folks is," she said.

The families who had been left behind as the agricultural economy changed in the Delta were in a dire situation, she said. "We have children who never had a glass of milk. We had children who had never saw a toy." The federal poverty programs were crucial, she added. "If we had to wait on our officials to bring a program, we would still be in bad, bad shape in the state of Mississippi."

When Kennedy's turn to question Blackwell came, he went beyond seeking program recommendations. He asked, "Is there hunger in the area that you are talking about?"
Blackwell responded that there was hunger, and it was getting worse because of the shift from commodities to food stamps.

"What happens to those people that don't get commodities?" Kennedy asked.

"They starve," Blackwell said.

"Is there some of that taking place now in the Delta area?" he asked.

Blackwell then addressed the indifference of Mississippi officials to the suffering of her neighbors. "Well, some folks say as long as you are eating a piece of bread and drinking some water you are making it," she said. She then went on to tell of threats and harassment leveled against poverty program organizers in Sharkey County. "We need some kind of protection, you know, to get programs started. . . . Now, the hunger, it's no possible way that we can overcome it unless we come under some free food stamps or still send the commodities until we can get some of these people trained," she said.

Kennedy followed up. "Is the hunger spreading now?" he asked.

"It's spreading," she said, estimating that 95 percent of the children in her area did not have enough to eat.

◆ ◆ ◆

When the subcommittee paused for lunch, Kennedy did not join his fellow senators for a meal. Instead, he exited the Hotel Heidelberg and climbed into the front seat of a local college student's car. He was headed to nearby Millsaps College for an impromptu talk in the school's auditorium

Affiliated with the Methodist Church, Millsaps was a small, private liberal arts college that had been in Jackson since 1890.It had about 881 students that spring, and the school had a good many moderate faculty members and students. In 1965, Millsaps College was the first all-white school in Mississippi to integrate, and it had occurred with little fuss or fanfare. Two years later, when

Kennedy came to speak, it had a few African American students and one African American student had graduated, but most of those attending were still overwhelmingly white.

On a lark, Millsaps student Ron Greer, a sophomore religion major from Louisiana, and a couple of other students had driven down to the Hotel Heidelberg the night Kennedy arrived in hopes of meeting him. Greer wanted to become a Methodist minister, and he admired Kennedy for both his work on civil rights and his growing focus on poverty. However, the young men arrived after the press conference in the hotel foyer. By that time, Kennedy and the other senators were finishing dinner with the Senate subcommittee staff and about a dozen community, religious, labor, and civil rights leaders.

A bit disappointed, Greer and his friends decided to hang around the lobby watching to at least get a glimpse of Kennedy. When Peter Edelman happened to come out to make a telephone call, Greer stopped him and asked if they could meet Kennedy. Edelman agreed. Then, excited at his success, Greer plunged forward with a new, even bolder request, one that he had not cleared with college officials.

"Well, do you think it would be possible, while he's in town, that he could come out to the college and speak?" Greer asked.

"Well, we'll ask him," Edelman said.

As the dinner ended, Edelman brought Kennedy over. To Greer's surprise, Kennedy seemed genuinely interested in the young men.

"We had his complete attention," Greer recalled nearly fifty years later. "He was listening to you, taking you seriously, and he was *enjoying* you," Greer said. Kennedy agreed to speak if his schedule allowed. Coordinating with Edelman, Greer then hastily called Dr. Benjamin Graves, the college president, who gave his permission. Greer promised to pick Kennedy up and take him to the campus, and, since he didn't have a car, recruited his friend Jerry Duck to drive them. Kennedy and Edelman climbed in for the ride. Despite the Jackson police's concerns before Kennedy arrived, no police officers or marshals accompanied them.

When Kennedy arrived at Millsaps, the school's main auditorium was full of college students. A banner reading "Welcome Bobby" stretched across the balcony facing the podium, and the audience gave Kennedy a long ovation.

Kennedy, who enjoyed speaking to college students, was relaxed and casual. The school newspaper reported that when he greeted the crowd, students "reacted to his well-known New England accent. "You people sound funny too, retorted Kennedy."

He began with a joke about finding a few young men from Millsaps "hanging around the hotel" claiming to be there "to meet U.S. Senators."

Saying he didn't have any formal remarks to make, Kennedy quoted the German writer Goethe: "The future of a nation, the future of a country, is determined by the opinions of their people under the age of 25, and I think the future of this part of the country and the future of the U.S. is going to be determined more and more by our young people." Kennedy went on to urge the students, regardless of their political persuasion, to get involved. "Whether they be Democratic. Or Republican. Or liberal or conservative, or whatever they may be," young people should be willing to devote some of "their time and some of their effort and their energy and talent" on behalf of their fellow citizens. "That's what's going to make a difference for this country," he said.

When he opened the floor to questions, the first one dealt with the controversy around the integration of the University of Mississippi.

"Oh God," he joked, " . . . I didn't have anything to do with it!" to loud applause and laughter. The questioner pressed on, asking him to just clarify the issue once and for all. "Oh hell, I've already done that. You can't really want to hear all of that again? But stand up, and we'll discuss it. Do you really want to hear all of that?" he asked.

The student mentioned the ongoing race for governor in the state, which included Ross Barnett on the ballot.

"I understand, "Kennedy said, "but I think maybe you're asking that question to get me involved in that struggle. I would just say, in brief, that the arrangements were made about sending James Meredith to the University of Mississippi were arranged with the concurrence and approval of the governor of the state at that time. . . . We worked it out together. Is that enough for you?"

More questions about his position on Vietnam followed, and Kennedy expanded at length on his reasons for calling for an end to the bombing of North Vietnam. Other questions touched on Communism in China and Cuba and relations with the Soviet Union.

One student asked him how effective he thought the poverty programs in Mississippi would be "with anything less than complete cooperation from the whites and Negro race."

The ideal, Kennedy responded, would be cooperation between the races, but he added that he didn't think that the programs should be ended if they lacked that kind of collaboration in some parts of the state.

Kennedy answered a few more questions and then, as was his habit, began to question the students. In response to his questions, most of the students raised their hands to support the escalation of bombing in Vietnam. According to the *Jackson Daily News*, an overwhelming number also indicated their support for college deferments from the draft.

Robert Kennedy gave an impromptu speech at Millsaps College during the lunch break of the poverty hearing in Jackson. Credit: Jim Lucas Estate.

"Now, how many of you raised your hands that you were in favor of draft deferments and escalation of bombing in Vietnam?" he asked. The newspaper did not report the corresponding show of hands.

Another student asked about the possibility of a Kennedy-Fulbright presidential ticket.

"I don't think it's got much future to tell you the truth," he said, beyond "some small support in the homes of our relatives, and I'm not sure even there," he said to laughter.

"I have none for the future other than I'm going to run for the Senate in 1970," he told the students. "But I haven't got any plans. Other than that, I support the national ticket in 1968."

Kennedy ended his talk to thunderous applause. As he made his way out of the auditorium, Millsaps students, almost all of them young, white Southerners, crowded around him, stretching to shake his hand and seeking autographs.

◆ ◆ ◆

A little later, Marian Wright, the young NAACP lawyer whose testimony in Washington a month earlier had prompted Kennedy and the others to travel to Mississippi, sat down alone at the witness table to testify. Trim and petite, the twenty-seven-year-old Wright was dressed in tones of light blue, which set off her smooth, caramel-colored complexion and was in striking contrast with the somber business suits of the senators and most of their witnesses. A paisley headband pulled her dark hair neatly off her face.

Despite her youthful appearance, Wright was poised and focused before the panel of senators, and, more importantly, she was well prepared. She quickly ticked through her points. The controversy swirling around the poverty programs showed these programs were having an impact, she told Kennedy and the others. Second, ensuring that the War on Poverty programs in Mississippi were integrated was a laudable goal, she said, but until the federal government could protect people from violence as they tried to exercise their civil rights, it was going to be hard for poor blacks and whites to feel safe enough to work together to help their children. Her third point went to the heart of one of Kennedy's key convictions. Poor people, and African Americans in particular, were experiencing self-governance for the first time as they participated in programs like Head Start. Consequently, the participation of the poor in developing and administrating the programs aimed at helping them must be continued and expanded. She believed that at that point, they would settle for nothing less than to "run things for themselves with dignity."

The chair of the committee, Senator Joe Clark, was eager to give Wright, who also severed as counsel for CDGM, a chance to rebut Stennis's accusations about the War on Poverty programs in the state. Noting Wright's law degree from Yale, he asked her view on Stennis's argument that bypassing local officials was not only ineffective, it ran contrary to the Constitution.

"Senator Clark, I would say, as a lawyer, that there are many constitutional principles, and I think that one of them is that all people in this democracy are to have a chance to participate on an equal basis. This has not been done in this state," she said.

Stennis had little right to complain about the effectiveness of efforts to help the poor, she added. "Senator Stennis, I think, has shown his lack of interest in poverty by voting consistently against the Poverty Act. I don't think he can now come in and scream when other people who are interested in doing something about poverty try to participate," she said. Mississippi's record on the issue spoke for itself, she said. "When Mississippi gets ready to do its job, I think we will all be very, very happy to participate with them."

Javits then asked Wright to respond specifically to the Mississippi senator's charges against the CDGM Head Start operation in Mississippi.

Wright minced no words. "He is wrong," she said simply and confidently. The audience, unused to a young, African American woman challenging a white US senator so directly, gasped. Then, citing the audit by the accounting firm Ernst and Ernst, she adroitly ran through the numbers. Any waste found—about 1 percent—was far beneath the amount generally allowed under federal programs, and "a miraculous achievement" for a program run by poor people with little experience, she said. "We feel we have nothing to hide. We think we have done a fine job," she said.

Wright was prepared for Stennis's attack and met it forthrightly, but she had another pressing concern. Tens of thousands of Mississippians were facing desperate, hungry days now that their main source of work, as meager as it had been, had disappeared. It had been weighing on her mind when she had testified in Washington in March. She had even surprised herself when, at that first hearing, she had so forthrightly demanded that the senators do something about the unfolding tragedy of hunger in the Delta.

Decades later, she would reflect on her initial testimony at that first hearing in March 1967 in Washington. "I thought I was going to testify on Head Start, but I don't know what moved me to talk about hunger. Because I guess I stayed out on the field a lot, and was often visiting poor parents, . . . and hunger, and even starvation, was increasing, and that's what came out of my mouth that day when the senators were there listening," she said. After her testimony in March in Washington, Wright heard that the committee was coming to Mississippi, but thus far she had put little faith in the chance that its most famous member would prove to be a helpful ally in her fight to bring aid to hungry children.

Wright had been active in the civil rights struggle in Mississippi for much of her adult life. In her mind, Kennedy was a ruthless campaign manager and arrogant anti-Communist crusader. As a civil rights activist on the ground in Mississippi, she also knew full well how Kennedy and his brother's administration had been slow to act at times and quick to calculate the political cost of civil rights progress. She had made calls about threats and very real danger to no avail. As a lawyer practicing in the state, she had also seen the consequences of their willingness to accommodate Mississippi's powerful congressional delegation with the appointment of segregationist judges. One of them, US district judge Harold Cox had even once forced her to sit at a table beside the men accused of killing the four civil rights workers in 1964.

Despite her prejudice, however, Wright found herself reconsidering her assessment after an encounter with Peter Edelman, one of Kennedy's top assistants. When Edelman flew to Mississippi two days before his boss was to arrive that April, his main priority was to seek out the young woman who had given such compelling testimony in Washington a few weeks earlier. Kennedy had asked Edelman to travel to Jackson ahead of time on a scouting mission. He was there to identify the key issues—the state of the Head Start program, the effectiveness of the War on Poverty job-training and education programs—and to find reliable sources of information. Kennedy liked for him to sketch out a list of questions for the witnesses before a hearing, preparation that he usually discarded after the first few questions once the testimony got going, Edelman had wryly observed. Marian Wright was one of the first names on his list to contact.

At twenty-nine, Edelman had been working for Robert Kennedy since the fall of 1963, when he signed on to work in the Department of Justice. Taller than Kennedy, with broad shoulders, Edelman wore his dark, wavy hair combed short off his brow. He had a strong jaw and a quick smile that softened the severity of his black frame glasses, which gave Edelman's face a serious, bookish look.

Marian Wright had grown up in small-town South Carolina enduring the realities of racial discrimination on a daily basis. In contrast, Edelman's comfortable childhood and adolescence in Minneapolis brought him little experience with poverty, racism, or even African Americans. In fact, until he left for college, he had known only three black people: two men who served with his father on the city's Council on Human Relations and a young man who transferred into his high school and subsequently won election as class president.

He was close to both of his parents, but his mother, an intelligent, quiet woman who, Edelman has written, loved music and "distrusted country clubs and wealth," had died when Peter was only fifteen. The boy did well in the public and Hebrew schools he attended, dabbled in student council politics, and learned to play the clarinet.

However, he wasn't completely insulated from the concept of racial or ethnic discrimination. He did develop "an instinctive but undeveloped liberalism derived from my father's Democratic-Farmer-Labor Party politics and from being Jewish in a historically anti-Semitic city."

Marian Wright's years in college were an awakening for her, a time spent in an invigorating atmosphere of civil rights philosophy and activism. For Edelman, his focus at college was mostly academic. He earned his undergraduate and law degrees at Harvard and, in 1961, was looking to start his legal career. "The lunch-counter sit-ins in the South were a universe away. The closest I came to the action was being a witness to heated debates at the Law Review about whether civil disobedience was justifiable," he wrote.

After clerking for a federal judge and for US Supreme Court Justice Arthur Goldberg, Edelman decided to take Goldberg's advice and spend a year or two in public service before joining a law firm. He took a spot in Kennedy's Department of Justice, although he only met Kennedy twice in meetings during that time.

When Kennedy left to run for Senate in 1964, Edelman signed on to work for his campaign. Kennedy began to notice Edelman as he used his research skills to ferret out inconsistencies in Kennedy's opponent's voting record.

After Kennedy's victory, he surprised Edelman by forgoing a formal interview and asking him, "Are you going to come to work for me?" Caught off guard, Edelman stammered about his lack of experience practicing law. Kennedy, who had weathered criticism for his inexperience when his brother nominated him for attorney general, responded with a characteristically wry remark, Edelman recalled in his memoir. "I had that problem too," Kennedy said. "I worked it out."

As Kennedy's aide in the Senate, Edelman did research, wrote speeches, and accompanied Kennedy on some of his fact-finding travels. It was a heady time. The pace was hectic; the demands on Edelman's time and skill were almost overwhelming. There were too many phone calls and too much mail that needed a response.

Edelman went with Kennedy as he met with Cesar Chavez and learned of the plight of farm workers in California. He watched as the new senator pushed for thirteen counties in New York to be included in Appalachian economic development programs and spearheaded the Bedford-Stuyvesant project. More than just a job, Edelman's time with Kennedy was an education. Kennedy did travel a lot, but Edelman said he was attentive to his duty in the Senate as he also attended hearings, meetings, and voted on legislation.

"Some have suggested that he was bored with the Senate. That misses the point. He wasn't the least bit uninterested. He was just interested in so much else at the time," Edelman later recalled.

Edelman had watched as Kennedy's interest in poverty grew, but he realized that Kennedy was an experiential learner with a deep curiosity about the way other Americans lived, but with an unusual perspective for a politician. "RFK always saw poverty through the lens of children and young people, and he always saw the connection of race to poverty. He always looked for opportunities to learn by seeing and hearing firsthand," Edelman recalled.

Edelman did not know it at the time, but the trip to Mississippi would provide Kennedy his most devastating glimpse into the lives of some of the nation's poorest citizens. It would also change the trajectory of Edelman's life and career.

Upon arrival, Edelman called Marian Wright and asked for a meeting, but Wright was a bit brusque and dismissive. She had important work to do. She was preparing a brief on a deadline, and she was too busy to meet, she said. Wright later wrote that she wasn't prepared to like Kennedy and expected Edelman, as a one of Kennedy's aides, to be "a cigar-chomping, arrogant know-it-all."

Edelman was undeterred. Fair enough, he acknowledged, briefs are important, but "you have to eat dinner," he told her. She reluctantly agreed to meet him for a meal, selecting a Jackson restaurant where a mixed-race couple eating would not attract unwanted attention. She expected to get a quick bite and get back to work.

However, the two lawyers, one who spent his days in the heart of the nation's government focused on policy, speeches, and legislation, and the other, who spent her time fighting so that African Americans could live as full citizens in the heart of the nation's most violently racist state, found themselves talking late into the night. "It was a decidedly pleasant conversation, even though the conversation was in large part about decidedly unpleasant topics," Edelman observed later.

This young woman was smart and attractive. With her rich, South Carolina-tinged voice, she was slim and almost birdlike in her movements. Her passion and commitment to her work in Mississippi, despite so many threats and obstacles, impressed him. For her part, Wright liked Edelman, too, but she still wasn't sure about Kennedy.

Even though they had talked until midnight, Edelman and Wright found a reason to meet again the next morning so Peter could collect some documents she thought were helpful. Then, once the senators arrived, Wright and Edelman had more time to discuss the issues facing Mississippi (as well as take each other's measure as they worked in a professional environment) during a working dinner at the Hotel Heidelberg with the committee members, their aides, and a small group of other activists working in Mississippi.

The trip into the Delta would bring them more time together, but there at the hearing in Jackson, Edelman watched as Wright gave a passionate plea for the nation's attention to the crisis in Mississippi. When Kennedy's turn came to question Wright, he again focused on hunger. Together they went through the costs to participate in the food stamp program—two, four, eight, or ten dollars per month—even for families with little or no income.

"For the reasons you discussed, first, there is widespread hunger and malnutrition, as I understand it. . . . And for the reasons which you have described, there is really not the kind of progress that needs to be made to deal with the problem?" Kennedy asked.

"It is not, and I think that it is the essential point that ought to be made, that so far the poverty program has done nothing to change the basic economic structure, which has to be changed, or really deal with the root problem that is causing poverty," Wright said.

Kennedy pressed on. "Do I understand that really for many of these families, it is a question of starvation or trying to leave and go to some other part of the country?"

In response, Wright said, her voice low and resonant, her tone matter-of-fact, "They are starving." Leaning forward across the table toward the microphone, hands clasped at her collarbone, she looked right at Kennedy, and punctuated her words with emphatic little nods.

"They are starving, and those who can get the bus fare to go north are trying to go north. But there is absolutely nothing for them to do. There is nowhere to go, and somebody must begin to respond to them. I wish the Senators would have a chance to go and just look at the empty cupboards in the Delta and the number of people who are going around begging just to feed their children. Starvation is a major, major problem," she said.

The next day, Wright got her wish.

◆ ◆ ◆

The hearings at the Hotel Heidelberg continued well into the afternoon, and as William Dunlap studied Robert Kennedy for each stroke of his pen, the young artist struggled to capture the growing weariness in the tilt of the senator's head, the tired look in his eyes. Dunlap wasn't the only one to notice. Dr. James Hendrick, a Jackson pediatrician attending the hearings, also thought Kennedy looked worn down.

Hendrick was at the hearing in support of Head Start. He had signed on in 1965 as medical director for one of Jackson's first Head Start centers, despite the objections from local officials. During the 1960s, his other acts of quiet compassion and Christian conviction had occasionally prompted lost business and generated hate mail. As senior partner of the state's largest pediatric group, for instance, he had integrated the practice's waiting room as soon as he earned senior status. When a younger partner said, "[D]on't you want to sleep on that, Jim?" he had replied, "I've been sleeping on it for 15 years."

Hendrick knew that Kennedy had been in the committee meeting all morning and afternoon. He also may have known that during the lunch break, the senator had given an impromptu speech to a packed crowd of college students on the campus of nearby Millsaps College, and his day wouldn't be over with the conclusion of the hearing. Kennedy was slated to attend a dinner and reception later in Jackson that night, and Hendrick and his wife were included on the guest list.

Kennedy wasn't staying at the Hotel Heidelberg but was instead housed at the Downtowner Inn several blocks away. Crowds were milling around, and many people pushed in to talk to Kennedy after the hearing ended. Security officers were wary and watchful, worried because of the hostility toward Kennedy in the state.

Hendrick knew something about that kind of hostility. Someone had even bombed the home of a rabbi in his neighborhood who supported better race relations. However, Hendrick, half-joking, half-serious, told friends he wasn't worried about a bomb. He was "protected," he said. A leader in the Citizen's Council lived just next door.

As the hearing ended, Hendrick pulled Kennedy aside. The senator looked like he needed a quiet place to rest, the doctor told him. Would he like to get away from the crowds and come to his house for a nap? Kennedy gratefully agreed. They slipped out and drove to Hendrick's home on Crane Drive. No one else was home. Mary Farrell Hendrick, usually a gracious hostess, was at her garden club. Their three girls were in school. The well-kept house was cool and quiet as Kennedy slipped into the front bedroom. Outside the windows, Mary Hendrick's carefully tended garden was a riot of spring blooms. Inside, though, for a while at least, Kennedy rested in peace.

◆ ◆ ◆

Before Senators Robert Kennedy and Joseph Clark set off for the Mississippi Delta the next morning, they were scheduled for dinner and a reception at the home of a politically progressive local couple. However, as the sun was setting on the long day he had spent in the hearings, Kennedy rode to Tougaloo College to meet with students and make a few remarks. Abolitionists had founded the college just north of Jackson in 1869 as a teachers' training school. Over the decades, the independent school had served as a haven for African Americans striving for a career beyond the menial work usually available to them in Mississippi. As the civil rights era unfolded, faculty and students provided leadership and support for the movement, and the campus provided crucial space for civil rights leaders to recruit and organize for their operations.

Ed King, the chaplain at Tougaloo, had organized the meeting with Kennedy for student leaders, including student body president Constance Slaughter. Known to her friends and family as Connie, Slaughter grew up east of Jackson in Forest and was one of six sisters. Her parents were both educated and educators. As such, they had shielded their daughters from much of the virulent racism in their native state, she said.

College, however, was an eye-opening experience for her, Constance Slaughter Harvey recalled decades later. "Once I got to Tougaloo," she said, "they couldn't protect me anymore." Tougaloo in the 1960s was a crossroads of intellectual currents, and a wide variety of civil rights thinkers and leaders came to campus speak, teach, and recruit students. As a freshman in 1963, Slaughter Harvey had met Medgar Evers not long before he was assassinated. His death had shocked and inspired her to set her sights on a law degree from the University of Mississippi, even though an African American woman had yet to graduate from that school. Later that year, she wept with other students when news of John F. Kennedy's assassination reached them.

By the time Robert Kennedy arrived, Slaughter Harvey was close to graduating with honors. The young woman was anxious to see Kennedy. She had long respected him and his family. Even at a young age, she took a pragmatic view about the Kennedy administration's uneven record on civil rights in Mississippi.

"I think that anyone who was aware of the political realities understood that in order to get anything done for black people, they were going to have to make deals, like the deal they made with Ross Barnett concerning James Meredith," she said. "That was the way you did business back then."

The Slaughter family admired the Kennedys because they were wealthy, but chose to be compassionate. "They were not flaming liberals, but they were compassionate. My mother taught us that the Kennedy family was a good family, and my mother was very seldom wrong about anybody's character," she said.

As the young woman chatted with Kennedy, she was surprised by the intensity of his interest in her and her fellow students. He peppered them with questions about their hopes and goals and what problems they thought he could address. They hashed out tough subjects like police brutality and racism. "He was kind. He was intelligent, and his smile was contagious. He was unlike any white man here in Mississippi. Here in Mississippi, you were not accustomed to intelligent politicians," she said. Later, Slaughter noted that hunger never came up during their conversation about current issues. Slaughter viewed news reports of Kennedy's visit to the Delta on the following day and was herself surprised to see that there was destitution on such a broad level in her home state.

After the meeting with students, Kennedy made a few remarks in Woodworth Chapel to an enthusiastic audience. However, his time at Tougaloo was brief because he had a dinner and reception set for later in the evening. The local papers didn't cover his speech and barely mentioned his visit there.

As Kennedy left the chapel, a press of students surged toward him, pushing one freshman, Constance's younger sister, Charlotte Slaughter, so close that she could pluck his handkerchief from his coat pocket. Made of fine linen and marked with his iconic RFK monogram, it was a keepsake that she cherished and still has.

The next morning, Kennedy and Clark departed for the Mississippi Delta, but the students at Tougaloo had another prominent guest speaker on the way. That night, a loud and lively crowd of students packed the same chapel to hear twenty-five-year-old civil rights activist Stokely Carmichael (later known as Kwame Ture). Carmichael, a stirring orator, had since 1966 embraced views that were controversial even with some of his fellow civil rights leaders. To further increase the tension surrounding his visit, African American college students in Nashville had rioted for two nights after Carmichael spoke in the city just three days before his arrival in Jackson.

A year earlier, Carmichael had taken over as the chairman of SNCC. Carmichael's ascension marked a distinct shift in tone and convictions for the group. As one of the Freedom Riders, Carmichael had been jailed (with Kennedy's tacit acquiescence through his deal with Senator James Eastland) in Mississippi's brutal penitentiary at Parchman during the summer of 1961. He also knew the Delta well, having served as project director for voter registration and other activities in the area for SNCC during the early 1960s. These experiences had extinguished much of Carmichael's faith in nonviolence. Instead, he and others like H. Rap Brown saw it as only one of many tactics rather than a foundational principle in the quest for civil rights.

Carmichael "does not advocate violence, but neither does he believe in turning the other cheek," wrote reporter Gene Roberts in a May 1966 *New York Times* article about the changes in SNCC's leadership. An eloquent, well-read man, the organization's young new leader also took rhetorical aim at the inequality he believed was built into American institutions because of white supremacy. Carmichael stood in stark contrast, Roberts wrote, to the group's original focus under his predecessor John Lewis and others, who had "dreamed of integration as an end itself" and "believed it could be achieved by love, conscience and morality if people were willing to risk their lives in non-violent protest."

Although the idea of black power was not new, Carmichael's public embrace of the slogan had resonated with surprising velocity after a rally in Mississippi the year before Kennedy's arrival. In June 1966, Carmichael, along with Martin Luther King, came to Mississippi to complete James Meredith's March against Fear. Meredith had proposed to walk from Memphis, Tennessee, to Jackson, Mississippi, in protest of continuing racism and intimidation in the Mississippi Delta, but a sniper shot Meredith a few miles into his walk.

As the marchers stopped to rally in the Delta town of Greenwood, Mississippi, following a dramatic conflict with a local resident and law enforcement, Carmichael had publicly articulated his philosophy of "black power" and taught the group to chant the phrase for the first time. Riled up that night, according to a *New York Times* report, he had shouted, "[E]very courthouse ought to be burned down to get rid of that dirt." "This is the twenty-seventh time I have been arrested," Carmichael continued, "I ain't going to jail no more. The only way we gonna stop them white men from whupping us is to take over. We been saying 'Freedom Now' for six years and we ain't got nothin'.' What we gonna start saying now is Black Power." By the time the march was wrapping up ten days later, reporters were writing analyses about the emerging philosophy of "black consciousness" that was "sweeping the civil rights movement," producing angry, at times even bloody, rhetoric and driving a growing divide between its younger supporters and older leaders like King, who continued to deplore division and call for cooperation between the races.

Carmichael's rhetoric rattled established African American leaders of groups like the NAACP, whose leader, Roy Wilkins, called "black power 'the father of hatred and the mother of violence.'" In the Delta, white friends of young journalist Curtis Wilkie, most of them with progressive views on race, fretted over it at dinner parties. It also put law enforcement and the white power structure even further on the defensive than it had been. Carmichael embarked on a speaking tour of colleges in the South in the spring of 1967. The scheduling of Carmichael to speak at Vanderbilt University on April 8 sparked vigorous complaints from city leaders, trustees, and alumni. During his speeches in Tennessee, Carmichael called on students to organize and "take over the city" and disparaged other black leaders as "vote deliverers" for white politicians. The next day, April 9, a dispute in a local restaurant erupted into conflict with an escalating police presence. During the two nights of violence, hospitals treated more than a dozen people, windows were broken, and molotov cocktails exploded in several local businesses.

Two days later, Carmichael was in Jackson as Kennedy left from Memphis to return to Washington. At the same podium in the Tougaloo chapel where Kennedy had stood the day before, Carmichael mocked the senator: "I understand that I'm following the 'Great White Father' Bobby Kennedy," he said, a sarcastic twist to his mouth. Carmichael took issue with some of Kennedy's advice to the students. "When he said, 'the world belongs to you,' that comes from a great *black* man, Frederick Douglass!"

Kennedy, Carmichael noted, had urged the group to stand up and speak out against injustice. "Well, we could tell him," he said, growing louder and punctuating his words with a pointed finger, "that we don't need anybody to tell us to stand up any more. . . . We are going to right the wrongs of our people in this generation." Carmichael, his shirt collar unbuttoned and his tie undone, banged the podium to loud shouts of approval and applause.

After a dramatic pause: "Our generation," Carmichael went on, "has the memories of the unpunished murders of Chaney, Goodman, and Medgar Evers. There are going to be no more unpunished murders! "he with an emphatic gesture. "No more!" he said, his voice rising over a cascade of cheers.

The crowd went on to chant black power slogans for more than ten minutes later in the speech.

Although Carmichael appeared to be joking about newsmen on the front row being CIA agents, two days later, an engineer for Jackson television station WLBT passed along a tape of Carmichael's speech and a photograph to the Mississippi State Sovereignty Commission, the taxpayer-funded state agency set up to spy on citizens and others working for civil rights. That same day, a Mississippi congressman, Thomas Abernathy, publicly condemned the Tougaloo speech criticizing the draft of African Americans to fight in Vietnam. Abernathy called for President Johnson's Justice Department to "bring court action" against Carmichael for "treasonous conduct."

◆ ◆ ◆

The summer heat savages Mississippi. Autumn is usually disappointing; the winters, drab and dreary. April evenings in the Magnolia State, however, are enchanting. The air sparkles. Fragrant spring blossoms abound. Soft twilight breezes temper the day's warmth.

Patricia M. Derian, known as Patt to her friends and family, was a natural choice to host Senators Robert Kennedy and Joseph Clark on their last night in Jackson. An experienced and gracious hostess, Derian knew that an intimate dinner on her screened porch would be a welcome respite for Kennedy and the others after the intensity of the Senate subcommittee's hearing in Jackson. And, because Derian had been active for years in progressive politics in the state, she knew how to pull together an impressive cross-section of the state's liberal and moderate activists, educators, journalists, and officials to meet Kennedy and Clark at a reception following supper at her house.

A Virginia native who was a registered nurse, Derian was married to Paul Derian, an orthopedic surgeon at the University of Mississippi Medical Center. The couple had three young children, and it wasn't long after the family's move to Jackson from Virginia in 1959 that she threw her support behind desegregation efforts in the city schools.

A willowy woman with a direct, intelligent gaze and a quick, warm smile, she helped to form Mississippians for Public Education, worked with the Council on Human Relations, volunteered to help in Head Start classrooms, and shrugged off the disapproval of her Mississippi neighbors. She carried on, even when a cross was burned in her yard.

By 1967, she was active in Mississippi Democratic politics as part of the Mississippi Freedom Democratic Party, which included African Americans like Fannie Lou Hamer and Unita Blackwell and a few white allies. (The

Freedom Democrats pushed for the national party to reject the state's regular party apparatus and delegates because it was based on a system that excluded almost all black voters.)

Winifred Green, a Jackson native and one of Derian's best friends was one of the first people added to the guest list for the April 10, 1967, dinner. Even though there was an eight-year age difference between the women, Derian and Green had become fast friends when they met in a Shakespeare class at Millsaps College in 1963. Derian was auditing the class, and Green had returned to school after dropping out to get married. The two bonded immediately.

"I thought Patt was glamorous. She [was] very smart. Beautiful. Interested in politics. Plus, she really hated the racist system of government we lived under and was determined to do something about it," Green said. Derian invited her new young friend to a meeting with a few other white women who were interested in supporting the integration of the state's schools, which were still segregated a decade after the US Supreme Court's ruling in *Brown v. Board of Education*. The group, which became Mississippians for Public Education, fought against plans for the state to abolish its public education system rather than integrate it, a possibility that wasn't just a hypothetical threat. Virginia had closed some of its schools rather than desegregate, and beginning in 1959, Prince Edward County in that state had closed its schools and diverted education funds to private academies for white children for five years.

Green was a fifth-generation Mississippian, and her childhood in Jackson had kept her comfortable and sheltered from racial strife. However, when she traveled to Boston as a teenager for an Episcopal Church conference she encountered intelligent, well-educated African Americans her own age. This experience triggered an epiphany of sorts. "It was revolutionary. I knew somebody had not been telling me the truth," she recalled in an oral history years later. While working with Derian, she met and became friends with Marian Wright during Freedom Summer of 1964. Green soon got a job with the American Friends Service Committee, which cooperated with Wright and the NAACP Legal Defense Fund. Green's new job meant that she traveled the rural roads of Mississippi seeking black families who would risk enrolling their children in all-white public schools. Her work, at least for a time in the 1960s, caused a breach with her family. When her mother once asked her, "[W]here did I go wrong?" Green responded that her grandmother had taught her the children's church song that went "[R]ed and yellow, black and white, they are precious in His sight."

"I thought that she meant it," Green said simply.

The night of the party, the Derians' home in the comfortable Eastover neighborhood in northeast Jackson was in perfect order, Green recalled. The single-level home on a tree-lined street was only a few years old and reflected refined mid-twentieth-century modern tastes. The entryway and spacious living room filled a central A-frame section. A beamed, cathedral ceiling soared above as light spilled in from high windows, which offered glimpses of the sky and early spring leaves. White walls set off several pieces of modern art (including an Andrew Wyeth painting that the artist sent to Paul Derian after the doctor set Wyeth's broken wrist in Virginia and refused to take any payment). Deep red, lacquered brick floors gleamed in contrast to several fine oriental rugs. Furniture with clean, contemporary lines in soft neutral colors, except for a blaze of orange on two chairs, awaited guests.

After drinks in the living room, the Derians led Kennedy, Clark, Wright, Green, and others out to the large screened porch on the back of the house. Green took her seat beside Kennedy. The tables set for sixteen offered a view of the pool, where a fountain splashed and fresh flowers floated in the spray. Green had lobbied her friend for the coveted spot next to Kennedy because even though she was well aware of the Kennedy administration's shortcomings in the eyes of her fellow civil rights workers, she still admired him. A few weeks earlier, when Patt Derian had told Green that she was hosting a dinner for the senator, Green had said, "'well, I'm sitting by him,' and she said, 'well, Winifred, he only has two sides,' and I said, 'Patricia, how many best friends do you have?'"

In a subdued mood, Kennedy chatted quietly with his tablemates during dinner about lingering segregation in the state. Even though the 1964 Civil Rights Act had barred segregation in public places, Jesse Parris, a Head Start director from Natchez told Kennedy that he had money in his budget to take the children in his centers to the dentist, but he had not used it, Green said. The children had to go up the back stairs past a sign that said, "colored entrance," Parris told Kennedy, who looked up sharply at this information. Peter Edelman and other aides for the subcommittee were in the master bedroom working the telephones, Green recalled. "When he said that, Kennedy summoned an aide to the table and said, 'get that man a dentist!' And the crush I had on him deepened 5,000 times," Green said, laughing at the memory.

Later that evening, about twenty-five more visitors arrived for an after-dinner reception. The list included journalist Bill Minor of the *New Orleans Times-Picayune* and newspaper editor Oliver Emmerich; Joshua Morse, the dean of the Law School at the University of Mississippi; Benjamin Graves, the president of Millsaps College; several Catholic priests; Jim Hendrick, the local pediatrician who had offered Kennedy a nap; Blair Batson, chairman of pediatrics at the University of Mississippi Medical Center; and Oscar Carr, a wealthy planter from the Clarksdale area. Carr later recalled that during the meal, Kennedy struck him as a "very shy man" who still asked many questions. Once the after-dinner crowd gathered to hear a few words from him, Kennedy, however, "exuded confidence," Carr said. "The minute Senator Kennedy began to speak on the subject in which he was so involved . . . his image and his aura completely changed." Although they were Democrats, Governor Paul Johnson and Allen Thompson, the mayor of Jackson, sent their regrets.

As the party thinned out, reporter Bill Minor found himself sitting on the couch chatting with Kennedy. Minor reminded him of their first meeting a decade earlier in Los Angeles when Kennedy was courting the Mississippi delegation for his brother's unsuccessful bid for the vice president's spot on the Democratic ticket. At this encounter with Kennedy, Minor noticed a difference in his manner from their meeting a decade earlier. Kennedy's reputation for brashness had been on display while campaigning for his brother in Los Angeles. "But what struck me that night (in Jackson) was the amount of humility he had. He didn't want to draw conclusions until he got more evidence on what the conditions were," Minor said. As Kennedy surveyed the room, he quietly asked Minor about the authenticity of the witnesses who had testified earlier that day. Who might be embellishing the story? he asked. Kennedy, Minor said, had not yet seen for himself the desperation that awaited him in the Delta. That night, he simply wanted to know whom he could trust.

Chapter 5

Wherever One Looks in This Land, Whatever One Sees, That Is the Work of Man

T he airplane carrying two of the four visiting senators, their aides, and about a dozen newsmen took off from the Jackson airport about 9:00 a.m. for the short thirty-five-minute flight to Greenville. Before they left Jackson, Robert Kennedy and Joseph Clark had briefly toured one of the state's first Head Start operations at Richmond Grove.

As the DC3 headed northwest, the photographers smoked and played cards. Marian Wright, in a red-and-white dress with a line of white buttons to her hem, sat next to Senator Joseph Clark. Kennedy settled in and donned his reading glasses to scan the newspaper. As he did so, he chatted with George Lapides, a reporter for the *Memphis Press-Scimitar*, continuing a conversation they had begun the night before.

On Monday night, after Lapides, who lived in Memphis, had finished writing, he found Kennedy, who was also staying at the inn, sitting alone by the pool having a drink. Kennedy invited Lapides to join him. Lapides had a cousin active in New York politics whom Kennedy knew. The young reporter also covered Arkansas politics, where Republican Winthrop Rockefeller had just won election in 1966 with a significant portion of newly enfranchised black voters. Rockefeller, from the wealthy family of John D. Rockefeller, had fled a playboy's life in New York a decade earlier to take up politics in Arkansas. "He [Kennedy] was fascinated by Winthrop Rockefeller and why

Robert Kennedy surveys the landscape that shaped the fortunes of many of the people he met in the Delta. Credit: Jim Lucas Estate.

he would be living in Arkansas," Lapides later recalled. Kennedy also knew Rockefeller had a drinking problem and wanted to know how he was faring. Kennedy, who had earned a varsity letter on the Harvard University football team and had even famously played with a broken leg, also questioned Lapides about southerners' obsession with college football. "He knew that the people were very passionate about it and wanted to know what it was like going to the games," Lapides said.

The next morning on the plane, however, as he read the sports page, Kennedy had another question on his mind for Lapides: Why were the New York Yankees not better? Even though the team had had a strong start the day before with an 8–0 win over the Washington Senators on opening day, the senator from New York was concerned, Lapides said. Kennedy thought they were being mismanaged and should be better. "That was very frustrating

Robert Kennedy, along with Peter Edelman (at left) and Ken Dean, leave a home outside of Greenville, Mississippi. Credit: Jim Lucas Estate.

to him. He thought the New York Yankees should always be great," Lapides said. Outside their windows, in occasional glimpses through the gray cloud cover, Kennedy could see the Delta spread out below in the pale April morning light.

◆ ◆ ◆

In the spring, the land in the Delta lies shimmering with life, a swath of brown and green along the wide, muddy Mississippi River that made it. Vast fields of turned soil in shades of cocoa, coffee, and nut spread out under the warming sun or soak up cloudbursts of silvery showers. The Delta runs for roughly seventy miles east from the twisting riverbed and for two hundred miles along its path. The flat, alluvial plain begins just south of Memphis, Tennessee, where sandy bluffs rise up along its eastern boundary. The Yazoo River marks the region's southern border as it flows westward, sluggish and muddy, into the big river just north of Vicksburg.

In April, the ground waits, split open, for seed. Redwing blackbirds flit from stalk to stem in the narrow green strips of grass, yellow and white wildflowers, and native plants that border the fields. The season's rain collects in shining paths between the furrows or seeks a low spot, where it widens into pools large enough to attract migrating waterfowl—geese, herons, egrets—for a few day's respite from their continent-spanning journey.

Roadside ditches fill quickly and drain slowly, their muddy water breeding mosquitos and nourishing the knobby roots of cypress trees festooned with twisting kudzu vines. Single houses or a strip of three or four, often little more than shacks, stand bare, leaning and vulnerable to the elements on the edge of field-side roads. At the homes of the more prosperous residents, spreading oaks and pecan trees, dusty with the spring's yellow pollen, shade the long, long driveways and shelter the tastefully appointed homes. The cities, or even large towns, of the Delta are few. In the many even smaller rural communities, the buildings huddle together, their backs to the land and the sky.

Although the sky looms wide over the fields of the Delta, it is the earth that dominates the senses. The land, flat and wide, rises gently to the horizon in all directions. The landscape dwarfs our human scale; standing in a freshly tilled field gives the impression of being rooted to the earth, like a seedling in an immense garden plot. At night, a sea of darkness covers the land, which was once the bottom of a prehistoric inland sea and where plows still sometimes turn up sharks' teeth.

Warmed by the vernal sun, the fields give off a primal smell, an earthy scent that reveals hints of the Delta's ancient origins. Until the last half of the nineteenth century, the Mississippi River, wild and swollen with snowmelt and seasonal rains, had for millennia risen from its bed, rolled over this land, and left the detritus of a continent in these fields. The sediment deposited in the alluvial beds, coupled with the region's humid, nearly tropical climate, created a lush and teeming wilderness of dense forests, canebrakes, and swamplands. As the seasons came and went, this wilderness laid its own deep layers of organic matter that crumbled, rotted, and fermented its way into a rich soil almost unparalleled in its fertility. As one government report noted of the Deer Creek area of the Delta in 1880: "Taken as a whole, the plant food percentages in this soil are probably unexcelled by any soil in the world thus far examined." Philosophers and historians have often observed that geography is fate, and it was this singularly abundant topsoil that dictated the destiny of the Delta's land and many of its human inhabitants.

Although the rural Delta of the modern era can be a place of natural beauty, it is no longer a natural landscape and hasn't been for a long time. Instead, the terrain is one wrought by man, one that required a brutality to man and nature alike to wrest it from its original state. Native American tribes, including the Chickasaw and the Choctaw, had roamed the region for millennia, hunting and developing complex trade routes, until their forced removal in the 1830s.

◆ ◆ ◆

Early explorers in the late 1700s and early 1800s thought clearing the Delta an impossible task, believing that the annual floods and dense, primeval forest made the land worthless. However, they underestimated the desperate desire of Eastern planters for soil of such incredible fertility and the lure of cotton, which had, with the advent of the cotton gin, become the most valuable commodity in the world. As the nineteenth century progressed, plantations in Virginia, the Carolinas, and Georgia began to wear out just as the Industrial Revolution took hold. The mills of the North and Europe that had spun and woven their way into the heart of the nation's economy still demanded an ever-greater supply of cotton, and planters, who had grown used to their luxurious lifestyle that cotton, produced with cheap or free labor, provided, were eager to provide it. Those who doubted the Delta's potential for cash crops, as historian James C. Cobb has pointed out, failed "to take into account the determination, rapacity, and cruelty that humans could exhibit if the proper incentives were in place."

Although the region was intensely rural, even still wild in places, isolated and far from the world's capitals of commerce, through cotton, the Delta's fortunes were intricately woven into a vast tapestry of global capitalism.

This "empire of cotton," as author Sven Beckert argues in his book of the same name, touched countless millions over hundreds of years. In the nineteenth and early twentieth centuries, the effects of cotton threaded their way through much of the world's agriculture, industry, commerce, culture, and government, enriching some of those it touched and devastating others. "Countries fought wars for access to these fertile fields, planters put untold numbers of people in shackles, employers abbreviated the childhoods of their operatives, the introduction of new machines led to the depopulation of ancient industrial centers, and workers, both slave and free, struggled for freedom and a living wage," Beckert writes.

The land of cotton has long been associated with "old times not forgotten," but this worldwide system of enterprise, which encompassed the growing, evaluating, transporting, spinning, weaving, sewing, and selling of cotton across oceans on multiple continents, shaped much of our current economic system.

According to Becker, "The empire of cotton was, from the beginning, a site of constant global struggle between slaves and planters, merchants and statesmen, farmers and merchants, workers and factory owners. In this as in so many other ways, the empire of cotton ushered in the modern world."

Driven by the prospect of rich topsoil hundreds of feet deep in many places, the region's early settlers, most of them planters or planters in the making, first clustered around waterways that would take their cotton to market. However, most of the Delta's interior remained uncleared until well after the Civil War. Then, as the nineteenth century drew to a close, techno-logical and engineering advances such as the railroad and canals made the transportation of crops easier, and a levee system made it feasible to drain and clear the land. Just as slaves had on the early settlements, laborers in the postwar Delta hacked their way through canebrakes and felled hardwood forests thick with trees six feet or more in diameter. However, the workers themselves were often felled by diseases like malaria, yellow fever, cholera, and typhoid fever or perished from inhumane working conditions or, at times, even murder.

The levees they built walled in rivers and streams, taming their twisting seasonal wildness and leaving now-parched swamplands ready to be claimed by land-hungry cotton planters. Delta writer David Cohn, who grew up in Greenville around the turn of the twentieth century, acknowledged that the land he knew and loved was a land that whites ruled with unchallenged authority and impunity, even though they did not create it themselves. Instead, he wrote, the Delta was wrenched from nature by the sweat and blood of Afri-can Americans. They "brought order out of primeval wilderness, felling the trees, digging the ditches and draining the swamps. . . . Wherever one looks in this land, whatever one sees that is the work of man, was created by the toil-ing, straining bodies of the blacks."

In the years just after the Civil War, newly freed slaves and poor whites were no more immune to the lure of the Delta's rich soil and its economic promise than the sons of the wealthy planters they followed. As historian John Willis points out, in the post-bellum decades, "the prospect of riches in this cotton economy drew tens of thousands of immigrants to the area. For-mer slaves, former masters, foreign-born merchants and northern men with entrepreneurial schemes all flocked to the region."

Because much of the rich soil was still cloaked in a thick tangle of hard-woods or swampland that flooded frequently, Willis wrote that by the early 1870s, planters had, because of necessity, modified their approach to their labor needs. They chose to "encourage black initiative (not repress it as many had while slaveholders)" in order to clear more land for cotton growing.

Newcomers, many of whom had formerly been slaves, jumped at the chance to rent such potentially profitable land, even if it required backbreaking work to clear it. And for a while, it paid off financially. According to Nan Woodruff, author of *American Congo*, for almost twenty years, the untamed Delta served as "frontier of opportunity" for many African Americans and others.

In fact, Woodruff points out, "Indeed, by 1900, more than three-fourths owned land. According to one study, African Americans were from 55 to 80 percent of landowners in seven of the nine Delta counties. Overall, black farmers made up 66 percent of all Delta farm owners at the turn of the [twentieth] century."

However, cotton farming is always a gamble, often requiring capital (sometimes borrowed) upfront for a payoff delayed until the bales are sold. The economic turmoil of the late 1880s, along with inexperience, predatory lending practices, and unscrupulous dealings, caused many of these farmers to lose their land as the next few decades progressed. Furthermore, the intensifying efforts of white political leaders to strip African Americans of the rights they had gained through the Thirteenth, Fourteenth and Fifteenth Amendments after the Civil War made the struggle even more difficult.

More land was cleared, levees built and swamps drained in the Delta, just as the Industrial Revolution accelerated the demand for raw materials and British, European and American capitalists were expanding their capitalistic empires. This made the land that was in African American hands suddenly much more attractive to the white planter class, as well as outside investors, and they moved to acquire control of the land through legal and illegal means. In response, African Americans attempted to organize, form cooperatives and align themselves politically with poor whites. These efforts threatened the profits and power of both the plantation owners and the region's merchant class, which met them with brutal violence, the state-sanctioned theft of their rights as citizens, and a growing cultural emphasis on white supremacy.

Using violence, intimidation, and even lynching, they prevented African American and white Republicans from voting until they had elected enough white Democrats to seize control of the legislature. They then began to systematically disenfranchise and then segregate African American citizens, making little secret that their actions were based on a vigorous conviction of white supremacy.

If they even bothered to justify their actions, they did it by clinging to the myth of black inferiority and amplifying the white population's fear of retribution from the black population, which outnumbered them in several Delta counties. In their ruthless pursuit of re-establishing their political dominance, the white leadership terrorized and punished African Americans who showed an interest in civic participation. Their intent was enshrined in law by 1890, when the Mississippi legislature called a special constitutional convention. With the express intent to disenfranchise African Americans and enshrine white supremacy, the delegates rewrote the state's post–Civil War constitution, which had been in place since 1868.

The US government's waning lack of commitment to enforcing Reconstruction-era promises further emboldened the white planter class. As Woodruff emphasizes, far from just being a local, state or regional matter, "legal disenfranchisement of black people was sanctioned by the U.S. Supreme Court, forcing African Americans to enter into an unequal bargain with employers for whatever social space they could obtain in civil society." During the last decades of the nineteenth century and the first ones of the twentieth century, the cash crop of cotton indeed grew to be king in the Delta, and huge profits were possible. Author Paul W. White points out that "between 1900 and 1904, the number of cotton spindles increased by 12 percent worldwide. By 1904, cotton prices went to 17.5 cents a pound, four times the price of six years previously."

The large plantations emerging in the early twentieth century Delta were not agrarian utopias, instead they were "organized along corporate lines and they operated according to the principles of scientific management, which required the close supervision of a routinized and disciplined labor force—in this case, African Americans sharecroppers and day laborers," he writes.

As more and more black residents of the Delta lost their farms and went into debt to the large landowners, the sharecropping system of labor grew to dominate the Delta more than any other part of the South. Under this system, the workers farmed a set number of acres in exchange for a share of the crop eventually produced there. The landowner would provide the seed, equipment, and usually housing for the workers' families. Because African Americas and poor whites could not get credit from independent merchants, the plantation owner often also operated an on-site commissary, generally with inflated prices, where the sharecropper could purchase food and dry goods on credit. At harvest time, the plantation owner would deduct what he determined was the cost of the supplies and commissary items from the portion of the harvest's profits that he owed the laborers. Many of the African Americans who worked the land were poorly educated, if at all. But even if they caught a mistake or realized they were being cheated, there was little recourse for them to dispute the tallies. It was clearly a system rife with the opportunity for abuse, and before long, sharecroppers were mired in debt, with little to show for their work at the end of each year.

Their deepening exploitation was possible only because of the political conditions. The wealth generated by cotton resulted in a lack of economic diversification and the growing power of the planter class, combined with the Jim Crow laws of segregation and disenfranchisement, ensured that generations of blacks in the Delta remained tied to the land with almost no access to education, inadequate to nonexistent medical care, no recourse at the ballot box or in the courts, and little protection from (and very often abuse by) law enforcement. It is a story of loss, disillusionment, and oppression, themes that influenced the blues, a Delta-grown musical tradition that many migrants took to new audiences as they left Mississippi.

These worsening conditions in Mississippi and the labor demands of industrial expansion and World War I defense jobs that opened up in the North and the West drove the first wave of the Great Migration of African Americans (1910–1940) to cities such as Chicago, New York, and Los Angeles. The second wave lasted until 1970. Altogether, more than 6 million African Americans left the South.

During the early migration era, Delta planters were at times almost desperate to keep their labor force from leaving the region. Local train and bus officials in the Delta often would not sell tickets for north- or west-bound routes without permission from the worker's supervisor. To supplement their workforce, they experimented with bringing in groups of Italian, Chinese, and Lebanese workers.

This form of control played out on a grand and deadly scale in 1927, when the worst river flood in American history stranded thirteen thousand African Americans on the high ground of an unbroken levee in Greenville for days. Conditions were brutal and deteriorating: no clean water, little food, poor sanitation. In *Rising Tide: The Great Mississippi Flood and How It Changed America,* author John M. Barry recounts how local planters realized that evacuating the black men, women, and children crowded on the levee would move them beyond the landowners' control, freeing them to join the Great Migration. In the process, it would devastate the Delta's workforce. One of the most powerful planters, former US Senator LeRoy Percy overruled his son William Alexander Percy's plan, based on his humanitarian urges and sense of noblesse oblige, to move the refugees to safety: "Most of them had with them on the levee the little they had been able to salvage before the flood washed their homes away. All that remained were their debts to the planters. It could take years to replace the croppers. They might never be replaced." White families fleeing the flood were evacuated, but the African Americans were forbidden to leave and given substandard food. However, "the most serious grievance penetrated to the soul. The blacks were no longer free. The National Guard patrolled the perimeter of the levee camp with rifles and fixed bayonets. To enter or leave, one needed a pass. They were imprisoned," Barry writes.

◆ ◆ ◆

The New Deal policies and jobs programs in the 1930s brought a few improvements into the lives of poor people in the Delta but as James Cobb has shown in his book *The Most Southern Place on Earth*, planters still wielded a great deal of political and social power. This meant they often managed to shape programs intended to help the region's poor population into benefitting themselves or to just block them from the Delta altogether.

A prime example of this was the power wielded by Oscar Johnston, who was the Roosevelt administration's top cotton policy expert. Throughout the Great Depression, Johnston held several positions with the Agricultural Adjustment Act of 1933's cotton program while presiding over a thirty-eight-thousand-acre plantation, the Delta and Pine Land Company, which at the time was the world's largest cotton plantation.

The AAA paid planters thousands of dollars to reduce the number of acres that they farmed to boost cotton prices and lower expenses. However, the policymakers paid little more than lip-service to the impact on sharecropping and tenant farmers. Usually the bulk of the money stayed in the planters' hands instead of passing on to those who worked the land. Cobb writes that "the most influential officials of the AAA cotton section argued that paying the planter and presuming that he would live up to his 'moral obligation' to his tenants was the most pragmatic course of action." They believed that paying the tenants directly would upset the balance of power between them and their landlord, risking "social upheaval" that threatened to turn the South's powerful congressmen and senators against the program. As cotton acreage fell, it reduced the need for labor, pushed many families off the land, and made it easier to buy the new tractors that were coming on the market, accelerating the out-migration of African Americans from the area.

During the midtwentieth century, especially as soldiers returned home with a fresh perspective after serving in World War II, more African Americans in Mississippi began to actively challenge the rigid system of segregation and try to assert their rights as citizens. As John Dittmer pointed out in his excellent analysis *Local People: The Struggle for Civil Rights in Mississippi,* even though civil rights leaders came to Mississippi from outside the state in the 1960s, they were only building on the brave work of hundreds of Mississippians already risking their lives by seeking to be treated as full citizens and human beings. Furthermore, these local activists were often left unsupported by federal officials, including at times the Kennedys, who feared the political impact on their own agendas if they offended Mississippi's powerful senators and congressmen.

During the midtwentieth century, a swirl of economic, political, and technological currents swept through the Delta, washing away much of the old patterns of work for black farm workers and white farm owners alike. Mechanization, chemical herbicides and pesticides, skip-row planting methods, new federal "set aside" programs, and (starting in 1967) the War on Poverty's farm worker's minimum wage all had an impact on the type and number of workers needed to successfully farm cotton in the Delta.

In 1933, the *New York Times* reported, Delta farmers were amazed by a demonstration of a new harvesting machine, which picked as much cotton in an hour as a man could pick in a week. As the equipment continued to improve, beginning in the 1940s, farmers began to embrace advances in tractors and harvesters, which reduced their reliance on mules, that required more labor for their care, and eliminated the need for most manual cotton picking. The changes shrunk the number of man hours from 165, with mules and humans tending the crop, to fewer than 35 with mechanized equipment.

In 1964, for example, machines picked 68 percent of the Delta's cotton. The next year, they harvested between 85 and 90 percent, dropping the number of people working in the harvest from 10,500 to 6,938, according to news reports. Research on new chemical fertilizers, herbicides, and pesticides also advanced. Pre-emergent herbicides, sprayed on the ground to prevent weed growth, became widely available in the Delta in the mid-1960s. Soon after, a new round of postemergent sprays came along.

According to Billy Percy, whose family has farmed in Washington County since 1840, the new chemicals meant that he and other farmers only occasionally needed a few people to hoe the weeds around the young plants, or "chop the cotton." This meant the cotton could be left alone almost until it was "laid by," or tall and vigorous enough to outgrow the weeds.

In addition, by 1966, increased efficiency from mechanization had yielded such a cotton surplus that the federal government cut the state's allotment by 30 percent. This meant that many fewer rows of cotton were to be planted in 1967. Billy Percy remembers the change as a substantial one that lasted several years. "And by substantial, I mean probably a 25 to 40 percent reduction, so if you were normally planting 1,000 acres, then you would be planting about 600 acres," he said. Furthermore, new recommended agricultural practices, called "skip-row planting," reduced the acreage under production. That meant that farmers would plant only four of eight rows, leaving the other four rows fallow.

By the mid-1960s, mechanization and other changes had mostly ended the sharecropping system. And although many farm workers still lived in shacks on large plantations, either for little or no rent, they were usually paid by the day. Additional day laborers were often procured, transported from town, supervised, and paid by African American contractors. For example, Billy Percy recalls that prior to the minimum wage law, he paid day laborers six dollars a day, which was more than the going rate of three to five dollars in the area, and "those were long days, particularly in the summertime," he said.

His tractor drivers made eight dollars a day. The new minimum wage of one dollar an hour, which took effect in the winter of 1967, caused a good deal of worry among cotton farmers initially, Percy said.

A July 1967 article in the *New York Times* put it more bluntly. The minimum wage requirement meant that "the demand for seasonal labor promptly collapsed." A survey of farms in the Delta by the Mississippi Employment Security Commission and the Delta Council found that spring, at about the time Kennedy arrived, that "54,830 people had been 'affected' by the cutback in employment," a number that included 24,756 children under sixteen.

Despite the concern of the Delta's planters in 1967, they soon found that even at $20,000 each, the new tractors, which were much bigger, better, and more reliable than the old ones, farmers could pay fewer people more per hour and still come out ahead. "It was cheaper to buy the new equipment and to farm with the herbicides than to continue paying the day labor, and that would have been true, I think, even if the minimum wage had not come along," Percy said.

◆ ◆ ◆

With diminishing work prospects, many of those workers joined the ongoing Great Migration of African Americans. Bus stations were crowded with families leaving the Delta for cities, either in the region, like Memphis or New Orleans, or further afield in the North or West. Just between 1950 and 1960, the eighteen counties of the Delta had a net loss of African American population of around two hundred thousand people. Between 1960 and 1965, another sixty thousand people had left the state, the bulk of them from the Delta. This time, however, no one tried to stop them.

In fact, by 1967, advocates for the poor in Mississippi believed there was an unofficial policy by elected leaders to make life so uncomfortable that they would leave. The Voting Rights Act of 1965 had wiped away most of the weapons like poll taxes and literacy or interpretation tests used to keep African Americans from gaining any political power. For the first time in their lives, white officials would have to court black voters and take their agendas seriously, a daunting prospect for politicians who had made careers out of standing up for their "Southern Way of Life." Consequently, as Ken Dean, the executive director of the state Council on Human Relations, told Kennedy and Clark during the Senate subcommittee meeting in Jackson, many leaders in Mississippi's white power structure hoped by resisting aid, they could force the state's black population to migrate.

According to Dean, one candidate in the state's ongoing governor's race had argued that segregation had to be maintained until the black population shrank to around 15 percent. Although thousands did leave during those years, other African Americans in the Delta were so poor that they lacked the resources to move, or they chose to stay on, hesitant to leave the only home they had known to live far away from friends and relatives.

Many of the farm workers who remained in the Delta in the mid-1960s managed to survive with some seasonal day work on the farms supplemented during the off season with food from the federal commodity program, which drew on agricultural surpluses to provide food staples such as cheese, flour, and cornmeal to poor families. But by the spring of 1967, as Marian Wright, the young NAACP attorney from Mississippi had told the Senate panel, well-intentioned policies, such as the new farm worker's minimum wage and the switch in some counties from the commodity program to the new food stamps (which at that time had to be purchased for several cents on the dollar) left many poor families in the Delta hungrier than before and without work. The realities of their destitution, and particularly the suffering of their children, would soon move Kennedy profoundly and inspired him to action.

When Kennedy arrived at Freedom City outside Greenville, Catherine Wilson (in striped dress) was optimistic about the cooperative farm's prospects. Marian Wright (at far right) looks on. Credit: Jim Lucas Estate.

Chapter 6

I Just Couldn't Make a Living

As the sedan carrying Robert Kennedy slowed to a stop outside a white, weathered clapboard store, the group of more than a dozen African Americans waiting on the porch moved toward the west side of the porch. Some of the women who came forward had babies on their hips and were dressed in the best they had to offer, others were in work-day clothes. Preschoolers, some of them with dirty faces, backed up against their mothers, looking warily at this white man surrounded by cameras. An older girl in braids, about ten, sucked her thumb when she thought no one was looking. Catherine Wilson, eighteen and wearing a colorful head kerchief, stood to the side of the group, arms folded, head cocked, watching. As the others stood around and behind her, a woman with graying hair pulled back in a knot stayed seated on the edge of the porch and gazed wearily at Kennedy and the men and women with him. A toddler climbed in and out of her lap.

When Robert Kennedy arrived at Freedom City on April 11, 1967, Catherine longed to believe in a bright future for the cooperative farm emerging from the Delta mud, but she had seen enough during the turbulent 1960s Mississippi to know that it wasn't assured. For Catherine, the economic and political changes that were at work in Mississippi were not abstract trends, but direct and powerful influences on the course of her young life.

The second to the youngest of eight children, Catherine had spent her early days near Indianola, another Delta town, where, under the punishing sun, she learned to help her mother and siblings chop and pick cotton. Her father worked in a nearby chemical plant. The family had always struggled, but, in the early 1960s, her parents separated, plunging her family further into poverty and uncertainty.

From then on, the family of six boys and two girls moved often, as her mother, Ora Dell Wilson, found work and food where she could. Meals were unpredictable. Sometimes they would have a little money from her work or a welfare check, and other times they ate commodities or relatives shared what they had. But it was never enough, Catherine remembered. Most often they ate syrup and bread. Sometimes they had grits and an egg or two. But there were many nights Catherine went to bed hungry. On those nights when she had no food to give them before they tried to sleep, her mother would gather the children around her on the floor and hold them, crying and praying. Maybe the next day, their prayers would be answered, she always said.

In 1964, the trajectory of Catherine's life changed. Civil rights workers in Mississippi for Freedom Summer moved in next door. The house where the young, idealistic volunteers who had come to Mississippi to register voters and teach the state's African Americans about their rights were staying had no indoor plumbing, so Catherine's brother Sammy Lee began taking them water.

This was not without danger, though. Catherine had seen the glare of the flames when the local Ku Klux Klan burned down one of the Freedom Houses that summer. But despite the dangers, Ora Wilson and her children were soon attending a nearby Freedom School organized by volunteers in the area. Even though she was a teenager by this time, Catherine had had little schooling. The many moves made it difficult to keep up, and the Wilson children rarely had enough shoes and clothes to attend school.

The Freedom Schools, where she learned for the first time about black history and the guarantees promised in the Constitution, were a revelation for Catherine and her family. For the first time ever, she thought of herself as a citizen with rights and found a framework—the fundamental racial discrimination that dominated the South—for understanding her family's destitution. As she watched for Kennedy's car, she knew he was the brother of a president, but she had little hope he really understood their destitution, nor did she have faith that he could, or would, actually do anything about it.

That morning in 1967, Kennedy's car was just one in in a caravan of ten vehicles that had rolled the eleven miles southeast of Greenville toward the patch of farmland where a group of thirteen families of displaced farm workers were trying to build a new kind of community. Senator Joseph Clark was the only other senator from the previous day's hearing to travel with Kennedy into the Delta. Marian Wright, who had organized most of the trip's itinerary along with Ken Dean, executive director of the Mississippi Council on Human Relations; local civil rights workers such as Owen Brooks and Thelma

Barnes; Senate and committee aides; and newspaper and television reporters also made the trip.

Wright and Edelman rode in the car with Kennedy. Federal marshals provided security for the group, but the state of Mississippi had insisted on providing additional manpower. Over the objections of federal officers who favored a more unobtrusive approach, the state sent uniformed officers in marked cars to escort the entourage. "We're protecting Mississippi," state officials told Kennedy's advance man, Les Finnegan.

Regardless of whatever imagined threat Robert Kennedy posed to Mississippi in the heads of the state's white leadership, the potential for harm to Kennedy, at least, was real. It could not have been far from everyone's mind that morning. The message had been stark and to the point. "Bobby Kennedy Will Be Murdered" the headline read on a right-wing pamphlet a man had handed Kennedy as he boarded the plane in Jackson for the short flight northwest to Greenville. When Kennedy disembarked less than an hour later, a member of the Ku Klux Klan tried to give Kennedy some Klan literature, but he was hustled away by Greenville's police chief.

The city's chief of police was not the only city official on hand for Kennedy's arrival. In contrast to state officials such as Governor Paul Johnson Jr., who had turned down an invitation to join Kennedy for dinner in Jackson, Greenville's mayor, Pat Dunne, greeted Kennedy with a warm handshake, as did the superintendent of the city schools, W.B. Thompson. One of the city's leading businessmen, Jesse Brent, hosted a luncheon in the visitors' honor later in the day.

◆ ◆ ◆

In some parts of the state, associating with Robert Kennedy would have been political suicide, but Greenville was different. Although by no means liberal in the national sense of the word, leaders like Mayor Pat Dunne, W. B. Thompson, and Jesse Brent had long cultivated the city's reputation for moderation. A bustling river town of about forty-one thousand, Greenville benefitted from the notoriety of past residents such as LeRoy Percy, a planter and former US Senator who had publicly confronted the Ku Klux Klan during its rise in 1922 and kept it from organizing in Greenville.

Decades later, with civil rights conflicts simmering, another local police chief got tired of hearing about nascent Klan activity in Washington County, according to Hodding Carter III. According to Carter, the police chief found out that the main Klan agitator was at a honkytonk outside of Greenville one evening, and the police chief and one of his lieutenants "went out and beat the crap out that guy, and said, 'you're not doing this any more,'" Carter said. The episode never appeared in the press, but talk of the Klan organizing beyond a few individual kooks in Washington County ceased, he said.

Carter's newspaper the *Delta Democrat-Times*, set the tone for the city's moderate reputation, beginning in his father's tenure. It printed spirited condemnations of violence and consistent calls for increased educational opportunities for African Americans. The elder Carter, though not a vigorous advocate for desegregation, consistently challenged Mississippi's treatment of African Americans, and his paper contributed a progressive counterbalance to the extreme conservatism that dominated most of the rest of the state.

By 1967, Carter's son, Hodding Carter III, was the editor of the paper. Greenville was indeed different from much of the rest of Mississippi, a view confirmed to him by one of the state's most powerful opponents of civil rights. Tom Hederman, the owner and publisher of Jackson's two unashamedly racist newspapers, said as much to the younger Carter at an editor's convention in Washington, DC. "He said to me, 'you understand—Greenville, Mississippi is the only place you Carters could have even SURVIVED in this state.' Well, he wasn't too far wrong," Carter said.

Greenville's leadership also benefited from the diversity of experience and viewpoints from the residents at the nearby air force base, which operated from the early 1940s through 1965. The town also had a long-standing and thriving Jewish community with a synagogue and more than more than seven hundred Jewish residents. The arts flourished in mid-century Greenville as well; the town had its own symphony orchestra and an active theater guild.

And even though planters were still a powerful force both financially and socially, the city's economy was diverse enough to loosen their grip. Businesses that relied on outside ownership or markets, such as textile factories, gypsum production, and thriving river barge operations such as Jesse Brent's business gave leaders a degree of freedom from the kind of economic pressure arrayed against racial moderates in other parts of Mississippi.

This meant that Greenville differed from other towns in the state in several distinct ways. For example, blacks had been voting in Greenville since 1940. The city, which had a population of 48 percent African American, had also hired a black police officer as early as 1950. During the beatings and arrests that characterized much of Mississippi law enforcement's reaction to the influx of civil rights workers as the 1960s progressed, Greenville's police force had protected them and had even prosecuted Klan members for burning a cross during the intense civil rights agitation of Freedom Summer 1964.

◆ ◆ ◆

The impact of Robert Kennedy's visit rippled through the Delta, sometimes in unpredictable ways. As Robert Kennedy asked questions at job-training programs at the old air force base, Jesse Brent's wife, Ruth, was at the Downtowner Inn, putting last-minute touches on the luncheon for Kennedy, Clark, and the others. Brent was not usually an anxious hostess. Her position as the wife of one of the wealthiest men in Greenville, as well as her own many social, church, and political activities, made her a veteran of a venerable southern tradition—luncheons.

With a polished smile, stylish clothes, and carefully coiffed hair, Ruth Brent looked like many other southern matrons in the Delta. However, Ruth Brent differed from most of the other women of her race and social status in the Delta in significant ways. A devout Methodist, her conviction that all people were children of God had motivated her to work with African Americans in Mississippi to improve race relations and to improve the lot of poor children. Brent was one of the few local white members on the locally controversial Delta Ministry's board directors. She had also started and operated the city's first daycare center for African American children of working mothers.

Ruth Brent knew that this luncheon also different from the typical civic noontime affair. Not only would the guest list include two US senators (one of whom was used to visiting the White House), but also there would be about two dozen reporters from newspapers, wire services and television networks around. However, what worried Brent most was navigating the complicated realities of race relations in this Mississippi River town. This luncheon would be the first integrated public luncheon in Greenville, and she was determined to make it a success, despite the predictions of disaster from her friends and neighbors.

When word got around that she would host the luncheon at the Inn, and that African Americans such as Marian Wright and other civil rights activists would be on the guest list, several people called Brent to try to talk her out of it, her daughter, Betty Jo Boyd recalled. City officials and civil groups had worked hard to lure the Downtowner Inn to Greenville a few years earlier. Since its opening, it had thrived. The modern hotel drew its customers from across the Delta, even hosting statewide and regional conventions.

The callers to the Brent home were sure, they told her, that if blacks and whites ate together there, it would mean financial ruin for the business. Brent was undeterred. She invited several local officials and civil leaders in the white community. If they balked, she countered one southern tradition—segregation of the races—with the dictates of two other powerful cultural forces—hospitality and respect for authority.

"Now these are U.S. Senators," she said to them. "They are coming to our town. And we owe them our hospitality and respect. We *will* welcome them," she said firmly.

Despite the flurry of worries around town, the luncheon went off smoothly. Thelma Barnes, a pleasant, soft-spoken African American member of the Delta Ministry's staff, had worked tirelessly to help the residents start Freedom City and was central to the civil rights organization's work in and around Greenville. Barnes remembered that one planter at the luncheon was upset because he was to be seated beside her. He started to fuss about it, but Brent and Barnes quietly suggested that he sit down and eat his lunch, Barnes recalled. "So he settled on down and ate his meal," she said. The planter, as well as the Downtowner Inn's business, survived.

Outside the hotel, a few of the reporters covering the Delta trip hung around the pool, smoking and chatting while they waited for the luncheon to end. Mississippi native and University of Mississippi alumnus Curtis Wilkie, on assignment for the *Clarksdale Press Register* looked up to see Kennedy, who was usually comfortable with reporters, walking out toward the group of newsmen. Wilkie greeted the senator and asked him if he had enjoyed his visit to the Ole Miss campus the year before. Kennedy visibly brightened and asked if Wilkie had been in the audience. When Kennedy discovered that the young reporter had covered the event, he told Wilkie that he and his wife, Ethel, had expected a hostile reception, but, instead, the Ole Miss visit was one of the most surprising and warm receptions he had ever encountered.

◆ ◆ ◆

In another part of Greenville, one popular local businessman, Clarke Reed, did not appear on the guest list for the luncheon at the Downtowner Inn to meet Kennedy and the others. In fact, Reed's reaction to the news in the *Delta Democrat-Times* story of the senator's impending arrival was little more than a shrug, for Kennedy was a Democrat. To Reed, who was chairman of the state's Republican Party, Kennedy's visit was little more than a political stunt, just another bid by Democrats to siphon off the support of newly enfranchised African American voters from their traditional allegiance to the Republicans.

Since the early 1950s, Reed's single-minded focus had been to build a viable Republican Party in Mississippi and the South (a vision he eventually realized as he served at the highest levels of the national party in later decades). Reed, a businessman deeply concerned about the Cold War, believed that the development of a true two-party system would strengthen the region. He deplored the tight grip that the Democratic Party held on Mississippi and the South.

Throughout the 1960s, Reed frequently hosted national figures in Greenville in an effort to boost local interest in the Republican Party.

With this goal in mind, the day before Kennedy's visit, the well-connected Reed had hosted a reception for the daughter of the new conservative governor of California, Ronald Reagan. The story of her visit appeared on the morning of Kennedy's arrival in the Memphis, Tennessee, newspaper, *The Commercial Appeal*, which had a wide circulation in the Delta at the time.

Wearing a tomato-red dress and a tiny silver elephant necklace, Maureen Reagan Sills, who was twenty-six at the time, was visiting Greenville to shore up support for Phyllis Schlafly as a conservative candidate for president of the National Federation of Republican Women. The article about her visit reported that the entire Mississippi delegation for the group planned to take her advice and support Schafley. The governor's daughter enjoyed her visit to the Delta, the news report went on to say. Reagan Sills responded to a question about what she thought of her time in Mississippi with outstretched arms: "It's God's country," she said.

◆ ◆ ◆

When Kennedy, Clark, and the others arrived to tour the Greenville Manpower Development Center at the former Greenville Air Force Base, Mayor Pat Dunne felt confident enough in his political milieu to greet them with a quip about the animosity many Mississippi officials felt toward the US government. "A lot of people down here say federal money has a taint. I agree. 'Taint enough."

Dunne was a savvy politician who knew how to work both ends toward the middle, according to Hodding Carter III. Meeting Kennedy would have few political costs for Dunne, the newspaper editor said in an interview years later. "Number one, they weren't going to kill him in Greenville, and number two, it was extremely useful to be seen as a guy willing to meet and accommodate all sorts of people since he was sure as hell going to do what he wanted to do. He was running his own show." For example, Dunne knew that the civil rights activists from outside Mississippi had alienated some of the local African American pastors and community leaders with their grassroots organizing.

"Nobody in the civil rights movement really trusted him at all, but he was as slick as they came. And he worked with a lot of black folks. . . . Carefully cultivated, you could split the community if you really worked at it by saying 'these outsiders . . .' If, of course, you aren't picking the pocket of the black guy while you're saying it. You had to be producing something."

War on Poverty job-training programs provided instruction in drafting and clerical professions. Buildings at the Greenville Air Force Base, which closed in December 1966. Credit: Jim Lucas Estate.

Yes, Greenville was moderate, but only in the context of the reactionary extremes of the rest of Mississippi, and the city's elite often took a paternalistic approach to the race issue, rather than one that would have actually empowered the African American community. African Americans could vote in the city, but only a small percentage of them did vote, and they still had to navigate past the state's byzantine literacy test, pay the poll tax, and worry about losing their job or business if they did register.

The schools for black children were better than elsewhere in the state and included a well-run Catholic school for African American children, but they were still separate and not equally funded. Major employers were still open and complacent about their discriminatory hiring practices. The Greenville Carpet Mill, for example, would only hire black men for menial tasks, employed no African American women, and had segregated lunchrooms and break rooms. Despite a small but active middle class, blacks in Greenville and the surrounding region were still desperately poor. Furthermore, despite the lack of overt racial violence in the city, African Americans were well aware of the steady stream of reports of state-sanctioned beatings, fire bombings, and shootings aimed at their fellow citizens when they sought to exercise civil rights in the state.

It was against this backdrop that the National Council of Churches, motivated by religious conviction and stirred by the moral questions raised by the civil rights movement, began looking for a place to launch its own civil rights operation. Mississippi, with arguably both the greatest need and the stiffest opposition, was a logical choice. The council, which represented much of America's mainstream denominations at the time, including the Episcopalians, Presbyterians, and Methodists, created the Delta Ministry in 1964. Once it opened an office in Greenville, selected because of the city's reputation for tolerance and the relative lack of racial violence, the Delta Ministry had ambitious goals. The lay and clerical staff hoped to take on racial reconciliation, voter registration, relief for the poor, economic development, and education. However, despite support from churches across the nation, the Delta Ministry's path was not a smooth one.

Greenville's surface civility and moderation masked a still-deep racial divide, and the Delta Ministry's arrival shook the city's complacency on the issue. The organization lost its lease downtown, for example, when it offended neighboring business owners by refusing to move Thelma Barnes, its African American secretary and the only one in town, out of the front office where she could be seen from the street. Delta Ministry workers also had trouble finding housing, and clergy from the white churches in the area were often reluctant to work with them, even if some of them privately sympathized with their goals.

As the passage of the Civil Rights Act of 1964 and the Voting Rights Act in 1965 began to remove many of the official obstacles to civic participation, the Delta Ministry's staff increasingly focused on economic issues, a move that pushed the organization into more controversy. The staff continued to provide food aid, operate Head Start centers and offer literacy training. However, any program that aimed to move African Americans toward full equality eventually ran up against the barriers that helped to keep them poor, like the racist hiring practices of the Greenville Mill and the low wages for farm work. In these conflicts, the Delta Ministry reflexively sided with the poorest residents of the region, even when the actions of the poor were ill advised. This often created a divide between the ministry and many of the black community's traditional leaders and alienated many of Greenville's white moderates as well.

After supporting and encouraging an ultimately unsuccessful (and some said, ill-advised) farm workers' strike in rural Washington County in 1965, the Delta Ministry staff was left scrambling to house the workers and their families, who were soon joined by other displaced workers from the area, including Catherine Wilson's family. Starting with a tent city on a nearby African American–owned farm, they moved the families to a series of makeshift homes before they, along with other displaced farm families, eventually

landed at Mount Beulah, a former college near Jackson that the Delta Ministry used for a Head Start program, conferences, and training programs.

◆ ◆ ◆

The winter of 1965–1966 proved to be a bitter one for many of the poor
farm workers of the Mississippi Delta. Temperatures were much colder than
usual—Bruce Hilton, a member of the staff of the Delta Ministry, remembers
the mercury going as low as -5 degrees and more snow than usual falling.

Even before the minimum wage for farmworkers took effect in February
1967, advances in mechanical cotton pickers and new chemical weed and pest
control options were roiling the Delta's labor markets. One federal program
created by the Food and Fiber Act of 1965 meant that participating Delta
farmers had to take between 12.5 percent and 35 percent of their land out of
cotton production. Hilton recalled the advent of widespread chemical farming in the Delta and its impact: "Late in 1965, the long-promised pre-emergent
weed killers—which could be sprayed on fields by airplane before the cotton
stalks came up—were perfected and on the market. These liquids, whose sour
smell hung over the Delta in the spring . . . eliminated at once most of the
part-time "chopping" with which the Delta's old folks and children stretched
family incomes."

Thousands of people in the Delta were left essentially without any income,
which also meant that many of them lost their homes. Under the old system,
the farm workers and sharecroppers and their families could stay in their
shacks for little or no rent through the winter on the plantations where they
had worked. However, in the winter of 1966–1967, many of the planters did
not advance money to their tenants as they had before to pay for electricity, gas, and groceries. This had dire consequences in the poorly constructed
homes. For example, on January 27, Hilton writes that the local newspaper
reported that an elderly woman and man were found frozen to death in two
separate Delta communities.

Two days later, the Delta Ministry hosted a "poor people's conference" at
Mount Beulah that attracted about seven hundred people. Upset about federal food aid that had not materialized that winter and looking for outside
recognition of their plight, they sent a telegram to President Lyndon Johnson
asking for help. After waiting three days for a reply, the group grew impatient
and decided to take action.

Early the next morning, the few remaining guards at the decommissioned
Greenville Air Force Base watched in shock as nearly fifty poor people rushed
past the gate. Breaking a lock on one of the empty buildings, they brought in

mattresses and blankets. They came at the urging of civil rights workers, one woman with three children told the *New York Times*. "It was snowing in our house," she said. "And it's a whole lot warmer here."

"People are hungry," Isaac Foster, one of the Delta Ministry staff, said to the *Times*. "They believed Mississippi had some free food and wasn't delivering it. So at Mount Beulah, they voted to come over here."

After about twenty-four hours, federal officials, with a promise to speed up the aid planned for the state, had military police forcibly remove the kicking, biting, and scratching protestors. Many ended up back at Mount Beulah, leaving the Delta Ministry again struggling to meet their needs. It was the families' precarious circumstances that winter that sped up the Delta Ministry's idea for a cooperative farm. The plans for the farm, which the families dubbed "Freedom City," aimed to offer displaced farm workers power over their future and the chance to stay in the Delta rather than migrate to already volatile northern cities, where employment options for uneducated, unskilled workers were shrinking.

❖ ❖ ❖

The chance to stay close to home and be a part of a new and idealist effort to remake Mississippi appealed to Catherine Wilson and her family. But the truth was, they also had very few other options. Since Freedom Summer three years earlier, they had become increasingly involved in civil rights activities in Mississippi, but this involvement came with a price. Catherine and her mother and brother were jailed for twenty days after protesting for voting rights in Jackson at the state capitol in 1965. The Wilson family were never beaten themselves, but while in jail, Catherine said she watched, trembling, as guards beat and kicked a pregnant woman until she miscarried. When local officials in Indianola found out about her mother's part in the protest, they cut off her welfare check. "They said that if she had time to protest, she had time to work," Catherine would later recall.

When her mother later found work in Indianola as a teacher's aide with the newly emerging Head Start program, she awoke early one morning to find a waist-high, charred cross in their front yard. It wasn't long before Ora Wilson felt too frightened to stay in Indianola, so they joined the striking workers at Tent City, then moved on to Mount Beulah, where they joined the brief protest at the Greenville Air Force Base. Soon after, they found themselves in rural Washington County, trying to build a new community unlike any other the Delta had ever seen. The initial idea for Freedom City had some of its origins in the kibbutzim of Israel. In fact, Marian Wright, who served on the commission of the Delta Ministry, admired the collective agricultural communities when she visited Israel and wrote in support of establishing something similar in Mississippi. Another member of the Delta Ministry staff, Warren McKenna, also saw possible solutions in the kibbutzim, which would combine private ownership of land that would be worked collectively with some light industry to employ other members living on the farm.

Although the organization had trouble finding anyone to sell land to them in Washington County, with a $71,000 loan from a Rhode Island philanthropist and other funding, the Delta Ministry made a down payment in the spring of 1966 on four hundred acres southeast of Greenville when a white farmer moving out of state finally agreed to sell. Ambitious plans called for a total of fifty families to eventually live there and own their own plots that would be farmed collectively. They would be trained to build their houses and receive literacy and vocational training.

But there were problems from the start, and by the time Robert Kennedy arrived, Freedom City was in tenuous financial shape. The land the group had bought was wet, and the soil was heavy and difficult to farm. So many years of dependence meant that the group had little experience with decision-making, and they had trouble agreeing upon what to plant and setting up regular work patterns. The first soybean crop in 1966 went in too late and was soon choked with weeds. They knew little about the modern machinery that came with the land and had trouble with operating and maintaining it.

However, the residents were still optimistic. Eighteen-year-old Thomas Hoskins told the *National Observer* in December 1966 that "at least we eat here most days." Catherine Wilson's mother, Ora D. Wilson, who served as the group's secretary, told the *Observer* reporter that she was happy to be working for herself after working in the fields for nearly fifty years. "For the first time in my life, I feel like I'm gaining something. For the first time I'm able to have some say-so in my life," she said. Working out the logistics of the group's new-found independence could be difficult, she acknowledged.

"We're the funniest bunch of people you ever saw," she told the *Observer*. In the Delta, the three main crops grown were rice, soybeans, and cotton, she pointed out. "You know we ain't going to plant cotton. We can't plant rice because we don't have the [irrigation] pumps. That leaves soybeans. But we argued two weeks over what we were going to plant before we could settle on soybeans. We argue over what we're going to eat. We decide on chicken. The cook doesn't want to cook chicken. He goes on strike. We end up with salami," she said.

By the time she moved to Freedom City, Catherine had already picketed to integrate the library in Indianola and protested for voting rights in Jackson, but she was about to be on the frontlines of the civil rights movement once again.

Once Catherine and her family settled in Washington County, she and thirty-three other children from Freedom City registered to attend nearby Riverside School in Avon. They would be the first black children to attend the school, which drew its students from the surrounding rural, blue-collar, white population and had a rough reputation. Further complicating matters, several white families had moved their children to the school, hoping to avoid integration.

Catherine's brother Sammy Lee, who was thirteen, told the *National Observer* that he was happy to be going to school regularly and not picking cotton. "I used to go to the fields with my mama. We got up when it was still dark. We worked all day, except when we had lunch. We came home when it was dark," he said.

Catherine's first few days at the school, however, were tough. The teachers and principals at the school, for the most part, were kind and helpful, Catherine said. But some of the students were hostile. "From the first day we were there, they were saying 'look at all them niggers coming up here.'" However, the racist comments didn't disturb Catherine too much. She had heard worse when she marched in front of the Indianola library. "We didn't pay that any attention," she said.

In the gym, several of the boys threw spitballs at her, and she tried to keep her cool. However, after a few days, a set of twin white boys stepped up and ordered the other boys to leave her alone. But the harassment wasn't over. Soon after, another boy punched her as he walked past her in class. "We were in the classroom, and I guess he just didn't like me or something. He just came up and hit me," she said.

But he soon regretted it.

"He realized he shouldn't have. I jumped that boy. He was bleeding, and they thought I had cut him, but then they suspended him. Everyone knew he started it," she said.

The threat of racial violence was always around her. The Klan had even ridden up to Freedom City one night looking for one of the residents, but some of the men had shooed them away with shotguns. Her brother was beaten up with chains outside of school, she said.

One day, the burden of such fear became too much for her to carry one more step. It began with three white girls who started following her around at recess and in the cafeteria. One of them carried something sharp, and Catherine was afraid they were planning to cut her. After a few days, she sat down, tired and resigned to whatever was going to happen next.

"I didn't know what they were going to do. I don't know why I did it, but I just sat down on the sidewalk. I wasn't going to walk no further. They just stood there, and then one of them sat down beside me and started talking to me," Catherine recalled.

The two girls, one black, one white, started talking about school, and the other girls joined them.

"We talked about school, math, spelling and our different subjects. I think they thought that most black children couldn't spell too hot. But when they found out I could spell, they questioned me and started asking me to spell different words. So, I began to spell for them," she said with a shrug. The girls soon became friends, and life at school improved.

School improved, but the comforts of a real home, the stuff of her dreams, were still out of reach. Catherine and the other families at Freedom City passed that first year in uncomfortable and even dangerous living conditions. No local electricians would wire the tentlike insulated plastic houses bought to house them on the property. The indoor plumbing didn't work. The temporary houses were mistakenly placed in a slow-draining spot, so they were surrounded by mud much of the time.

However, as flawed as their new living quarters were, Catherine was happy with the house, which was new and better than almost any other home she had lived in. She settled in, pleased that for the first time ever, she would have furniture with drawers where she could keep her own things. But then, in a final blow, a fierce storm blew through in November 1966, destroying the Wilson's house, damaging the other homes, and badly frightening Catherine and the other families. In his book, about Freedom City, Bruce Hilton describes the families after the storm, "surrounded by their rain-soaked belongings, ruined furniture, and useless houses." However, instead of dooming the little settlement, Hilton writes, "the disaster got the people cooperating; there was a community kind of spirit of a kind the group hadn't achieved before." When the storm blew apart their house in November, the *National Observer* article noted, the first thing the family saved was Sammy Lee's schoolbooks.

When Kennedy walked up to their porch in April 1967, the men, women, and children waiting to meet him had spent the winter, including Christmas, in makeshift housing in a converted barn and a few of the remaining tenant shacks. But despite the many obstacles they had faced, that spring they had reason for some hope for the future of Freedom City. A winter wheat crop had just generated enough money to pay the mortgage on the land, and the Delta Ministry had recently received a Ford Foundation grant that would provide funds for the fifty houses, the training, and other programs.

As the cameramen caught up with him near the porch at Freedom City, Kennedy, in a dark grey suit with a sober black and maroon striped tie, stood with his hands in his pockets, head tilted slightly, comfortably chatting with the women and children. He asked questions about what they ate, if they had heard of federal antipoverty programs, and, if they worked, how much they made.

"Why did you leave [the plantation]?" Kennedy asked one woman.

"I couldn't make a living," she answered. Another woman, Ida Mae Lawrence, told him she left "because I was sick and tired of it. I decided that I wasn't going to work in the fields for $3 a day."

At Freedom City, the families existed on grits, rice, soybeans, and donated food, Ministry officials told Kennedy and Senator Joseph Clark. The forty-eight children living at Freedom City rarely ever had milk, eggs, or juice, Kennedy heard. Also, their parents seldom had the two dollars per month for food stamps, and, because they used common kitchen facilities, they could not get welfare from the state.

Kennedy listened carefully to the families as he toured their operation. Always attuned to children, he smiled at them and patted their heads as they scrambled and pushed for a spot to see him. Catherine Wilson's nephew, Rufus Donald, who was three at the time, remembers him picking him up for a moment.

At one point, Kennedy stood listening as the Delta Ministry workers made introductions. As he reached up to grasp a woman's outstretched hand, his slight, almost shy, smile suddenly widened into a warm grin as their hands and eyes met. However, by the time he left the homes he visited in Cleveland, the next city on the itinerary, Kennedy was no longer smiling.

◆ ◆ ◆

With a federal marshal at the wheel, Kennedy, Wright, and Edelman settled in for a thirty-eight-mile drive to Cleveland, Mississippi. They had been riding together since the airport in Greenville, and Wright found Kennedy, who rode in the front, to be a surprisingly pleasant companion.

"He was sort of relaxed; he was funny; he was honest," she would later recall.

Kennedy teased her about having to open the door for her since she rode in the back of the marshal's car, which was used sometimes to transport prisoners. "I'm the star, and you let me open the door for you? What would you do if I hadn't come?" he joked.

Always curious, Kennedy quizzed her about her life in Mississippi and what motivated her to work in such a troubled place. He asked what she was reading, and they discussed her selection, *The Confessions of Nat Turner*, and moved on to how to encourage children to read. She was firm with her boundaries, though. When he turned his questions to her personal life (When was the last time she went to the movies? When had she last gone on a date?) she quickly told him that it was none of his business.

Kennedy then shifted his attention to the attitudes of Mississippi people, black and white, toward the federal government. He also quizzed Wright about the ongoing shift in rhetoric toward black power, which SNCC activists such as Stokely Carmichael had first embraced publicly just a year earlier not too many miles from where she and Kennedy were traveling in Mississippi.

Though reasonable enough, these questions touched a nerve in the young NAACP lawyer. Wright was not naïve. She knew full well the political considerations Kennedy had wrestled with as attorney general: the need to placate powerful southerners in Congress; Cold War intrigue; the concerns about public opinion after a razor-thin victory in the 1960 election; and his role as his brother's protector, just to name a few. But Wright knew something else, something that was more powerful, more visceral, more painful, than her intellectual understanding of a complex political situation.

Marian Wright knew the reality of Mississippi jails. Secret trials. Beatings. Lynchings. Snarling dogs loosed on children and old people. Medgar Evers, dying in front of his children from a sniper's shot. James Meredith writhing on the highway. Vernon Dahmer, the flames and smoke from a firebomb searing his final gasps for breath. James Chaney, Mickey Schwerner, and Andrew Goodman, holes in their heads, buried under tons of Mississippi mud. To many of the people helping African Americans in Mississippi struggle to exercise their rights as ordinary citizens, the Kennedy Department of *Justice* had been, in fact, no such thing.

The failures of the Kennedy administration's approach were clear to her from her first visit to the state as a young law student in 1961. The first night she was in Greenwood, someone burned down SNCC's house. The next night, someone shot at another house where they were staying. The third day, she watched police beat people both young and old who were rallying for voting rights. Officers arrested them and locked her out of the courthouse and tried the protestors without a lawyer. Frantic, frightened, and outraged, she called Justice Department attorney John Doar just before the telephone lines going out of town were cut.

"I said, 'John, you really don't know what's going on here,' and I described this whole scene. John's first words—which, in retrospect were right—were infuriating at the time—'Stop being emotional and talk like a lawyer!'" Wright would later say as she recounted their conversation.

"All I could say was, 'what the hell are you going to do?' . . . I never had felt such a feeling of total isolation in my life . . . just total helplessness. I had told John what was going on; he was very calm, you know. 'We'll send somebody in to investigate,' which is the word I got to hate worst of all," she said.

Wright knew that it was this kind of bitter disappointment that had fueled the anger and shift toward black power within the ranks of SNCC. So many of those workers were, early in the movement in Mississippi, "the most ideal-istic, the most trusting; they really believed they could change the world," she would later say. They had hoped in the promise of a Kennedy administration, which, instead, had left them too often at the mercy of their oppressors.

◆ ◆ ◆

It was spring, and in the fertile fields of the Delta outside her car window, a cycle as old as time was beginning anew. This year, though, thousands of the people who had worked so hard on the land with so little to show for it were not needed and had nowhere to turn. Oh, there was so much to say. In that moment, however, Wright instinctively drew upon a southern tradition, one that ran deep in both the black and white communities in her native region: she told Robert Kennedy a story.

In 1964, a young girl who had attended a Freedom School wrote a fable, one that Wright had read in a newsletter and never forgotten. As Kennedy listened, the caravan of cars rolled down the long, straight roads of the Delta. Marian Wright, her straightforward, unflinching manner contrasting with her soft, South Carolina vowels, told him about "Cinderlilly."

Once upon a time, the story went, a little black girl in McComb, Missis-sippi, watched as the grown white folks went to a beautiful ball at the armory downtown. Wide-eyed as any child at the splendor, Cinderlilly asked her mother if she too could go to the ball. Her mother, knowing the truth about Mississippi but not wanting her dear child to be disappointed, would put her off, saying, "No, Cinderlilly, you're too young."

Years passed, but Cinderlilly did not forget her dream. She persisted, but her mother would always find some excuse. Finally, though, the day came when the girl was obviously old enough to go to the ball. Her mother reluc-tantly agreed. "All right," she said, "but you really can't go because you haven't been invited." Cinderlilly, however, was undeterred.

"Oh, yes. I've got my invitation," the girl responded, "I'll take the 14th Amendment to the Constitution, and that'll get me in the ball." Her mother wasn't sure that would work, but Cinderlilly replied, "Oh, I think it will, but if that doesn't work, I've got a new card. I've got the Civil Rights Act of 1964. Surely that will get me in the ball."

The mother thought of another obstacle. "Maybe you're right, Cinderlilly, but who is going to take you? You can't go to the ball without an escort."

Her daughter had answer for that too. "Oh! Prince Charming, Bobby Kennedy, is going come and take me!"

"And the mother said, . . ." Wright went on with the story, as Kennedy listened intently, "'You're sure he's going to show up?' And the little girl said, 'I'm sure he's going to show up,' So sure enough, Prince Charming promised her he would come and take her to the ball. And the night came. And the little girl's mother pressed her pretty little clothes, and she was going down to the ball. And she was very excited."

"At the last minute," Wright continued, "Prince Charming called and said he couldn't come. The little girl was crushed. She was terribly scared, but she said, 'I'm going to go anyway.' And she took her little Fourteenth Amendment, and she's packed up her little Civil Rights Act of 1964, and went down to the ball," Wright told him.

When Cinderlilly arrived, the doors were closed to her, but she could hear the ball going on inside. Summoning her courage, she knocked and knocked and kept knocking.

"Finally the doors opened," Wright said. "They looked at her . . . The people at the ball stopped and everybody looked at the little girl and said, 'What are you doing here?' She said, 'I've come to the ball.'"

"They said, 'Where's your invitation?' So she pulls out the 14th Amendment and she gives it to them. And the doorman started laughing, and said, 'this won't get you anywhere,' and he passes it around the room, and everybody starts laughing."

Cinderlilly began to cry. But then she remembered the new Civil Rights Act in her pocket, and gave that to them. "And everybody kept laughing and kept laughing," as Cinderlilly stood at the door, just outside of the ball, her hopes crushed, tears rolling down her face.

As Wright concluded her tale. Kennedy said nothing. Then, after a moment, Wright broke the silence and said, "It's a cruel story, but I think it's as much as anything how little children and how people down here view the disappointments in the federal government. You know, Prince Charming simply didn't show up."

Kennedy remained quiet. "[H]he felt very badly. He really . . . really felt very badly. And there's not much you can say to something like that," she said after his death.

◆ ◆ ◆

Outside the car, the muddy fields of April rolled on by as they sped toward Cleveland. The sun had come out, and the greening landscape was punctuated by the occasional white clapboard church, corrugated tin farm building, or houses—the unsteady, gray unpainted shacks of the farm workers contrasting with the pleasant, well-cared for homes of the planters. Along the way, the ever-present, half-starved dogs of the Delta peered around corners or stood on thin legs nosing through litter tossed near the roadside. Later in the day, one of the cars in Kennedy's entourage ran over one of them. Insisting they stop even though they were running late, Robert Kennedy scolded the police escort for its carelessness and bent to comfort the boy who had lost his pet.

In Cleveland, Mississippi, fifteen of the Dillard children lived in one house with their mother and grandparents when Kennedy visited. Charlie Dillard (at far left) was nine years old. Credit: Dan Guravich.

Chapter 7

A Terrible Reflection on Our Society

Nine-year-old Charlie Dillard's life was filled with uncertainties—his grandfather's unpredictable temper, his mother's frequent and often frantic search for work—just to name two. However, some things were certain. His grandparents' three-room home in Cleveland, Mississippi, which he shared with his eight brothers and sisters, as well as various aunts, uncles, and cousins, would be cold in the winter. It would be sweltering in the summer heat. And there would be nights that he would go to bed hungry, even days in a row when he would have almost nothing to eat. There would be times when, with his growing legs aching, his stomach hollow and gnawing, he would lie awake and weep.

At the time of Kennedy's visit, Charlie lived on Chrisman Avenue in the Low End section of the East Side, a poor, black neighborhood a few blocks from the center of the former railroad town. The rail line that ran through the heart of town had shaped both Cleveland's history and the racial landscape of the city, acting as a dividing line between mostly all-white upper- and middle-class homes and the East Side, where closely packed, weather-beaten, often crumbling shacks housed much of the city's African American population.

It was the rail line and depot built in the decades following the Civil War to move the cotton from the newly cleared land of the Delta that grew the community. The town incorporated as Cleveland in 1886. Roughly halfway between Memphis and Vicksburg, Cleveland was a logical place to change railroad crews. With the influx of railroad personnel after the Yazoo and Mississippi River Valley (later Illinois Central) built a roundtable there in 1910, the opening of a state teachers college (now Delta State University) in 1925, and industry such as Baxter Laboratories in 1949 meant that Cleveland, like Greenville, had a more diverse economy than many Delta towns and was less dependent on the planter-controlled agricultural economy. However, Cleveland, with about ten thousand residents, was still a rigidly segregated community, with few opportunities beyond menial work for African Americans, which made up about 38 percent of the city's population.

Charlie's grandfather, Joseph Dillard, had grown weary of always owing the landowner, and in 1960, he gave up sharecropping and moved his family to Cleveland, where he found work at the county road barn. His daughter, Pearlie Mae, had stayed in the country with her own growing family to work in the fields. Chopping and picking cotton was all Pearlie Mae Dillard knew. Because her parents needed the help of all their children in the fields, she had rarely ever gone to school. Starting late after the cotton-picking season and leaving in the spring for planting and weeding meant she was always behind in her studies. Overwhelmed and struggling, she gave up attending school. Then the babies started coming, first Rob and then Charlie and his twin brother Charles, and then six others, all delivered by midwives in tenant shacks deep in the rural Delta, far from medical care. One of the babies died from pneumonia after only a few months of life, as his mother watched, helpless to save him.

As the 1960s unfolded, waves of change began to sweep over the Delta. The fieldwork grew scarce and unpredictable, and Pearlie Mae, who remained a single mother, struggled to care for her children. Charlie never knew his father, and his mother moved him and his brothers and sisters often, until, a short time before Kennedy visited, they landed at her father's house in Cleveland. Pearlie Mae had heard that there was work in Florida in the vegetable fields for more money than she could make in Mississippi, and she headed down there to find out.

The addition of eight hungry children to his household weighed heavily on Joseph Dillard. He already had a few of the youngest of his nine children still with him, and some of them had babies of their own. By April of 1967, there were fifteen people living in the small house, and his county wages were hardly sufficient to feed, clothe, and care for all of them. Angry over Pearlie Mae's departure, Joseph Dillard was often harsh with her children. His wife, Fanny, however, always insisted that they take their grandchildren in and loved them all in her quiet way. A deeply religious woman, she often gave up her own meals for them. At times Joseph would order her not to feed Charlie and his brothers and sisters if the food got scarce. However, if his grandmother had something, she would share it with the children when her husband left the house. When the family did eat, it was usually a meager meal of molasses and bread or cornbread and beans, supplemented with vegetables from the garden during the summer. Occasionally they might have salmon croquettes, but they almost never had meat. Sometimes, their neighbors in the close-knit East Side community, poor as they were themselves, sent whatever leftovers they had to help Fanny Dillard feed the children.

With no money for toys, Charlie and the other children spent most of their time playing together in the grassless yard outside their grandparents' home. He was playing there that April afternoon when he looked up and saw the newsmen aiming their big black cameras at a man in a suit coming toward his house. Kennedy, escorted by Amzie Moore, a local civil rights stalwart, was walking the unpaved streets of the East Side.

To Charlie's surprise, Kennedy approached the Dillard home, but stopped to talk with the children before going inside. Kennedy greeted Charlie, delighting him by shaking his hand, a shocking thing for a white man to do in 1967 in Mississippi. Kennedy asked Charlie about school, which he was not yet attending, then asked what he had eaten that day.

"Molasses," Charlie answered simply.

As Kennedy talked with the other children, Charlie ran inside the shack to tell his grandmother about the visitors, and Kennedy followed, climbing the unpainted steps to a screened-in porch. Charlie watched from the corner behind his grandmother.

"How do you feed all of these children?" Kennedy, who was the father of ten children at the time, asked. It was hard, but they got by, Fanny Dillard told him. Opening the door to the screened porch, Kennedy greeted Fannie Dillard quietly, almost shyly. Dillard, a sturdy woman with expressive eyes, had her hair tied up in a ragged scarf and wore a worn housedress. The senator asked her about her family's meals that day.

"No, didn't have no meat, sir," she was quick to answer.

Then what *did* they have to eat? Kennedy wanted to know.

"Bread and syrup," Fanny Dillard replied.

Kennedy struggled to understand her Mississippi accent.

"Bread and what?" he said.

"S-y-r-u-p! S-y-r-u-p!" she said, her voice rising.

"Syrup . . . and bread," Kennedy repeated, slowly. "What did . . . Did they have any lunch?" the senator asked.

"No, I ain't given 'em no lunch," Charlie's grandmother said, frowning and glancing down. Then, looking up again to meet Kennedy's gaze, she added, "I won't feed 'em again 'til the evening,"

"But they, but they . . ." Kennedy stammered.

" . . . I can't hardly feed 'em but twice a day," she said, raising her voice a little as she talked over his objections.

Silenced, Kennedy blinked, and then his eyes widened momentarily in surprise. He looked over her shoulder to Charlie, who stood leaning on the rail in the corner of the porch, his head resting on his thin arms. Kennedy's gaze shifted then toward the yard where other children from Cleveland's East Side milled around the newsmen.

He nodded to Mrs. Dillard and looked down. With a small, rueful sigh, Kennedy turned to go.

Charlie's grandmother stood still on the porch, her left hand on her hip. She stared into the middle distance, biting her lip as he walked out.

As Kennedy came out of the Dillard home, some of neighborhood children stood outside, lined up against the weathered boards of the screened-in porch. Flies buzzed around them. They wore ragged, grubby hand-me-downs that were too small or too big. All but one of them were barefoot, and their feet and legs were grey with dust. One little boy, maybe as old as three, with a running, unwiped nose and a shirt full of holes, ignored Kennedy and stared into the news camera with sad, worried eyes.

Kennedy stopped in front of Rob Dillard, Charlie's eleven-year-old brother. "What did you have for lunch?" Kennedy asked.

"Didn't eat lunch yet," was Rob's quiet response. He looked up and smiled shyly at Kennedy, who smiled back at him reassuringly.

"You haven't had lunch yet, eh?" Kennedy said, even though it was well into the afternoon.

"No," Rob said, and looked down at his siblings. Kennedy watched him, his smile fading. Looking suddenly grave, Kennedy bit his lip and turned to go, caressing the boy's cheek as he passed, and then touching Charlie's sister Gloria's cheek gently with the back of his hand as he went by.

As the father of so many children, Kennedy was well versed in what made preschool children happy.

As he walked by the line of children, he came to a girl of about three wearing a tattered, dirty dress and dusty, too-large cowboy boots. She was backed up against her brother, watching Kennedy warily.

"Nice boots!" he said, with a quick smile.

Her face lit up as she returned his smile with a shy half-smile of her own. She looked down at the boots and wiggled her feet in them happily as Kennedy moved on.

◆ ◆ ◆

Robert Kennedy delights a boy by helping build a tower. In Cleveland, the Head Start teachers went from house to house to gather enough presentable clothes for their students to wear to meet Kennedy. Credit: Jim Lucas Estate.

The two senators, Kennedy and Clark, continued walking the streets of the East Side, making an occasional unscheduled stop to chat with the people. At Reverend Sammie Rash's United Baptist Church, Kennedy and others slipped into the sanctuary to observe a Head Start classroom. In 1967, Rash was a minister in his twenties who worked closely with his mentor, local civil rights leader Amzie Moore. About one hundred children attended makeshift Head Start classrooms set up in the church's main sanctuary. That afternoon, the little children, some dressed in their best, others in hand-me-downs, greeted Kennedy with renditions of songs they had learned in Head Start, such as "All of God's Children" and "Mississippi Wants Freedom."

Their teachers, including Frances Smith, had spent the days before his arrival searching out decent clothes for the children to wear. Smith's work was rewarded, she said, when Kennedy picked up and held some of the children.

"You know, we had everybody really clean that day," Smith said. "I'm telling you, we had to go out and pick up little pieces (of clothing) from here and there for them to put on because they were going to see the senator and maybe talk to him. That's what I told them." The children were shy, Smith said, around this white man who bent down to talk with them, smiled, and tried to put them at their ease.

When Marian Wright and Ken Dean began to set up the itinerary for Kennedy and Clark, they knew that Amzie Moore was the man to call in Bolivar County. No one in Cleveland was more closely connected to the people in the city's poorest neighborhoods than Moore, who had worked with the NAACP since the early 1950s. With close-cropped graying hair, a wide face, and a warm smile, Moore's sturdy figure was a familiar one in the East Side. Moore, fifty-five, knew firsthand how little the families there had to eat, how few opportunities they had to improve their lot, and how many obstacles stood in their way.

Moore was a successful businessman who owned a filling station and rental property. But it was his job at the post office, which he had held since 1935, that had propelled him, the son of a sharecropper, into the tiny black middle class of the Delta. His federal job also served to insulate him somewhat from the economic penalties usually brought to bear on African Americans in the South who pressed too hard for equal rights. However, he had still faced threats and boycotts of his service station for his refusal to segregate the restrooms as the White Citizen's Council grew in power during the 1950s.

Moore had been concerned about economic development and the plight of the region's African Americans in the wake of mechanization in the Delta for years, but he had not always felt motivated to help others. Prior to his service in World War II, he believed that whites were somehow naturally superior and were meant to govern African Americans. The only way to mitigate the hardships of the Jim Crow South, Moore believed was to acquire enough personal wealth to be self-sufficient.

However, his experiences during the war, where he chafed against the hypocrisy of American messages about freedom to segregated troops and saw entire civilizations run by people of color changed his mind about the destiny and abilities of African Americans, and soon after the war he became involved with the NAACP. As president of the Cleveland branch, he grew the local chapter to more than six hundred members, investigated the Emmett Till murder in 1955, and spoke to audiences across the country about racial violence, the injustice of Jim Crow, and daily deprivations and degradations faced by blacks in segregated Mississippi.

As important as his push for civil rights for African Americans in the Delta was to Moore, he had remained mindful of the economic component of attaining equality. Years earlier, it had been the suffering of a local family that moved him beyond achieving his own financial security to improving the lot of his race. While searching for property to buy in rural Bolivar County, he had met a mother and her fourteen children whose destitution remained etched in his memory. The children, naked from the waist down, were burning cotton stalks in an old metal barrel to keep warm.

"Not a single bed in the house. A few old raggedy quilts were used to wrap the kids up to keep 'em as warm as possible, and no food. Well, don't misunderstand me, I'd been hungry in my life," Moore recalled in an oral history interview. "It was an experience that carried me back to my youth, and I could tell how a hungry child felt, because I knew how I felt. Just looking at that I think really changed my whole outlook on life. I kinda figured it was a sin to think in terms of trying to get rich in view of what I'd seen, and it wasn't over seven miles from me." By 1967, Moore had seen great gains in terms of the legal dismantling of Jim Crow, voting rights, and civil rights, but not much had changed for many of the Delta's hungry children. When he heard Robert Kennedy was coming to Cleveland, he knew exactly where to take him to illustrate this point.

◆ ◆ ◆

Even by the standards of Cleveland's East Side, where most of the residents, like the Dillards, had trouble meeting their basic needs, Annie White was desperately poor in 1967. Struggle and want had shaped her childhood in south Mississippi and still filled her days. A tall, big-boned woman with a wide face and a serious, direct gaze, White and her children—five sons and a daughter—lived in what was little more than a shack, a rickety shelter tacked together from unpainted boards greyed from the years of hot summers and cold rain, but that provided only scant relief from those same elements. There was almost no furniture in the front room, only one faucet with no hot water. The family's toilet, nothing more than a hole in the floor, sat open in the back, its inevitable stench mingling in the dark rooms with sweat, diapers, old cooking smells, and wood smoke from the stove.

Life in the Delta in 1967 was hard for Annie White, but then life had always been hard for her. Annie Mae Wilkinson White was born in 1928 in rural Amite County about two hundred miles south of Cleveland near the Louisiana state line.

Her parents, Charles and Pinkie Wilkinson, were tenant farmers near the rural community of Smithdale. Far from the modern world, Annie's early life was ruled by the seasons. In the spring, they planted cotton. As the summer heat intensified, they chopped the weeds away from the growing stalks. In the fall, they picked the cotton. Work began at sunrise and ended when twilight fell, though there may have been a break during the hottest part of the day. Once Annie could sit up, she sat on the cotton sack as Pinkie pulled it from row to row or stayed in the house minded by an older sibling. As the youngest of eight children, with five older brothers and two older sisters, there was always someone to look out for Annie.

Although Charles and Pinkie regularly registered their children for school, the family's survival depended on the work that every member, even the children, could contribute. Consequently, Annie only went for a half day when she wasn't needed in the fields. Even if Annie had gone to school regularly, she would not have had access to a quality education. In the best of times, Mississippi provided very little training for teachers of African American children and very few books, school buses, or anything else, and the Depression made it worse. Annie struggled along for a few years, but her schooling ended after the third grade. By the time Kennedy met her, she was thirty-nine years old and could read just a few words and sign her name, a skill she had learned only after her oldest son and daughter had taught her when they began school.

In her early teens, the relentless demands of the cotton fields once more determined the course of Annie's life. The fields always needed work, and they were hot and dusty in the summer and cold when the cotton was ready for picking in the fall. But they held other dangers as well. One day as Pinkie worked, she felt a sharp, biting pain. A rattlesnake had struck her, pumping its venom into her veins. Frightened and hurting, she told her husband, but Charles didn't believe her at first. There was much to do, and he needed every hand he could get. He accused her of trying to get out of working, and she kept on as best she could. However, by the time it was evident that the deadly poison was indeed coursing through her veins, it was too late for help, medical attention the family could have barely afforded anyway. As her frightened children cried, Pinkie died a wrenching, painful death.

After their mother's death, Annie's oldest sister, Olivia, who was twelve years her senior, raised her and her nearest brother, David. Although Pinkie had been a good cook, she had had little time to teach her youngest daughter. It was Olivia, or Ollie as they often called her, who taught Annie how to grow a garden, cook, and clean house as she grew into a young adult. Other than working in the fields, these would be the only skills that Annie would have to earn her living and support her children. Unmarried, Annie White bore her first child, a son, in the early 1950s, but a childless relative took the boy to raise.

Soon after, Annie married Willie White and continued the life she had known in rural Mississippi. In 1953, aided by a midwife as she labored at home, Annie delivered their first baby, a healthy boy they named Willie Jr. But then, like so many other poor women in Mississippi past and present, Annie twice lived the heartbreak behind the state's dismal infant mortality rates. With little to no access to pre- or postnatal care, White bore two more sons who died as infants before her daughter Edna was born in 1957.

By the late 1950s, though, Annie's marriage was an unhappy one, and she took a big step. She, Willie Jr., and Edna followed her two older brothers, Jack and Jesse, to Cleveland, which must have seemed like a bustling city after her life in rural Amite County. With her brothers' help, she supported herself and her little family by doing day work in the cotton fields surrounding Cleveland. She worked every day it didn't rain, Edna remembered, as her son Willie helped and Edna rode behind her on the sack she dragged.

She also worked a few days a week for a white family in town, the Richardsons, cooking, cleaning house, and caring for their three young children. The relationship between white families and their African American domestic employees in the South is one that was based on an inherently unequal balance of power. It is one, therefore, ripe for misunderstanding and misinterpretation. Often white families perceived the relationship as a close and loving one, but their employees viewed it through a very different lens. However, Annie White's daughter, Edna White Brisby, recalls her mother's relationship with the Richardsons as a legitimately close one. They were not wealthy, but helped her when they could and "she loved their children, and they loved her," Brisby said. If Annie White felt a wrench of longing as she walked the few blocks each week from the Richardson's comfortable home and well-fed children to the home she struggled to make for her growing, always hungry brood, she kept it within her own heart.

The difficult lives of Annie White (shown here in a portrait painted by a family friend a few years later) and her six children in 1967 moved Robert Kennedy profoundly. Credit: Photo by Will H. Jacks.

By 1967, White's work at the Richardson's home was the only income she had, about fifteen dollars a week. As mechanization and the use of herbicides and pesticides had increased during the early years of the decade, the work in the fields that once supplemented her income had dried up. White had been twice to the local welfare office to apply, but she had been turned away both times. There was less work and little money, but she had more mouths to feed. Charles, Michael, David, and Lorenzo were all born in Cleveland during the 1960s, two of them at home. Willie, who always knew when his mother was about to give birth because the house would be scrubbed clean, fetched the "granny," as the midwife was known, and boiled water. Edna, hearing her mother cry and moan in labor, tried to peek through the keyhole.

Annie White's options for birth control, prenatal care, and medical care were limited in Mississippi. Medicaid, a federal program that provided health care to the nation's poorest residents, began operating elsewhere in 1965, but the state of Mississippi refused to participate until 1971. However, a local white pediatrician in Cleveland did treat Annie's children if they got sick. "He would say, 'put it on Annie White's bill' when we were there," but he never sent us one," her daughter, Edna White Brisby said.

The children's father or fathers were "Out. Never in the picture," Brisby said. "When we asked her, she would say, 'I'm your mama and your daddy,' and we just left it alone."

Annie White rented the cheapest house she could find, a shack on Ethel Street on the East Side. It had one faucet for running water in a sink in a back room, but no flush toilet, just a hole in the floor on the back porch and no electricity. She paid three dollars a month for rent, which later went up to five dollars and then seven dollars a month.

The house was one of the worst houses in the worst part of town, but Annie White did her best to make it a home. White had a green thumb and loved flowers, especially roses. Wildflowers are free, and she filled old jars with them to brighten the dreary rooms, even though they had almost no furniture. If she was lucky, she found morning glories in her favorite shade of blue. She trained wild honeysuckle vines so they twisted up the side of the weathered doorframes to mask the stench from the open-pit toilet. She was one of the only families on Ethel Street, an unpaved track that locals called "the alley," to sweep and rake the dirt in her grassless yard.

She cooked, and the children kept warm as best they could with a wood-stove, heated with wood her brothers cut for her, although sometimes she could afford to buy a little coal. The children helped keep the stove running, chopping kindling and passing the wood to her through the window on the porch. In the front room, divided by a curtain that their mother had sewn, they did their homework or read books from the bookmobile by oil lamp. Their mother couldn't help them with their reading or check their work, but she could encourage them. "Her message to us was always, 'Go get it. Do bet-ter than me,'" Edna White Brisby said.

Each morning before school, White would wake well before her children and get the stove going. If there was food in the house, she would cook them breakfast, perhaps some biscuits or rice, or, in the unlikely event there was food left from supper, she might serve them leftovers. Annie did what she could to provide food for her children. She always planted a garden and sweated through the hot days of the Mississippi summers in her little kitchen, canning and preserving anything her growing family didn't eat fresh.

Before Bolivar County switched to food stamps for purchase, Annie had often received food from the federal commodity program: canned salmon, meal, flour, beans, and cheese. In the winter, her brothers worked for large hunting camps owned by white planters in the area. They were allowed to hunt the property for themselves, and they shared what they killed with their sister and her family. They ate just about any kind of wildlife you could eat—deer, blackbirds, game birds, possum, raccoon, squirrel—and were glad of it, Annie White's children said.

But there were many mornings when Annie awakened her children knowing she had nothing to fill their stomachs for the day. Most of the time, they could not expect to get much at school because it still did not participate in the federal free lunch program, Edna White Brisby remembered. However, the teachers always bought one extra meal ticket, and they would give it to a different child who had no lunch each week. Fifty years later, Edna's face still lit up when she recalled the gift of a hot lunch every day for a week.

If Annie had to go to work that day, her sisters-in-law, who lived just a few blocks away, kept her babies. But regardless of what else she had to do, if her children went to school hungry, she made sure that she had something to feed them when they got home. If Annie had no money on hand, she would spend her morning going from house to house, borrowing or trading for an egg or some rice or grits, whatever her friends or family could spare. Despite her lack of resources, Annie was a talented and generous cook, according to her children.

"My mama, she could make a meal out of anything. I'm not bragging on her; she really did. You might go to school, there's not a whole morsel in the house. We would come back, and you can smell my mama's cooking way down the street. Everybody would say, 'Ah, somebody cookin'! That ain't nobody but Miss Annie!'" her daughter recalled. In a neighborhood like Cleveland's East Side, her children were hardly the only hungry ones, and, as little as they had, Annie's children said she never turned away any of their playmates at mealtime. She often made rice and beans or a little cake of cornbread or pan bread flavored with bacon grease or molasses. The starches were immediately filling, but they lacked protein and brought little nutritional value to her children's growing bodies, deficiencies that were painfully obvious to Kennedy, the parent of a thriving family himself, when he visited that day in April 1967.

On the afternoon that Kennedy arrived, White, dressed in a worn cotton housedress—she always wore dresses—was scrubbing dirty clothes on a washboard in the back of the house. She stitched almost all of her own clothes by hand, as well the blankets and quilts they slept under, and many of the clothes her children wore. Often as she worked, she sang along to hymns like her favorite "Take My Hand, Precious Lord" on the gospel stations out of Memphis that she listened to on a small radio. With six children at home, the laundry kept her busy. She lived on an unpaved road that was dusty in drought, muddy in the rain. Even though each child only had one or two outfits, she had two sons still in cloth diapers, and it was hard to keep them all clean.

That day her youngest child, Lorenzo, only three months old, lay on the neatly made bed—really just a mattress set on a few bricks—in the back room sucking on a bottle when Kennedy arrived at her home. Her daughter Edna was visiting Annie's brother a few blocks away. Her remaining four sons—Willie, Charles, Michael, and David—ranging in age from thirteen to nearly two, sat on the floor among the remains of one of those after-school meals of beans, rice, and cornbread when the senator and his companions arrived.

As Kennedy and the others entered, they passed through the White's front room, which had no furniture at all, and then walked past the baby on the bed. Kennedy bent down to greet the boys and handed each of the older ones, to their astonishment, a silver coin, a half-dollar with John Kennedy's image on it. To Willie and his brothers, fifty cents was a fortune, more than they had ever had to spend on their own. They rushed out of the little shack to Miss May Bee's store on the corner to spend it immediately on candy and cookies.

As Annie White continued to talk with Clark and Wright, Kennedy's attention, as it often did when children were around, wandered to the little one left there on the floor nearby. At twenty months old, David White was small for his age and wore only a filthy, tattered shirt and a diaper. Important visitors and half dollars held no interest for him. Instead, he was focused on the remains of rice and cornbread scattered on the floor. His little hands scratched at the crumbs and bits of rice mingled with the dirt on the floor and slowly delivered each hard-won fragment to his mouth.

Kennedy spoke gently to the child. "Hello, hi. . . . hi, baby," he said, clucking to get the child's attention, but the boy remained intent on his task. Kennedy leaned down and tried again. When he got no response, he sank to his heels and then down on the floor, stroking the child's cheek to get a response, oblivious, as *Memphis Press-Scimitar* reporter George Lapides silently noted, to his expensive charcoal gray suit.

Marian Wright stood back, also watching quietly in the dim room. Her initial distrust of and resistance to this man, one whom so many other activists in the movement viewed with suspicion, was melting away. She found herself surprised to be near tears. His focus was entirely on this child, she noted. The darkness, the dirt, the smells, even the child's open sores—he let none of those things blind him to this baby's humanity. She had to admit that she would have hesitated before kneeling on that floor and touching that baby. Maybe, just maybe, Kennedy was for real.

Peter Edelman stood beside her as if struck by lightning. As he watched Kennedy's response to the toddler's little fingers searching for even a morsel of rice, he was undergoing his own epiphany of sorts. It was a moment that would stay with him for the rest of his life, like when he got the phone call saying his mother had died, he would later write. This was more than a need for better policy. Children, even babies, were near starvation in the heart of the richest country in the world.

One of Kennedy's sons, Max, was close in age to this child, and the profound difference between the two children must have struck him. Instead of a curious toddler on the move, this child's eyes were dull, his belly distended. Very little light filtered into the unlit room. Kennedy stroked the boy's face and touched his stomach. He continued talking to the boy for two minutes or more, but the child remained listless and didn't speak. He only looked at him with wide eyes. Kennedy finally stopped, carefully put him back on the floor and walked out White's back door, past the tiny baby on the bed and the open toilet. He paused as he ducked under the clothesline outside to brush away what looked to some observers like a tear.

No longer smiling, his voice somber and slightly constricted with emotion, he stepped up to talk to the reporters outside Annie White's home. Calling what he had seen so far "as great a poverty as we've had in our country," Kennedy pointed out that the nation had a gross national product of $700 billion dollars and questioned its priorities. "We spend some $75 billion on armaments, weapons. . . . We spend almost $3 billion a year on dogs in the United States," Kennedy said.

The television cameras were rolling, but most of the newspaper photographers had gone to file their photographs for afternoon papers after the Greenville stops. In Cleveland, Kennedy had asked that the photographers stay outside the homes of the families while he and Joseph Clark talked with them. Dan Guravich, a professional photographer based in Greenville, however, had stayed close to Kennedy as he walked the unpaved streets of Cleveland's East Side. Once Kennedy emerged from Annie White's home and began answering CBS news reporter Daniel Schorr's questions, Guravich apparently slipped unnoticed into the Whites' house.

Alone in a shaft of light from the open door, three-month-old Lorenzo White lay on a cloth spread over the ribbed bedspread pulled tight on the carefully made bed. He drank from a half-full bottle propped up on folded rags. As Guravich snapped two quick photos, Lorenzo watched him, his tiny

Robert Kennedy and his aide, Peter Edelman (in glasses behind Kennedy) visited several homes in Cleveland and found "awfully bare cupboards." Credit: Dan Guravich.

brow furrowed, a thin brown hand grasping at air from the sleeve of a well-worn cotton gown.

Just outside, in front of the television cameras, Kennedy's thoughts turned to the future awaiting little David and Lorenzo White and others like them. "We could be doing more for those who are poor, and particularly for our children, who had nothing to do with asking to be born into this world, no school to go to, insufficient clothes so that they are going to lead a very difficult, unhappy life through the rest of their existence. This is a reflection on our society, on all of us," he said.

Not everyone saw it that way. As he toured the East Side, Kennedy encountered a vocal member of the city's white civic leadership. Taking a pugnacious stance in front of Kennedy, local newspaper owner and editor Clifford Langford asked the senators just why they selected Mississippi to start their tour of impoverished America.

"Senator, just what do you think you're doing down here?" Langford asked with an edge in his voice.

The editor (in glasses) of the local newspaper questioned Robert Kennedy about why he came to Cleveland to see poverty. He denied that anyone was starving in Mississippi. Credit: Dan Guravich.

The editor had worked at the *Bolivar Commercial* for decades and had purchased it in the early 1940s.Langford was intimately involved in the community, active in the Chamber of Commerce and civic clubs and a member of the First Presbyterian Church.

Two years earlier, in 1965, Langford had invited Erle Johnson to speak at the Cleveland Exchange Club. Johnson was the head of the Mississippi Sovereignty Commission, the state-funded agency overseen by the governor and charged with protecting the state's sovereignty from "federal encroachment." It routinely spied on citizens active in promoting civil rights and had passed along information that led to the deaths of the three civil rights workers in Philadelphia, Mississippi. In fact, based on the number of records associated with him in the Sovereignty Commission files, Langford may have routinely communicated with the state's spy agency about civil rights advocates like Amzie Moore and their activities to the domestic spy agency from at least 1959 through 1965.

In addition to directing the news coverage at the paper, he also wrote a regular opinion column that ran on the front page. As the civil rights movement unfolded across the South, Langford, like many local editors in the state, was deeply conservative and vocal in his opposition to the movement and racial equality. Even his friends thought he was something of a hothead.

The day Kennedy visited Cleveland, Langford was in a confrontational mood. He took up his grievances with the senators as Kennedy walked the unpaved streets of the East Side. Kennedy had just stopped to speak softly to one of the young Dillard children.

Suddenly, Langford rounded the corner. Just what, he asked Kennedy, did he think he was doing there? Journalists gathered around them. Peter Edelman stood watchful at Kennedy's shoulder. Langford, who was shorter than Kennedy with glasses and his greying hair cut short, had his chest puffed out, one hand in his pocket, and an irritated look on his face.

"Trying to help people," Kennedy responded simply.

Why, Langford asked, didn't Kennedy and Clark take care of the hunger in their own states?

"I am. Why aren't you trying to help here?" Kennedy asked.

Kennedy listened to Langford's response, his head bent slightly toward the man, his fingers interlocked in front him. From time to time, his hand crept up to just below the knot in his maroon and blue silk necktie, or fumbled with the PT-109 tie pin he wore in honor of his brother. The editor went on with his complaints: Amzie Moore had deliberately chosen the worst part of the city, Langford said, pointing toward the Dillards' house.

Kennedy was a younger child in a fiercely competitive family, the grandson of rough-and-tumble Irish American politicians and had once been a little boy whose parents made him take boxing lessons to toughen him up. He was no stranger to conflict. He met Langford's glare coolly and with confidence.

Langford had clearly lived around families like the Whites and the Dillards for years, but as he talked to Kennedy, he showed little sign of recognizing the daily struggle to fill their children's growing bodies.

"What happens if you don't have a job?" Kennedy asked him.

Langford scoffed. "Well, anybody that wants a job can get it," he said.

"Can they?" Kennedy said, with a quizzical look.

"Yes!" Langford replied emphatically. "There's no problems with that," he said.

Kennedy said he had met people in Mississippi and elsewhere who couldn't get jobs. In fact, Mississippi officials had testified the day before that many people in the state lacked the education and training to get jobs, he pointed out.

At this, Langford interrupted him.

"I think basically most of our colored people here, even though they are very, very poor, some of them, have a lot of pride. They don't like to take a handout. They'll scrape around to get a few dollars to buy the food stamps. I think it gives them something to live for, rather than just 'I'll become a ward of the government.' That's the thing that disturbs us here," he said.

"Disturbs who?" Kennedy asked.

"Disturbs the people of this community. We want to help 'em, and we want to see that nobody goes hungry. I have a standing offer from my paper, that anybody who goes hungry, I'll put food on their table. . . ." Langford said.

With a sly grin, Kennedy said, "Well, here, I'll introduce you over here, . . ." as he gestured and took a step toward the Dillard children.

Langford, nodding, looked down, then back up at Kennedy, "I live with this every day . . ." he said.

"Well, I don't think that it's satisfactory," Kennedy replied. He went on to say that he wasn't trying to criticize Langford or the state of Mississippi. "I just don't, in the United States, think that it's satisfactory that that kind of situation exists," he said.

Senator Joseph Clark, who had shouldered his way to Kennedy's side by this time, asked Langford how many families like the Dillards were in the area.

"How many are like this?" Langford repeated. "There's no answer to that, sir."

Speaking to a group of reporters just outside Annie White's house, Kennedy was clearly still moved by the plight of her family as he addressed Langford's broader question about poverty beyond Mississippi. Starting out with a sigh, and looking as if his thoughts were focused elsewhere, Kennedy acknowledged "tremendous deprivation" elsewhere in the nation. But there was an important distinction between what he had just seen in the White household and elsewhere in the Delta and the poverty in places like Harlem and Bedford-Stuyvesant, Kennedy pointed out.

"In the large cities of the country, particularly in the North, where there is poverty, people can live on welfare so that the children don't suffer. Here, children, as well as grown ups, are suffering," he said, his voice low and grave, as he looked down and stuttered momentarily.

Looking troubled, he went on in a quiet, serious tone. In Mississippi, the housing, he said, was completely inadequate, and many of the children in the state could not attend school because they lacked sufficient clothes to wear, he said, glancing away, perhaps to where the neighborhood children were playing outside the focus of the camera. He let out a quiet sigh, and then looked back straight into the camera.

"So as I say, I think it's a terrible reflection on our society," he said in a more confident tone. With gathering energy, Kennedy then went on to emphasize how invisible poverty was for most Americans, whether it was in the cities or in places like the Delta.

"I think that one of the great problems is that for most of us, as American citizens, we don't run across it. . . . We don't ordinarily run up against—if you're doing reasonably well—you don't run up against this kind of poverty, and certainly people elsewhere in the country have very little personal knowledge or information about it. But it exists," he said, raising his voice a little and nodding for emphasis. Then: "And it seems to me that we should do something about it. It's long overdue."

A reporter started to interject a question, but Kennedy had another point to make.

"And I don't think . . ." Kennedy said more forcefully, talking over the reporter.

He went on, sounding more and more like a senator as he got going. "An inadequate poverty program, or a poverty program that's on the books, and sounds good, but is inadequately funded—it might salve our conscience. We might say that we're doing what we should, but the fact is that we're not doing what we should be doing in this country to deal with this problem."

Veteran CBS reporter Daniel Schorr paid close attention as Kennedy emerged from White's cabin. Schorr had known Kennedy since his days working for Joseph McCarthy during the Republican senator's anti-Communist witch hunts. He had also seen Kennedy's single-minded pursuit of the presidency for his brother and his fierce service as JFK's most loyal cabinet member as attorney general. His initial impression of Bobby Kennedy was not positive. Schorr later wrote, "I found him then intense, cold, and unfriendly—and 'ruthless,' the label many pinned on him."

Schorr then left Washington for a decade to cover the Soviet Union and Europe. When he returned in 1966, he was surprised when he encountered Robert Kennedy after John Kennedy's assassination. "It was a changed man I met ten years later," Schorr observed.

With Kennedy in the Delta, Schorr had noted in his national news report earlier in the day that the senator's manner thus far had been like an "inspector general" as he looked at War on Poverty job-training programs and asked about food aid. But, in Cleveland, Schorr wrote later, Kennedy was clearly touched by what he had seen. "Kennedy went from shack to shack, shaking his head and muttering, 'this is unacceptable . . . simply unacceptable.' At one point I thought he was close to tears."

Hodding Carter III had spent much of his life watching politicians shake hands, do inspection tours, and kiss babies. He was, after all, the son of a community newspaper editor. He had been a reporter himself and was now an editor. However, watching Kennedy interact with the children of the Delta, Carter was struck by a significant difference in how this senator approached the visit. "You can usually tell that they would rather be somewhere else. But he was different. He was right there with those children."

George Lapides, a reporter for the *Memphis Press-Scimitar*, watched through the doorway. The image would never leave him. "I can see him sitting on that filthy floor with that child . . . as clearly as I see you sitting here right now. I can't remember a lot of things, but I will never forget that. That is etched in my memory, and I will take that to the grave." Unita Blackwell, a veteran of the civil rights struggle in the Delta, had met with Kennedy, his aides, and other witnesses for a working dinner the night before the hearings and had testified in Jackson. She accompanied the senators as they toured Cleveland. "I saw the look on his face when he walked into those houses and saw the little children with the skinny legs and bloated stomachs and the whole thing," she later wrote. Kennedy was "shocked and hurt by the scene," she believed. A year later, when she saw him as he sought the presidency, he thanked her for her testimony. "He just kept saying, 'Unita, I thank you for helping me see the drastic needs of the Mississippi Delta people.'"

As they concluded their tour of Cleveland's East Side, Clark, Kennedy, and their entourage of aides, police, marshals, and reporters headed north on US Highway 61. Throughout the trip, Kennedy had found ways to move off the path that Marian Wright, Ken Dean, and local advocates had chosen for him. This was typical of Kennedy's approach, according to his former aide, Adam Walinsky. He sought answers for himself and liked to learn things through experience. Kennedy disliked, even resisted, being led to any one conclusion, Walinsky said.

Kennedy was intent on seeing how people lived on a plantation, so he insisted that the caravan pull off on a dusty road and stop at a cabin. As he stepped inside, he found a woman alone with a baby at her breast. The mother was unfazed by the famous man in her front room; she went right on feeding the baby while she calmly answered his questions.

Passing through tiny Winstonville, a few miles north of Cleveland, Kennedy called for an unscheduled stop at a rickety shack by the road. When he knocked on the door, an African American man named Andrew Jackson opened the door. "Are you really Mr. Robert Kennedy?" he asked with surprise. Kennedy grinned and said, "[Y]es, are you really Mr. Andrew Jackson?"

Flustered by the unexpected guests, Jackson's wife apologized for the state of their front room, which had a tattered ceiling; a calendar and a photo of the Glorybound Singers was all that decorated their walls. "This house sho' ain't clean," a local newspaper quoted Mrs. Jackson as telling Kennedy. She had been working in the garden and had not planned on visitors, she said. Andrew Jackson, who was thirty-nine, told Kennedy that mechanization had taken his job, and he had been put off the land where he used to work. Since then, he, his wife, and their family of six children had no regular source of income at all. They got by picking up odd jobs for ten dollars here and there. For the past two months, he told Kennedy, they had purchased food stamps, but only because a reporter passing through had given him twenty-four dollars to buy them. That morning, the children had eaten sausage for breakfast, and for lunch, they had eaten "light bread." Kennedy, whose ten children had a menagerie of pets, noticed the family's cat.

"How do you feed the cat?" he asked.

"Oh, we do," the woman said.

"Stew, eh?" Kennedy responded.

It was growing late, and Kennedy and Clark were concerned about missing their 6:30 flight that evening from Memphis. In a huddle before leaving Cleveland, they had discussed bypassing the planned stop forty-five miles north in Clarksdale. However, Kennedy wasn't finished seeing the Delta. There was a crowd waiting in Clarksdale, where a biracial coalition had crafted a thriving program with a holistic approach to helping the Delta's poor. The crowd's enthusiastic welcome would buoy Kennedy after his encounter with the bleak realities of Charlie Dillard and little David White's lives and send him back to Washington on a wave of passionate acclamation.

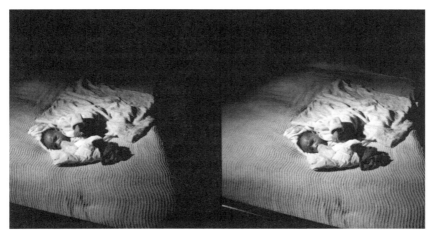

Three-month-old Lorenzo White waits for his mother to finish her washing. Credit: Dan Guravich.

The audience at Clarksdale, Mississippi, the last stop in the Delta, clamored for a few words from Kennedy. Credit: Courtesy of the *Clarksdale Press-Register*.

Chapter 8

We Need to Make an Effort Together

Ain't goin' let Mississippi,
turn me around,
turn me around,
turn me around,
Ain't goin' let nobody turn me around,
Goin' keep on walkin'
Keep on talkin'
Marchin' up to Freedom Land.

As the song rang out, hundreds of people outside Clarksdale's Neighborhood Center just off Highway 61 had been waiting for the better part of an hour for Kennedy's car. The morning's cloud cover had burned off and it was a very warm spring day. Standing in the afternoon Delta sun in an asphalt parking lot made it downright hot. Kennedy's entourage was late, but the crowd hung on, hoping for the promised press conference.

While the mostly African American crowd had waited, someone had organized an impromptu choir. Soon familiar songs about freedom and faith rang through the spring air, helping to pass the time and giving the event the air of a gospel meeting. They had not yet given up hope for a glimpse of this famous man, the brother of the slain president, a leader whom they had mourned along with Robert Kennedy. They wanted to hear what he had to say now that he had been to Mississippi, now that he had seen their world.

Eight-year-old Brenda Luckett was certainly feeling hot under the Delta sun that day, but she was determined to stay until she had seen Robert Kennedy. Brenda wasn't very tall, but she had claimed a prime position that helped her see over the heads of many of her parents' friends and neighbors in the crowd. Her uncle, Will Poindexter, had been in Clarksdale that morning selling spring vegetables—onions, greens, young lettuce—from her grandfather's farm, and he had stayed in town to see Kennedy too.

As Brenda stood on the tailgate of her uncle's pickup truck, she watched the road for Kennedy's car. She may have only been in the third grade, but she knew what Robert Kennedy looked like; her house was one of the few on her street in Clarksdale's small, tight-knit black middle-class neighborhood to have a television. She had seen him on the news, looking pale and stricken as he walked behind his brother's horse-drawn casket.

Brenda also knew the Kennedys were important to her family and her community. Her parents had John Kennedy's photo on the wall of their living room, right next to portraits of Jesus and Martin Luther King. Her mother helped Brenda keep a scrapbook, and one of her prized pages had John Kennedy's picture on it. When they visited Washington DC after the assassination, her parents had made sure they toured the White House.

President John Kennedy and Robert Kennedy may have frustrated civil rights activists by their cautious, often calculating approach to the issue. But Brenda's parents, J. R. and Edna Luckett, saw them through a different lens. In their minds, the Kennedy brothers were committed enough to equality to use the US Army to make sure a black man, James Meredith, could go to the state's best university.

"Like my mama and daddy used to say all the time, they [the Kennedys] were rich enough not to have to do what they did," Brenda Luckett later recalled. "They didn't have to support us at all. True enough, they tell us the background: that they [the Kennedys] did it for this purpose or that, but they didn't have to do it. It's the same thing with Abraham Lincoln. They say he didn't really care. But he didn't have to do it, and he did," she said.

As she watched for Kennedy's car in April 1967, there was also a shadow of fear that clouded the excitement in Brenda's mind. She hadn't forgotten the grief and shock that consumed her community when John Kennedy was shot in Dallas. In November 1963, the state of Mississippi did not offer public kindergarten, and black children in Clarksdale went to house kindergartens. Brenda was playing in her kindergarten classroom when the telephone rang. Brenda's teacher, Miss Minnie B. House, who had grown children living in Dallas, answered the phone, cried out, and then burst into tears. Her relatives had been in Dealy Plaza as the shots exploded out of the Texas School Book Depository. Brenda and her young classmates knew that John Kennedy was probably dead even before it was on her television, before most of the rest of the shocked world. The little girl watched as weeping mothers and fathers arrived to collect their crying children.

Three years later, she saw news footage of James Meredith, the man who had made them so proud when he graduated from the University of Mississippi, writhing in pain on the pavement from a sniper's shotgun blast. That was in Hernando, Mississippi, just sixty-five miles away. Brenda also knew that some nights, her father sat up through the darkest hours of the Mississippi night with a shotgun on his lap, one of the self-appointed guards who kept watch at Doc's house, the family friend whom Kennedy and so many others knew as Clarksdale's civil rights pioneer, Aaron Henry.

"To me, it was a scary time, because I did know (what could happen). Actually, in the 1960s we lived in terror. It was terror," she recalled.

But that day, the fear remained just a faint shadow in the bright anticipation of Kennedy's arrival. The crowd, pressed in arm-to-arm, kept growing in size and excitement as Bennie Gooden, another local civil rights leader, joked with some of the women Brenda knew. "I know some of you church women can't wait to see him," Gooden said. "I know you all think he's so cute," he said as the crowd laughed and teased.

Brenda had a prime position to see Robert Kennedy that day, and she occupied an unusually privileged position in her community, one that set her apart from many other little African American girls in the Mississippi Delta. Brenda's father was a fireman for the Illinois Central Railroad, and her mother taught eighth-grade English, science, and social studies at a school in nearby Jonestown.

Brenda's parents worked hard to expand her horizons. Unlike some of the children Kennedy saw in Cleveland, whose parents drew a strict line between what was grownup talk and what children could hear, Brenda's parents didn't send her away when talk about civil rights arose. Instead, Brenda, an adopted only child, was the light of her parents' life, and they took her with them everywhere they could in Clarksdale and beyond.

J. R. Luckett's position as a fireman on the *City of New Orleans* meant that his family could also travel by train to see the country. J. R. had worked around trains since he started sweeping out the train station as a teenager. His father had the job there, but he didn't show up some days, so J. R. would go so his father didn't lose the job that the family needed so much. J. R. Luckett dreamed of being an engineer, but that was an impossible dream for a

Brenda Luckett's parents, Edna and J.R., took their only child to see Robert Kennedy, just as they took her along to other civil rights activities in Clarksdale. Credit: Courtesy of Brenda Luckett.

young black man in the 1950s. However, over the years, he worked his way up through just about every job available to him at the station and the rail line and became a fireman.

For African American men in the South, a railroad job was one of the best careers available. Working for the railroad meant that J. R. traveled and spent time outside the South, a break from the oppressive atmosphere of Jim Crow. Even more significantly, however, it meant that his job wasn't dependent on local bosses, which gave him a little insulation against the economic retaliation that civil rights work often generated in Mississippi. Because of that very fact, Luckett became a charter member of the local chapter of the NAACP when his friend Aaron Henry, a fellow World War II veteran, organized it in the 1950s.

Edna Poindexter Luckett, however, knew her teaching job in nearby Jonestown was at risk if she signed the charter, so she didn't join. In fact, after the US Supreme Court ruled in *Brown v. Board of Education*, Mississippi did away with its teacher tenure laws and barred teachers from belonging to "subversive groups," a list that included the NAACP.

Edna Luckett loved teaching. She had grown up in Mattson, a small community outside Clarksdale. Her family, which claimed among its ancestors Mississippi's second governor, George Poindexter, were some of the few black farmers in the Delta. Throughout the ups and downs of the Delta economy and the status of African Americans, they had held on tightly to the farm, which had about fifty acres, for several generations. The youngest child, Edna was intelligent and loved school, but when she finished the local school at the eighth grade, there was no high school for her to attend, so she began as a boarding student at Coahoma Agricultural High School. She impressed her teachers, and the need was so great, that even before Edna had formally finished high school, she had been offered a teaching job in rural Coahoma County at Sandy Bayou.

The state provided no school building for black children in that community at the time, so her classes met in a local African American church. Edna did the best she could with the outdated, and sometimes damaged, school-books discarded from white schools. Attendance was unpredictable. Edna's young students came when they could, when they weren't needed in the fields.

There were no school buses, and many of the students walked long distances. In the winter, few of her children had shoes, and Edna fretted over their cold, bare feet as they came in each frosty morning. The young teacher felt so bad for them that one night, she left the fire banked in the little stove that heated the church so the rooms would be warm when the children arrived. However, that night, to her horror, the school burned down. For the rest of her life, Edna wondered if her concern for the children had caused the fire that cost them their church and school building.

No one held it against her, however, and by the time Kennedy arrived, she had been teaching for years. It was a stable job, but it didn't pay during the summer, so Edna and her husband supplemented their income with a cab license. She also jumped at the chance, during the Freedom Summer of 1964, to be the director of a summer preschool program that was a precursor for Head Start. Brenda joined her in one of the classrooms.

"It was fun. Some of the volunteers who had come from the North were there," Brenda Luckett recalled. "They had guitars. Those hippies, they taught us so much about history and government. I had grown up in a house with books, but some of those children were very poor and functioning at a lower level because they had never been exposed to that kind of thing before."

The Head Start program benefitted more than just Coahoma County's children.

"Head Start was a good thing for their parents too," she said. "She [Edna] would go to their houses and recruit the children, but it also gave jobs to their parents too, driving the buses, preparing the meals. It got some of those women out of the field. They got their drivers' licenses for the first time. Some of them went on and got their GED after that," she said.

The Lucketts' careers placed them in the very small minority of African Americans in Mississippi who could live the kind of middle-class lifestyle that dominated midcentury American culture. They were by no means wealthy, but they had stable incomes and a car. They lived in a small brick house with a wide front porch on Peacock Street, which J. R. remodeled himself (he worked as a bricklayer on the side), with all the modern conveniences. Their television brought the wider world into their comfortable living room. The Lucketts took vacations, seeing the sights of Chicago and teaching their daughter about history and government in the nation's capital.

Their circumstances did indeed mean the Lucketts' lives looked, in many ways, like other mid-twentieth-century middle-class Americans. However, because they were black and lived in Clarksdale, this comfortable existence was always tenuous. The lives J. R. and Edna worked so hard to build were set against the unforgettable backdrop of Mississippi's system of rigid segregation and racial oppression. They could only rise so far.

No matter how much money they made, if they stayed in Mississippi, segregation limited their quality of life in ways big and small. It meant the state spent far less on their education and teacher training. It meant that no matter how smart Brenda was, how much she read, how fast she could add and subtract, they would still have to look in her bright eyes one day and tell her she couldn't go to any of the best universities in the state. That's one reason why James Meredith's integration of Ole Miss, and the Kennedys' role in it, meant so much to her family.

Mississippi's legal and cultural commitment to segregation and disenfranchisement also limited the Lucketts' options for financial success. It meant it was hard, if not impossible, to get a loan from the local bank without a white person to guarantee it. If they tried to register to vote or publicly supported civil rights activities, they might lose their jobs or their white customers. No matter how much money they saved, they could not buy a house in the best part of town, where property values were higher, held their value longer, and increased at a faster rate.

If they got sick, even if it were an emergency, depending on where they were in the Delta, they might have to wait in the waiting room until all the whites, even those with only minor injuries, were treated first. The few hospitals that admitted black people would likely be of poorer quality than the white facilities. The fact that this could lead to their deaths wasn't just an abstract theory; African Americans had died in Mississippi waiting hours for care.

Even though they were the kind of family that many white residents of Clarkdale would have considered "good Negroes," it would have been dangerous for the Lucketts to ever forget that they lived in the Jim Crow South. This meant that everything they had, everything they worked for, even their very lives, could be destroyed in an instant if they crossed the wrong line, crossed the wrong person, or were in the wrong place at the wrong time. Emmett Till and Medgar Evers were two prominent examples of this vicious truth, but just in Brenda's short lifetime, twelve other people had been killed for civil rights activities in Mississippi.

The state's embrace of white supremacy also meant that the avenues of redress in the face of any such loss, threat, or injustice were limited. Calling the police was a dicey option. Some them were helpful and did their jobs, but others served as the brutal foot soldiers in the state's system of white supremacy. In the courts, no matter whether African Americans were plaintiffs or defendants, just asserting their rights carried risks both physical and financial. If they made it to court, it was likely they would face a white judge and an all-white jury, people who would resist taking the word of an African American over someone of their own race.

Most of the time for young Brenda Luckett, however, these difficult realties remained in the background of her life. She went to George Oliver Elementary School, which was segregated, of course, but her family did most of their business in Clarksdale's small-but-lively African American business district on and around Fourth Street. This meant she was treated well in most daily interactions. If they ate out with friends, they ate in the small city's black-owned restaurants.

But Brenda was an observant girl. She had never forgotten the look on her father's face when, once on a vacation trip to Chicago, they stopped at a restaurant in Carbondale, Illinois, and the owners insisted they only be served out the back door. Never, he said, would he stop in that town again. She also knew that segregation kept her from one of her dearest wishes; Brenda desperately longed to splash in the new Holiday Inn's pool as she sweated through the Mississippi summers, but, as her mother explained gently, little girls who looked like her could not swim there.

In the segregated South, all black parents came to the day, sooner or later, when they had to tell their children why they couldn't swim in a pool, ride a merry-go-round, or drink from the cold-water fountain. Martin Luther King had pointed this out with poignant eloquence when he wrote in his famous 1963 *Letter from a Birmingham Jail*: of a time "when you suddenly find your tongue twisted and your speech stammering as you seek to explain to your six-year-old daughter why she can't go to the public amusement park that has just been advertised on television, and see tears welling up in her eyes when she is told that Funtown is closed to colored children, and see ominous clouds of inferiority beginning to form in her little mental sky."

◆ ◆ ◆

The Neighborhood Center on Highway 61, where Brenda and the rest of the crowd waited in April 1967, was a natural choice for Kennedy to visit. The organization, Coahoma Opportunities, and the programs it housed played a central role in Clarksdale's response to the changes wrought by civil rights' gains and the mechanization roiling through the Delta in the 1960s. Many of the people waiting there for Kennedy knew firsthand about how the new federal programs were working because no other contemporary operation in the Delta strove to meet their needs more comprehensively.

Two leaders, one black, local druggist and civil rights leader Aaron Henry, and one white, prominent planter Andrew Carr, had come together a few years before to form a community action agency to help Clarksdale's poor. (Carr's brother, Oscar, had met Kennedy's group in Greenville and later pleaded with Kennedy and Clark in Cleveland not to bypass Clarksdale in their rush to the airport.) Their efforts took advantage of the new federal money available for poverty relief programs. Since 1965, their organization, Coahoma Opportunities Inc., had received more than $5 million in federal funds and more was in the pipeline.

Early in its history, Coahoma Opportunities, had been held up as a model of biracial cooperation. It was touted as an example for the nation by Kennedy's brother-in-law Sargent Shriver, who was head of the Office of Economic Opportunity in Washington, who went so far as to invite Carr and others on the board to the White House in 1965.

However, the path of Coahoma Opportunities had not been a smooth one. And although by 1967 no one saw it as a paragon of biracial cooperation, it was still operating with a vigor and vision that outstripped any other operation in the Delta, making Coahoma Opportunities' programs in Clarksdale arguably some of the most successful in Mississippi at the time. At the Neighborhood Center, Clarksdale's poor (most of whom had fewer than five years of formal schooling) could find someone to teach them how to read or help them sort out tangled legal relationships to get Social Security. They could find help with emergency food aid or medical care. They could put their child in a Head Start preschool or help their teenager find a summer job. They could get job training themselves and be paid for it, or they might even be hired to build or work in a new Head Start classroom. They could find a safe place for their money in a credit union or, if they were elderly, get help enrolling in Medicare.

Coahoma Opportunities was born out of struggle. During the early days of the War on Poverty, there were competing groups who wanted to get funded as the community action group for Clarksdale and Coahoma County. With about twenty-two thousand people, Clarksdale was a cotton town, wealthier than Cleveland and less cosmopolitan than Greenville, and was situated in a county where almost seventeen thousand more blacks resided than whites. The poverty endemic to the Delta was just as prevalent in Coahoma County, where per capita income for black males was only $758, and black women made less than half of that amount. Like other parts of the Delta, it had been hit hard by the displacement of workers by the new technology and farming practices.

Its white leadership was divided roughly into two camps, an upper-class set who generally eschewed rough, violent means, and working-class whites who embraced aggressive measures meant to keep blacks "in their place." They were both staunchly resistant to civil rights efforts and integration and, for the most part, rigidly enforced Mississippi's system of restrictive Jim Crow laws and daily humiliations for African Americans. However, even before the federal Voting Rights Act, a few blacks had been allowed to vote in Clarksdale, albeit only in small numbers. By manipulating the state's convoluted literacy test, the county circuit clerk had ensured that African American voters never threatened the white majority. And, unlike other parts of Mississippi, while the resistance to civil rights progress in Clarksdale included beatings and a few bombings, it had never turned deadly.

In 1965, when some of Coahoma County's leaders realized that millions of dollars of federal War on Poverty money would be available for Clarksdale and that they couldn't keep it out of the city, they moved to block a rival all-black group of applicants. The county's leaders created a community action board of their own, one they thought they could control. However, even though they had asked a few black residents to serve to meet the federal requirements, they pointedly left local civil rights leader Aaron Henry off the board. Then, when the few black members on the county's board resigned in protest, their efforts fell apart.

However, Washington officials weren't happy with either group and urged Clarksdale officials to come up with another more integrated board. After some pleading and maneuvering by Henry and Carr, the new board became the official conduit for federal funds. Ironically, a white lawyer who was opposed to integration chaired the new board. It had more than a dozen, mostly conservative, white members. But with Aaron Henry and Andrew Carr and an equal number of blacks on board too, this action was celebrated in Washington, where Shriver and other administration officials were eager to promote examples of interracial cooperation. But their hopes of trouble-free racial reconciliation were soon diminished by reality.

Within months, the conservative white members, dismayed by the scope and pace of the programs coming out of the War on Poverty initiatives, had resigned en masse. Faced with telephone calls from the press and the office of Mississippi senator John Stennis (who had worked to block the group's funding) anticipating the group's demise. Andrew Carr drove the back roads of Coahoma County for three days until he had enlisted twelve new white board members willing to serve.

It is no surprise that conservative whites would have initially tried to keep Aaron Henry away from the Clarksdale community action board and no surprise that his fellow African Americans and progressive whites would see him as essential. By 1967, Aaron Henry had emerged as one of the region's most well-connected, influential civil rights leaders in one of the Delta's most intransigent towns. President of the Mississippi chapter of the NAACP, he had brought Martin Luther King to Mississippi and served on the governing board of the Southern Christian Leadership Conference. He had organized voter registration drives and mock elections to demonstrate the potential power of black enfranchisement. When hardline segregationists had pressured the Clarksdale Chamber of Commerce into canceling the invitation of the black high school and community college bands from the Christmas parade, Henry had organized an effective boycott of downtown businesses.

His dignified demeanor and skillful diplomacy meant that he could bridge the gap between the often-contentious civil rights groups working in Mississippi at the time. These skills had served him well in 1964, when, as head of the coalition of groups that successfully brought more than one thousand college students and other activists to Mississippi for Freedom Summer. Later that summer, Henry led the Mississippi Freedom Democrats, a group of African Americans and whites who were protesting the state's all-white primary, in their efforts to be seated at the Democratic National Convention.

A native of rural Coahoma County, Henry was born on a plantation. However, his family's emphasis on education and the G.I. Bill helped Henry chart a path out of the grinding rural poverty his family had known for generations. After serving in the army, Henry earned a pharmacy degree from Xavier University in New Orleans. Along with a partner, he opened his own drugstore in 1950, which gave him some autonomy in a place where most African Americans lived in fear of losing at least their jobs, if not their lives, if they pushed too hard for change. His profession, however, did not shield him completely from retribution. His wife lost her teaching job. He faced threats to his business and to his safety. And Henry was under no delusions about the deadly potential of Mississippi's racists. It had only been four years since a white supremacist had killed his best friend and close ally within the NAACP.

A Delta native shot Medgar Evers, the organization's field secretary, the night John Kennedy had proposed comprehensive civil rights legislation. Over the years, Henry's pharmacy was bombed, his home was firebombed, and someone also fired shots into his house. But Henry pressed on. He faced arrests on trumped-up morality charges but was undeterred. As the 1960s unfolded, he learned how to use his contacts and rising profile on the civil rights stage to leverage the new War on Poverty funds to address the needs he had seen in the Delta all his life.

Henry was no stranger to Robert Kennedy. The civil rights leader had met Kennedy in Washington several times, and, at least once, Kennedy had rescued him from racist police officers, perhaps even saving Henry's life. In the spring of 1962, Clarksdale merchants were feeling the pinch of lost business because of the boycott and had been complaining to city officials. One evening in March, the Clarksdale police chief showed up at Henry's door without warning and arrested him. From the start, almost everything about Henry's arrest was highly irregular. He wasn't told of the exact charges against him. Police chief Ben Collins, an ardent foe of equal rights for African Americans, took him to the Clarksdale jail for interrogation, even though the alleged crime had taken place in Mound Bayou in Bolivar County.

At the jail, there was more irregular and unsettling activity. The Clarksdale mayor, the county attorney, and two Cleveland police officers questioned him about his whereabouts that day, then he was driven forty miles south to the Cleveland jail. When Henry's friends and family, frightened and desperate for information, arrived at the Clarksdale jail, they were told that Henry wasn't there, and they didn't know where he was.

At this point, R. L. Drew, the head of the local Voter's League, called Robert Kennedy. Kennedy immediately called the Coahoma County sheriff. According to an oral history of Henry, Kennedy told the sheriff in no uncertain terms that if anything happened to Henry, then the US government would hold him personally responsible. According to Henry, the sheriff "got busy, found out where I was being held, and notified my family."

The next morning, his friends arrived, and Henry discovered that he was accused of asking a young white hitchhiker to procure him a white woman for sex, and then, when the man refused, Henry's accusers claimed that he told the man that he would have to take her place. The charges alleged that Henry had groped the young man, who jumped out of the vehicle and fled. Henry was released to his relieved friends on a two-thousand-dollar bond.

Soon after Henry's release, a woman active in the Clarkdale civil rights struggle reported to him about an anonymous telephone call that she received. According to the whispered message, Henry was only alive because the caller did not "follow through on his part of an arrangement." The man claimed that he was supposed to hang Henry in the Clarksdale jail. The death would be called a suicide and attributed to his shame at being arrested on a morals charge. "We had no way of knowing if this was true or why he had failed to come through with his end of the bargain," Henry said.

Even though Kennedy may have been wary of acting too quickly on civil rights violations in Mississippi in his capacity as attorney general, he offered a level of personal support for Henry's work, the civil rights leader said in later years, just like he had done for Charles Evers after Medgar Evers's assassination. "Bobby Kennedy stayed in touch with me through most of the hard times. He would call me up and start the conversation with 'Hey Big Daddy South.'"

◆ ◆ ◆

Like Henry, Andrew Carr was born in rural Coahoma County, and his early life was shaped by the rhythms of a cotton farm. Although he came from a well-connected family of means, it was not a life of unmitigated privilege. The Depression was hard on most Mississippians, and, despite his advantages, Carr still knew what it was like to wake up in unheated rooms and to have only a few clothes to get through the week.

Yet from early on, the educational and vocational opportunities open to Carr differed vastly from those available to Henry. Carr graduated from the US Naval Academy and then entered the US Navy, finally returning home to Clarksdale just a week before the *Brown v. Board of Education* decision in May 1954. Once back in the Delta, though, he saw his home with a fresh perspective. The poverty was appalling. The race relations were worse. And, he noticed, blacks suffered intolerable indignities at the hands of local officials. He spent too much of his time, for instance, getting his farm workers out of jail in on "indecent exposure" charges, all because there were no public toilets in town for blacks to use. The arrests, Carr realized, were just part of the ongoing harassment of African Americans by the white power structure.

But beyond these realizations, it was an old loyalty that also moved him toward change. Carr's younger sister had been born without a soft spot in her skull, a birth defect that left her unable to speak, sit up, or feed herself, and her African American nurse had lived with Carr's family from the time he was nine years old. When Carr left for school and the navy, the nurse wrote him regularly, letters full of love and wisdom that sustained him through miserable times.

Carr maintained that this woman's letters and her loving care of his sister taught him the fullness of her humanity, regardless of race. It was this

Andrew Carr (left) was a plantation owner who, along with his brother Oscar, cooperated with civil rights leaders to get War on Poverty funding for programs in Coahoma County. Credit: Troy Catchings.

conviction, his growing awareness of the injustices around him in the Delta, and his Catholic faith that moved him to agree to be on the board of Coahoma Opportunities Inc. Carr worked, along with his brother Oscar (who had organized the First National Bank of Clarkdale, which was the first bank in the area to offer loans to African American farmers and businesses) for Coahoma Opportunities' success, regardless of pressure and resistance from white friends and neighbors.

In his position as board president of Coahoma Opportunities, Andrew Carr had traveled to Washington in March of 1967 to testify at the first round of hearings of the poverty subcommittee. One day prior to Marian Wright's appearance, he had told the committee that although he supported the farm workers' minimum wage, it had vastly reduced the work available to people in the Delta. The War on Poverty programs were an effective first step, he said, in helping the Delta handle this problem. "Such a program will never create sufficient jobs or business to meet the need, but it does provide the means for effecting change in traditional thinking, planning and action for social and economic progress of the total community," he said. Carr went on to praise an often-controversial component of the War on Poverty programs. The community action concept, with its stated goal of maximum feasible participation of the poor, was "the greatest innovation in social thinking, 'to insure domestic tranquility and to promote the general welfare' that has come about in 100 years. If this concept can be made to work, we can at long last realize our true democratic heritage on which this country is supposedly founded."

A month later, in April 1967, Carr was waiting in the parking lot with the crowd there to show Robert Kennedy Coahoma Opportunities' work in Clarksdale. Aaron Henry had traveled with the group as they went through the Delta. However, when Kennedy's car finally arrived that afternoon at the Clarksdale Neighborhood Center, the planned tour and press conference were already off the schedule. The senators had fewer than two hours to make it the eighty miles to the Memphis airport. "We're in a terrible rush," Senator Joseph Clark told the crowd from the back of one of the cars. The flight was leaving soon for Washington, he said. "And I'm going to catch that plane."

The largest crowd of the trip—more than a thousand people—many of them black, but some whites too—was awaiting them, and Kennedy was loath to let them go without a few words. He climbed on the back of his car. This visit to the Delta, he said, had been "most helpful." Kennedy sounded a note of inclusion and solidarity with his audience, "The problems of poverty are problems of all United States citizens. We need to make an effort together." Then, as if sensitive to the Cleveland newspaper editor's comments a few hours earlier, he reiterated that severe poverty could be found outside of Mississippi as well.

Kennedy turned his attention to dozens of children and young people in the crowd who had gathered after school let out. "Stay in school, and get as fine an education as possible," he told them. When he asked to see the best students, "a forest of arms shot up," local reporter Curtis Wilkie wrote, prompting Kennedy to laugh and say that Clarksdale must have the "smartest students" in the country. Brenda made sure to raise her hand and wave from her perch on her uncle's truck.

As he finished speaking, the crowd pushed closer, hands outstretched. Kennedy, with a slightly embarrassed smile, grasped as many hands as he could. Soon, his companions could wait no longer, and the car he was upon began to move, yet the crowd reached up for him still, hoping to touch him or have a smile or a nod directed their way, reminding one journalist of the biblical story of crowds "trying to touch the robes of Jesus Christ."

Slowly, the local police force cleared the way. Brenda Luckett marveled that she had actually seen Robert Kennedy and that the visit was so short. She watched as those in the crowd continued to call out and wave as Kennedy climbed in the car and headed for Washington.

At the airport in Memphis, Peter Edelman took his time telling Marian Wright goodbye. Both of them secretly hoped it wouldn't be for too long. As for Kennedy, before he boarded the plane home, he told Unita Blackwell that after his trip to Mississippi, he would never be the same again.

◆ ◆ ◆

Around 9 that evening in Washington, DC, Lisbeth Schorr waited at the airport gate for her husband, Daniel Schorr, to disembark. She was eager to hear about his trip. She knew Dan had pressed his producers at CBS to allow him to travel to Mississippi with Kennedy, and that he was proud to be the only network television reporter covering it.

The plane from Memphis arrived at one of the most remote gates at National Airport, and she soon spotted Dan, who was walking and talking with Kennedy. After greeting her, the two men continued deep in conversation as the three of them walked through the airport together.

"It was maybe a 10-minute walk, and during that time, Kennedy could not stop talking about what had happened in Mississippi and how moved he was," Lisbeth Schorr said in a 2017 interview.

"There have been a lot of stories about how that trip really changed him, and you could see that. He was just so full of what happened and what he had seen, and that he was going to do something—he was determined to do something about it," she recalled.

Lisbeth Schorr had met Kennedy before on one or two occasions, but the intensity of his reaction left an immediate and lingering impression with her.

"It had clearly become a passion, almost an obsession for him. That was what so striking. We weren't just having a chat while we were walking, I was hearing this man give expression to how moved he was, and what a difference it was going to make to him," she said.

Mississippi senator James O. Eastland had a plantation in the Delta and controlled the powerful Judiciary Committee. Although they disagreed on policy, he and the Kennedys were friendly behind the scenes. Credit: James O. Eastland Collection, Archives & Special Collections, University of Mississippi.

Chapter 9

You Don't Know What I Saw!

Dinner at Robert Kennedy's home, Hickory Hill, in McLean, Virginia, was always a lively affair, and, at times, even a bit chaotic. With ten children in the Kennedy family so far—their ages ranging from newborn to fifteen—how could it not be? But on this April night, the Kennedy children were even more buoyant than usual. It was Ethel's thirty-ninth birthday, and they were staying up late. After two nights away in Mississippi, their father was on his way home to celebrate with them.

As they waited, Ethel and the children heard Bobby Kennedy arrive outside and looked expectantly at the dining room door. But, as he entered, Kennedy paused on the threshold of the dining room of the old house, his progress arrested by the sight of his healthy, happy children. Standing in the doorway, the room's old-fashioned folding door only half open, he recounted his trip to Mississippi.

"It was an unusual entrance," Ethel Kennedy recalled. "Usually, he would ... I don't want to say 'bounce in,' . . . but he would come in like a normal person and give us all a hug and a hello and tell us something wonderful that had happened that day. But, no, this was totally different," his wife recalled, nearly fifty years later.

It was a lovely April evening, and the contrast between his well-appointed dining room, with its paintings of his children, a crystal chandelier, and the table set with fine china, and the bare, dark rooms he had just left in the Delta could not have been starker.

Her husband was obviously upset, Ethel Kennedy recalled. "His mind and spirit were still in Mississippi. He was emotional. Everything about him was, I don't know how to say it, but he was more in Mississippi right then than in Virginia," she said.

His children took notice too. It was not unusual for Kennedy to discuss his work and the day's issues with them at the dinner table. In fact, it was a Kennedy tradition he had carried over from his own parents' table. But as he walked in, ashen faced, from his trip to the Delta, he had a different intensity that night, both his oldest daughter, Kathleen, and second son, Robert, recalled. "He was shaking," Kathleen Kennedy Townsend recalls.

His visit to Mississippi had disturbed him, and it seemed especially important to him that his children understand why. Kennedy was "ordinarily not a preachy guy," but he seemed emotionally exhausted and to have something important he wanted to say, his widow recalled. "He was extremely affected by life in Mississippi, and he looked around at all the children, and he just wanted to imprint on them that some people live totally different lives from theirs, and that they could not imagine the difference," Ethel Kennedy said.

"Families there live in a shack the size of this dining room," Robert Kennedy told them. They didn't have shoes or enough clothing, and they were hungry. "The children have distended stomachs and sores all over them because they don't have enough food. Do you know how lucky you are?" he said. "Do you know how lucky you are?" he said again. "Do something for your country. Give something back," he said.

The atmosphere in the room had changed dramatically from the fun birthday dinner, Ethel Kennedy recalled. The couple's children responded to their father's description of what he had seen and asked him questions. "It became charged with care, learning, putting yourself in an entirely different place and frame of mind. You have got to love children. They are able to switch. He had their full attention. There was just something in his voice," she said.

In his oldest daughter's recollection of that night, his experience in Mississippi went to the heart of her father's view of social justice. "When he saw people living in such poverty with a country so rich, I am sure it struck him as unjust and unfair and unacceptable," Kathleen Kennedy Townsend said.

Later, Kennedy Townsend would write about that night for the *New York Times*, recalling that her father regularly made sure his children understood that not everyone lived as they did and that they saw these conditions in Harlem and Appalachia and on Indian reservations.

"But on that evening his outrage was especially obvious, his sense of injustice palpable. And he wanted his children to feel the desperation of those children the way he had—and to see the need to do something positive about it," she wrote.

Robert Kennedy was not prone to wait upon solutions. Once he saw a problem, he threw himself into addressing it, like he had with the urban renewal project he had initiated in Bedford-Stuyvesant after the riots of 1965. The situation in Mississippi was no exception. Ethel Kennedy was not surprised at the intensity of his efforts to help the children he had seen on his trip to the Delta. Her husband's struggles to keep up with his older brothers had helped shape his personality, she said. "Jack was a natural golfer, . . . but Bobby was a good golfer because he had fierce concentration. If he had to sink an 18-foot putt, you better bet on him. He knew how to focus," she said.

The morning after the Mississippi trip, he and Joseph Clark had an appointment with the US Secretary of Agriculture, and the entire subcommittee had agreed to write a letter to the president calling for emergency aid.

However, it wasn't just bureaucratic solutions he sought. When Kennedy had arrived at the office the morning after his return, Melody Miller, an intern who was answering the phones in his office, watched as he sat down at his desk. Rifling through his pockets to find scraps of paper with names and addresses, he laid them carefully out on the desk. Then he dialed wealthy friends and charitable agencies, one after the other.

"Could you please send a carton of soup to this address?" he said. "And could you please send blankets to this address?" During the calls, he told them of his trip to Mississippi. "I've just seen such horror, and I'm going to try to do something about it," Miller heard him say. "It's unacceptable," he said. Miller had not been working in Kennedy's office long, but she knew that when Kennedy said something was "unacceptable," he meant it had to be addressed, and addressed immediately.

◆ ◆ ◆

Even though he was doing what he could, Robert Kennedy was still wrestling with the emotional impact of his experience in Mississippi. After a frustrating and unproductive meeting about the people of the Delta with the secretary of agriculture, he flew to New York.

That night, he encountered the wife of Carter Burden, a legislative aide in his New York office. Amanda Burden was a delicate young beauty with luminous eyes, a heart-shaped face, and a pearl-like complexion. As the daughter of an heir to the Standard Oil fortune and the stepdaughter of CBS founder William Paley, Burden could have been at the very heart of New York City's social scene. However, she and her husband, who were awaiting the birth of their first child, were happy to spend quiet evenings at dinner with Bobby Kennedy when he came to town for his senatorial duties, Burden said.

"We were just kids, and we spent a lot of time with Bobby because Ethel was down with all their babies in McLean," she said.

Kennedy often let his guard down with the young couple.

"When he would tell you something, he was totally there. He would kind of lean toward you. You can see that even in the pictures, but not in the way that politicians usually lean toward you. There was this gentle, deep feeling that was so intense, especially if he were moved or angered by something," she recalled.

The young woman knew immediately, though, that something was different about Kennedy that night following his return from Mississippi, she told biographer Evan Thomas in 2000.

"He grabbed me," recalled Amanda Burden. "He said, 'You don't know what I saw! I have done nothing with my life! Everything I have done was a waste! Everything I have done was worthless!' He was so shaken, so self-deprecating about his life. Mississippi was the worst thing; he needed to dedicate his life to this."

The impact lingered beyond the days immediately following his trip to the Delta, Burden said.

"This seemed to refocus his life in a deep, profound, *personal* way. And he was as shaken by what he had *never* seen as by what he saw."

In conversation that night and subsequent ones, Kennedy asked questions of the Burdens and himself, she recalled. Raw poverty—why didn't he dedicate his life to that work? Why had he been focusing on all these other things?

"His passion for justice, for equality—he talked differently after Mississippi than he did before, about people, pain and suffering. It was as if he had this profound knowledge about this unfair society and people who could not help themselves."

Based on her observation, the intensity of Kennedy's reaction also influenced how he connected with voters once he began to run for president the next year, Burden said. It helped him touch a chord with voters from diverse backgrounds.

"And that, I think, was due to Mississippi," she said. "If you had seen him . . ." Burden said, her words trailing off as she recalled the encounter fifty years earlier. "He was just so wounded by the pain of others."

◆ ◆ ◆

Kennedy was by no means naïve about how Washington worked, but when he framed a problem as a moral imperative, he often developed a laserlike focus. It did not take long for him to realize that the officials who controlled federal money and policies did not share his clarity on the need to feed hungry children like little David White as soon as possible. And once again, a Mississippi elected official—in some ways perhaps the most powerful he had encountered thus far—would stand in the way.

On the morning after their return from Mississippi, Kennedy and Clark, eager to mobilize a quick federal response to the crisis they had encountered, had immediately called upon Secretary of Agriculture Orville Freeman, whose agency oversaw food aid programs including the commodity programs, the food stamp programs, and the school lunch program. Kennedy had good reason to consider Freeman a potential ally. He was one of the few members of Johnson's administration who had continued to be friendly toward Kennedy. Also, Freeman had worked closely with John Kennedy, who, moved by poverty that he saw while campaigning in rural West Virginia, had on his first day in office delivered on a promise to expand the commodity surplus food distribution. Furthermore, as agriculture secretary, Freeman was instrumental in early 1961 when the new president activated congressional authorization languishing since 1959 for a pilot food stamp program that his Republican predecessor, Dwight Eisenhower, had declined to act upon.

Consequently, Kennedy was unprepared for Freeman's resistance to their recommendation to send emergency commodities into the Delta counties immediately, and was surprised by Freeman's hesitation to act on Kennedy and Clark's request that the cost of food stamps should be waived for the nation's poorest residents. Although he was sympathetic to their concerns, Freeman was skeptical about their descriptions of families with no income.

"Bob, there aren't people with no income in this country. That couldn't be. How would they exist?" Freeman said.

Remembering Andrew Jackson in Winstonville and others whom he had met, Kennedy assured him that there were indeed some Americans with no income. In fact, he had met them only twenty-four hours before. After an extended discussion about regulations with little progress, Kennedy cut to his point. "I just don't know, Orville. I don't know why you can't just get some food down there," Kennedy said.

Freeman finally agreed to send some of his own staff to investigate further to travel with Kennedy's aide, Peter Edelman, and retrace the route through the Delta. As Edelman and Kennedy left Freeman's office, Kennedy said to his aide, "You know, I really like Orville Freeman, and I don't understand why he gets so mad. And I don't understand why, when we've seen hungry people, why they can't be fed." He was, Edelman recalled, nonplussed.

What Kennedy did not realize during that first meeting was the extent to which a man who now represented the people of the Mississippi Delta actually controlled Freeman's ability to help them. It was a lesson Kennedy would soon learn well, to his frustration, during the summer of 1967.

While Freeman may have been the secretary of agriculture for six years, in reality, Representative Jamie Whitten, who had represented Mississippi's Second District in Congress since 1941, was privately known in the capital as the Department of Agriculture's "permanent Secretary."

Whitten was a native of the Delta, and his district included a large portion of the impoverished agricultural region. As chairman of the House Agriculture Committee's Subcommittee for Appropriations for the previous nineteen years, the low-key, smooth-talking southerner controlled every penny that flowed into every part of the Department of Agriculture's $7 billion budget.

As journalist Nick Kotz observed in his book, *Let Them Eat Promises: The Politics of Hunger in America*, presidents and cabinet officials came and went, but Whitten remained. The energetic former prosecutor had a steely mastery of the complex funding streams and government expenditures that flowed through the department. Journalists at the time noted that agriculture officials, even the cabinet-level secretary, ignored Whitten's priorities and prejudices at their peril. The congressman from the Mississippi Delta could defund entire projects and eliminate hundreds of jobs with a stroke of the pen. "He's got the most phenomenal information and total recall," one official told a journalist at the time. "Once you fully understand his do's and don'ts and establish rapport with him, life is a whole lot easier."

For Jamie Whitten, those "do's" included the staunch maintenance and expansion of the multimillion-dollar farm subsidies that flowed into Delta planters' pockets. This included several of the programs that had helped accelerate the transition toward mechanization and the use of pesticides. His list of "don'ts" included implementing anything that smacked of integration or "social welfare." For example, in 1946, he had blocked a planned study examining the impact of returning black soldiers on the agricultural workforce that could have informed government strategies and policies for the changes poised to upend the Delta's farm workforce. To Whitten, a program to feed the hungry like that Kennedy and the other senators were urging was "a hound dog project," one longtime Agriculture official told journalist Nick Kotz, one that, "like a hound dog, "is always hanging around, useless, waiting to be thrown scraps."

Whitten feared that federal money might breed dependence in the poor families who received them, but farm subsidies carried no such apprehensions for him. During the 1960s in Whitten's district, as many as 59 percent of Whitten's constituents were mired well below the federal poverty line, yet received only $4 million in food aid. Within the same time period, the federal

Mississippi senator John C. Stennis, known as the "conscience of the Senate," was a vociferous critic of poverty programs in Mississippi. Credit: Jim Lucas Estate.

government paid a tiny .03 percent of the population in Whitten's district $23.5 million in farm subsidies.

And in 1964, despite Congress's approval of President Johnson's expansion of the school lunch program, Whitten and a colleague held up funding for a program that would have fed 5 million hungry children for more than two years. Furthermore, when Johnson authorized the Department of Agriculture to coordinate services and aid to rural families, including basic needs like food, water, housing, and education, Whitten, thought it "smacked of social experimentation and civil rights" and simply drained its budget and transferred its powers to a more conservative agency.

After meeting with Freeman, Kennedy tapped Peter Edelman to retrace their route through Mississippi along with the Department of Agriculture officials. Edelman wanted to help solve the problems, but his eagerness to return was something more than just professional. When he called Marian

Wright to tell her, her response was similar. As the couple drove through the Delta's fields, green with new growth, they found themselves holding hands across the front seat as the Department of Agriculture officials followed in a second car.

While Freeman's aides headed to Mississippi, Kennedy and Clark kept pushing on other fronts. Even Senator George Murphy, a conservative Republican from California, had seen enough just during the hearing in Jackson to move at the end of the hearing that the subcommittee write a letter to President Lyndon Johnson requesting immediate action on food aid to the region.

Johnson's aides were wary of Kennedy's involvement in the issue, and Edelman conceded in a later oral history that even the conservative members of the subcommittee "were quite united . . . Republicans were as eager to embarrass Lyndon Johnson as Robert Kennedy was," Edelman said. Because of the two men's history of ill will and distrust, Johnson interpreted Kennedy's attention to poverty as an effort to make the president look bad. Perhaps hoping to mute Robert Kennedy's criticism of some of the War on Poverty's problems by playing on the famed Kennedy family loyalty, the White House initially tried to refuse receipt of the letter, suggesting instead that it go to Kennedy's brother-in-law Sargent Shriver at the Office of Economic Opportunity. When Kennedy heard about this, "he just exploded," Peter Edelman said.

"You tell them to take the letter. The United States Senate can send a letter to the President of the United States," Kennedy said. However, White House officials never responded and routed the letter to Shriver's office anyway, which only issued a press release a few days later essentially blaming Congress for underfunding the War on Poverty.

Meanwhile, Kennedy's staff, along with Clark's and the staff of the subcommittee, wrote memos and letters and searched legislation and agency regulations to find ways to dispatch emergency aid to the Delta or to ease the restrictions on allowing food stamps and commodities in the same county. They made little progress. Behind the scenes, as usual, Whitten was unmoved, sounding a thunderous "No" to any of the proposed food aid reforms. Freeman, worried about the upcoming renewal of the nationwide food stamp program, begged Kennedy and Clark not to go public with their concerns so southern conservatives would not eliminate the food stamp program completely.

Retracing Kennedy's and Clark's steps in Mississippi, the two aides who had returned to the state with Peter Edelman were soon convinced that there were indeed families who could not find even two dollars a month per person for food stamps. A team of nutritionists that Freeman sent in a few weeks later found that poor families' "diet was worse than had been that of the average Southern family with less than $2,000 annual income in 1955—12 years earlier."

Two weeks after his return from Mississippi, Kennedy sought help from his fellow US Senators at an Agriculture and Forestry subcommittee hearing on food stamp authorization. When they allowed him onto the agenda, he urged the senators to expand access to food stamps and commodities. Kennedy discussed the details of several policy proposals under consideration and expressed concern about the impact that a proposed measure, which would require states to increase their contribution, would have in New York, as well as other states.

Then he transitioned to what he had just seen in Mississippi two weeks earlier.

"I saw conditions of extreme hunger and saw people who eat only one meal a day. . . . I saw widespread and extreme malnutrition and seriously inadequate diets. Farmworkers who in the past have had only a few months of work are now losing even that as mechanization removes their jobs," he said.

He strongly urged the committee to approve the bill before them without adding more complications to the food stamp program.

"I might just add on our trip to Mississippi, Mr. Chairman, we did see children with distended stomachs and with sores on their lips because of malnutrition, and who are really kept alive because of the food stamp program and the assistance they receive," he said.

After further discussion about policy details and questions from the committee members for Orville Freeman, who was there to answer questions for the Department of Agriculture, the committee chair thanked Kennedy, ready to move on to other witnesses.

Kennedy spoke up.

"Could I just take 30 seconds more of your time?"

He asked the senators to consider finding ways to help Americans with no income at all.

"Many of these people whom we saw during our poverty hearings have been thrown out of work and do not have access to any income, so that they cannot buy the stamps," he said.

"The result is that they are living on virtually nothing," he said. Then he focused on the most disturbing part of his experience.

"And the children are living virtually on nothing," he said, warming to his subject. "And as I say, there is a tremendous amount of hunger, not just among older people but among hundreds and hundreds of children whom we saw. And I say also, here in the United States in 1967 we saw a lot of children with swollen stomachs just as you see them in India or Africa," he said.

However, Senator B. Everett Jordan, the chairman of the committee and a conservative Democrat from North Carolina, was unconvinced that hunger was truly a serious problem. The children's bloated stomachs could just be from overeating, he said. "You cannot tell," Jordan said.

"No, no it wasn't," a frustrated Kennedy responded. "It's a serious problem as to how they are going to get any food."

Another senator jumped in, asking to go off the record. After a few minutes of discussion, Kennedy said, "I just bring it to the committee's attention.

Representative Hale Boggs of Louisiana, which also has several Delta counties across the river from Mississippi, asked Kennedy if the people with no income to buy food stamps could get surplus commodities. Freeman jumped in and explained that the law would not allow counties to get both types of food aid.

Boggs did not comment and focused on Kennedy's descriptions of what he had seen in Mississippi.

"I must say, Senator," he said. "It is a very, very pitiful sight.

Freeman interjected that his department was trying to find solutions to the issue.

Kennedy ignored Freeman's comment. Boggs's observation had resonated with him, and he responded.

"It is very disheartening when you see a child seven, eight, nine years old, an American child, and you ask him what he had for breakfast—molasses, and you ask him what he had for lunch and he didn't have anything, and you ask his mother what she expects to feed him for dinner—and you find out it is going to be beans. That is what he is living on all the time, and they do not go to school. They cannot go to school, because, of course, they do not have any clothes."

Boggs said he hoped Kennedy would have some recommendations for the committee. "Because it appears we are missing the ones we must cover, somehow or other."

"There is a great and most acute need," Kennedy said, simply.

No one responded to Kennedy's statement, and then the senator from North Dakota, which has cattle ranching interests, turned to Freeman and asked about the potential for the government to purchase surplus beef.

At this point, Kennedy thanked the committee and left.

The next day, Kennedy sought help from a different quarter: Martin Luther King Jr. The two were not close. Men of different temperaments and spheres of influence, they had not always agreed on the path toward change or its pace.

When John F. Kennedy began his run for the presidency, civil rights leaders like King were skeptical about his understanding of and commitment to the issue. They knew that Kennedy, running as a Democrat, would have to appease the southern wing of the party, a group who bitterly opposed any progress on civil rights. Furthermore, his positions were not much different from that of the Republican candidate. And Richard Nixon didn't have as many reasons to accommodate segregationists.

Andrew Young, who worked closely with King, recalled the hesitations about Kennedy. "At that time, the 1960s, the black community across the South were largely Abraham Lincoln Republicans. My parents were Republicans. And I was rather cynical about the Kennedy family, that they didn't know any black people. There was a deep-seated personal suffering that we had known in rural South. But Kennedy didn't know any of that," he said.

African American support, however, began to shift toward the Kennedys during the 1960 campaign. A few weeks before election day, Jack Kennedy called Coretta Scott King to offer support and comfort after her husband was arrested on a traffic charge and sentenced to hard labor. Robert Kennedy was so disturbed by the injustice of the arrest that after wrestling with the issues, he called the judge in the case to urge King's release, a seemingly impulsive act that risked losing southern support. For years, this version of events—two spirited brothers, carried away with sympathy and interest in civil rights, push past political considerations to do the right thing—remained part of the canon of Kennedy hagiography.

The calls certainly had an impact. In response, King's father famously said the calls had convinced him of the Kennedys' commitment and that he had "a suitcase of votes" for the Kennedy ticket. Black voters did vote in higher number for Kennedy than they did for the Democratic candidate in 1956, making a key difference in such a close race.

However, author Larry Tye, in his 2016 biography of Kennedy, sheds new light on the incident. A 1992 book by historian Jack Bass had uncovered that the call by Robert Kennedy to the judge was coordinated with Georgia's governor to give him political cover. What Tye has found was that the calls were part of a larger behind-the-scenes plan by Robert Kennedy to get King released and that he carefully tested the waters before acting.

John and Robert Kennedy may have been genuinely sympathetic to King's plight, but they were too focused on winning the presidency in a tight election to let their emotions push them into action. Far from being swept away by righteous feeling for civil rights violations, the Kennedys pursued their plan with careful planning.

Tye writes, "As soon as they heard about King's fate, Bobby and Jack started making calculations about how they could help him and themselves.... Standing up for King could cost them in the Peach State; doing nothing would cost them with black voters nationwide and Northern liberals. The solution was classic Bobby: Have it both ways."

◆ ◆ ◆

Once the Kennedys were in office and the civil rights movement rolled on, RFK and King often misunderstood or disapproved of each other's methods. Several examples prove this point: King was not amused the night Kennedy, with his characteristically dark Irish humor, made a joke on the telephone while King was in an Alabama church surrounded by a mob of angry white supremacists threatening to burn it down. And Kennedy was baffled and irritated when King told him that the Freedom Riders would remain in the jails of Mississippi to protest their unjust sentences rather than be freed on bail.

Furthermore, King sank into a "profound depression," his biographer, Taylor Branch, writes, after observing the Kennedy brothers' handling of James Meredith's integration of the University of Mississippi, which left him feeling that African Americans were only pawns in a political game. In private, King also voiced disappointment in John F. Kennedy's address to the nation that night. By giving so much accommodation to Ross Barnett and the state's position and talking about the school's football glory and traditions, King believed, John Kennedy had missed an opportunity to inspire Americans and had "summoned the nation to nothing more positive than a grim obedience to the law," Branch writes.

Alternatively, King's willingness to put children on the front lines of the movement, where they were attacked by police dogs and sprayed with fire hoses during the Children's Crusade civil rights marches in Birmingham, horrified Kennedy. For his part, King wondered why Kennedy was so blind to the threats to their future that these young people already faced.

The most divisive issue between the two men, however, was Kennedy's authorization, beginning in 1962, of the FBI's wiretapping of King, his lawyer, and others in his organization. Powerful FBI director J. Edgar Hoover hated King and was always looking for evidence, however flimsy, of Communist activity on the part of King and suspected King associate Stanley Levison of maintaining old ties to the Communist movement in America. Hoover, Robert Kennedy knew, also kept an extensive dossier on the president's extramarital and often risky sexual appetites, as Hoover made sure to remind the attorney general every chance he got. In addition, the attorney general may have been motivated to head off the political firestorm if the press discovered that advisors to King, their uneasy ally on civil rights, still had these ties. When Hoover asked for the wiretaps, Robert Kennedy reluctantly agreed.

However, much had changed by 1967. John Kennedy was dead from an assassin's bullet; Robert Kennedy had coordinated with King to help Lyndon Johnson pass several pieces of civil rights legislation, and he was no longer head of the powerful attorney general's office. Vietnam was worsening day by day. What was most pressing at the time for Kennedy, however, was that he had just returned from seeing those hungry children in Mississippi.

When he got back to his Senate office the day after the April 25 hearing of the Agriculture and Forestry subcommittee, Kennedy dictated a letter to Martin Luther King, which was typed up and mailed the next day. While in Mississippi recently, Kennedy wrote, he had seen "enough evidence of widespread malnutrition and extreme hunger to convince me that a way must be found to provide more and better food to people with low income—or people with no income—in this country. I cannot agree with you more that something must be done." Kennedy also wrote King that he had urged the Department of Agriculture to lower the costs for food stamps, especially for the poorest recipients, and that he had testified at the food stamps hearing the day before. Then, Kennedy, whose interactions with black civil rights leaders could, at times, be marked by arrogance, reached out to King. "If you have any suggestions," he concluded, "I would appreciate hearing from you."

Other than a May 4, 1967, confirmation of receipt from King's assistant, which promises he will be in touch when he returns to the office, there is, thus far, no further evidence of contact on the subject between the two men.

On the day that Kennedy dictated the letter to him, King was in the news. The day before, as Kennedy tried to convince the Agriculture and Forestry subcommittee that children in Mississippi were desperately hungry, King was holding a press conference. Although the civil rights leader reaffirmed his stand against the Vietnam War, he announced that he would not run for president as a peace candidate. "I understand the stirrings across the country for a candidate who will take a firm, principled stand on the question of Vietnam and the problem of the poor in urban ghettos," he said, "but I must add that I have no interest in being that candidate."

◆ ◆ ◆

Meanwhile, the inevitable publicity that followed Kennedy's trip to the Delta had its own impact. Coverage of his trip moved several charitable organizations, including the Field Foundation, to mobilize aid to the region. After reading about the Delta trip in the *New York Times*, Leslie Dunbar, director of the Field Foundation, contacted Dr. Robert Coles, a psychiatrist, author, and Harvard professor, and asked him to organize a visit to Mississippi to further examine the food and medical conditions there.

In Mississippi, the reaction to Kennedy's visit and the resulting press coverage of hungry black children was as reactionary as it was predictable.

Opinion writers in the state leveled scorn and criticism at Kennedy, recoiling with offended honor at the implication that they would let children starve. Seizing on the word "starvation," they claimed it was a gross exaggeration and flatly denied the existence of widespread hunger and malnutrition in the state. Three days after the hearings, the main editorial in the *Jackson Daily News* said that the charges of hungry children in the state just couldn't be true, otherwise it would indict every doctor, hospital, church, official, business, and individual in the state. "Who would stand idly by and permit starvation when there is so much plenty in the land?" Instead, the editorial called it "a gnawing from somebody's empty brain rather than a growl in an empty stomach."

The paper's vigorously racist writer Jimmy Ward, whose "Covering the Crossroads" column ran down the right side of the front page every day, was incensed that Stennis's accusations of waste were dismissed but accusations of starvation were accepted "as the gospel truth," with, he claimed, little evidence. "There are thousands of persons of goodwill who would cheerfully help any starving person in the state. As was to be expected and easily predicted, the anti-poverty hearing put another smear job on Mississippi."

On the same day that Kennedy and Senator Joseph Clark traveled into the Delta, *Clarion Ledger* columnist Tom Etheridge took aim at Clark, charging that he "often seems more hostile to the White South than to Red China." The next day, the headline on his column read, "Hearings End, but Stink Lingers On."

However, the reaction in the state's newspapers was not monolithic. One newspaper editor wrote of dining with Kennedy and Clark the night after the Jackson hearings at the Derians' home. Oliver Emmerich, editor of the *McComb Enterprise-Journal,* reported that Kennedy did not just bash Mississippi, but he was quick to point out that problems with poverty existed all over the nation. Invoking Marie Antoinette's "Let them eat cake" comment, Emmerich cautioned Mississippians against overreacting to the criticism that people were starving. "Instead of flaring up with provincial pride at the suggestion, responsible leadership at the local level should and must search out the truth and cope with it whatever it is."

Anthony Henson, a candidate for lieutenant governor, termed the reports of starvation "ridiculous." How could such destitution exist, he asked? He went on to cite median income rates in Washington County, where Catherine Wilson and her family struggled to build Freedom City. The county had a minority population of 55 percent, and a median income of $3,112 per year, he said. "The foundation for such outrageous claims that besmear the image of the State of Mississippi in the eyes of the world and those of fellow Americans has clearly and purposefully been manufactured."

Cliff Langford, the newspaper editor in Cleveland who confronted Kennedy outside Annie White's shack, remained unconvinced, calling Kennedy "a professional politician, preying on the sympathies of the people by being concerned with children." He went on, defensive and scornful of Kennedy and Clark's motives: "Of course, the senators were looking for headlines and the only place they could get them was by making derogatory statements about "POOR MISSISSIPPI."

Later, on a playground in Cleveland, Annie White's son Michael would stiffen and try to hide his embarrassment as a classmate teased him. The newspaper had said the brother of the president went to their house, which was "the dirtiest house in town," the child taunted.

In the halls of Jackson, outraged denials and conspiracy theories arose. The state's Democratic chairman, Senator Bidwell Adam, claimed that charges were made by northern senators who wanted to undermine Senator John Stennis's exposure of the "endless stream of golden shekels flowing into undeserving pockets."

Governor Paul B. Johnson Jr. was dismissive of the allegations by "four Socialist-minded senators." He went on. "All the Negroes I've seen around here are so fat they shine," he told Bill Minor of the *New Orleans Times-Picayune*. In the *Memphis Commercial Appeal* three days after Kennedy's visit to the state, Johnson went further. Incensed that they had highlighted the state's hunger and poverty, he again criticized "the four socialist senators" who visited the state. "Any Negro in Mississippi who can buy $5 worth of minnows can buy a loaf of bread," he said.

But there was more damming evidence to come about Mississippi, too often the quintessential state of denial. On Memorial Day weekend, a team of four doctors led by Dr. Robert Coles headed to Mississippi on behalf of the Field Foundation. Setting up in rural churches and Head Start centers, the doctors were immediately overwhelmed and appalled by the needs and condition of the children they encountered.

◆ ◆ ◆

Dr. Joseph Brenner, who had worked with the Field Foundation to establish a medical clinic for the poor in Cambridge, Massachusetts, flew to Mississippi with Coles and the others. This wasn't Brenner's first trip to the state. A soft-spoken man with a gentle manner and an impeccable British accent, Brenner had been in Mississippi as part of the Medical Commission on Human Rights to provide health care for the civil rights workers during Freedom Summer in 1964. However, his return in the spring of 1967 brought back bittersweet memories. During his first visit to the state, Brenner had grown very close to Mickey Schwerner, one of the three civil rights workers who were killed near Philadelphia, Mississippi, later that summer.

The doctors split up, and Brenner and another doctor traveled to a small community in the Delta, where they used an African American church as their base. There, on Sunday morning, Brenner found himself, a white, Jewish Englishman, in the pulpit of a black church in Mississippi giving a kind of sermon in front of what was almost the entire town's population. It was, he said nearly fifty years later, "a very astonishing experience." When he got up just to introduce himself and explain a little about what he was looking for there, the congregation urged him into the pulpit.

"Looking back on it, I thought I had a hell of a nerve, but I had no choice," Brenner said. "They forced me into the pulpit, and I thought, 'I'm here. I have to give a sermon and explain what we are trying to do in Mississippi for them.'"

As Brenner spoke about health care and the need for access to good food, the people in the congregation began to encourage him in the antiphonic "call and response" style of worship rooted in African cultural traditions. To Brenner's own surprise, he fell into the rhythm himself, drawing on skills that had made him a good mimic as an adolescent. "I rose to the occasion, I guess," he said, with a laugh at the memory.

After his talk, he and his companions visited the home of one of the local families for a dinner of grits and greens, another first for him. "It was, of course, ladled out with a great deal of good feelings," he said. Word had spread about their visit, so while they ate, local residents kept interrupting the doctors' meal in search of medical care for untreated wounds and illnesses.

After the meal, they met in the church hall to talk with families about their food and health care needs. But the local residents had something else in mind. Men and women, old and young, stood in a line that stretched out the door, all hoping for treatment for illnesses and injuries. However, Brenner and the others weren't licensed to practice medicine in Mississippi, so they were limited in how they could help. "It was a huge number of people, a bit overpowering," he said.

There were two young African American men, however, who were not eager to see the doctors. The men, in their early twenties, "were bothered that we came in like white knights riding on white horses trying to save them from their fate. They argued that it was their job to do something about their fate, and that we were going to disappear to the North and wouldn't help them one little bit," Brenner recalled.

The next day, Brenner left Mississippi, so disturbed by the plight of the people he saw there, he began making notes for his part of the report before the plane took off. While in Mississippi, the visiting doctors had encountered neither aid nor resistance from the state's medical community, but when Brenner began working on the report, he wrote to the Mississippi Department of Health for statistics. The staff there sent him a wealth of information on which to base his report. "It was very helpful, and very revealing," he said. That state agency had known the data points the report cited all along.

◆ ◆ ◆

When it was issued in the summer of 1967, the Field Foundation report was a devastating illumination of the suffering of thousands of children in Mississippi. The conditions of the children they saw in Mississippi shocked the team of four doctors, even though they were accustomed to treating children in crisis.

They examined nearly seven hundred infants and children in six Mississippi counties, including two in the Delta (Humphreys and Leflore). Many of the children they saw were sick and suffering. They found children with severe anemia; eye, ear, and bone diseases; and appalling tooth decay. Many of the babies and children had rickets, scurvy, and beriberi, which were unknown elsewhere in twentieth-century America. These pathologies stemmed from severe vitamin and other nutrient deficiencies and are usually only associated with undeveloped nations and famine, the doctors' report explained. The report noted that other children needed surgery immediately for heart, lung, and kidney disorders, yet were in such poor condition they would need blood transfusions just to survive surgery.

The doctors' description of what they had observed in Mississippi was direct and heartbreakingly descriptive:

> We saw children afflicted with chronic diarrhea, chronic sores, chronic leg and arm (untreated) injuries and deformities. We saw homes without running water, without electricity, without screens, in which children drink contaminated water and live with germ-bearing mosquitoes and flies everywhere around.
>
> We saw homes with children who are lucky to eat one meal a day and that one inadequate so far as vitamins, minerals, or protein is concerned.
>
> We saw children who don't get to drink milk, don't get to eat fruit, green vegetables, or meat. They live on starches—grits, bread, flavored water. Their parents may be declared ineligible for commodities, ineligible for the food stamp pro-

gram, even though they have literally nothing. We saw children fed communal-ly—that is, by neighbors who give scraps of food to children whose own parents have nothing to give them.

Not only are these children receiving no food from the government, they are also getting no medical attention whatsoever. They are out of sight and ignored.

They are living under such primitive conditions that we found it hard to be-lieve we were examining American children of the Twentieth Century.

We do not want to quibble over words, but "malnutrition" is not quite what we found; the boys and girls we saw were hungry—weak, in pain, sick; their lives are being shortened . . . They are suffering from hunger and disease and directly or indirectly they are dying from them—which is exactly what "starvation" means.

Even though Governor Paul Johnson had been dismissive in public state-ments of the reports of hunger and starvation after Kennedy's visit, when the findings of the Field Foundation report hit the newspapers in June, Johnson sent a private telegram to Senator James Eastland. "Have read with a great deal of dismay the wire service reports quoting a small group of physicians concerning the health of Mississippi negoes . . . They charge widespread dis-ease and starvation to exist in our (s)tate. As usual, the charges are general, nothing specific. I have appointed a committee to investigate thoroughly these alleged conditions and to give me the facts as they find them," he wrote. Once "this exhaustive study" was complete, Johnson promised to send it to Eastland as soon as it was available. The later report from Johnson's team of doctors, which got little attention in the press, found many of the same prob-lems as Kennedy and the Field Foundation doctors.

◆ ◆ ◆

The anguish of the children they saw in Mississippi spurred the Field Foun-dation doctors, just as it had prompted Kennedy, to action. In June, the team flew to Washington to alert officials in the Johnson administration, including Orville Freeman, to the crisis they too had found in the Delta. Freeman, who had by this time received confirmation of Kennedy's findings from his own staff's visit to Mississippi, did not encourage the doctors. However, Freeman made it clear to Coles and the others that, essentially, no matter the need, the political reality meant that Whitten ultimately controlled the flow of dollars. "We were told that we and all the hungry children we had examined and all the other hungry Americans . . . would have to reckon with Mr. Jamie Whit-ten, as indeed must the Secretary of Agriculture, whose funds come to him through the kindness of the same Mr. Whitten," Coles recalled.

Coles and the doctors received similar answers from the other federal officials with whom they met—the secretary of health, education, and welfare, Sargent Shriver, the head of the Office of Economic Opportunity. The message was that the powerful congressmen and senators who controlled such issues were from states like Mississippi and Alabama, "men hardly interested in advancing, as it was constantly put to us, our 'agenda'" according to Coles.

After several meetings, the group was feeling discouraged, defeated, and, frankly, disgusted with Washington politics, according to Coles. Most of the doctors headed home to their practices and lectures. However, before they left, two of them, Coles and Dr. Milton Senn, the head of the Yale Child Study Center, were surprised to get a call from Kennedy's office asking them to come talk with him about their experiences. Kennedy heard them out and then asked what they meant to do next.

"We've done all we can do," Senn said, bluntly.

"We've done all we can do . . ." Kennedy repeated softly, staring into the distance.

An uncomfortable silence fell in the room, Coles recalled. "He seemed to be musing—even as, for a moment, I wondered whether he intended irony, or meant to be sardonic and implicitly to reprove us."

Kennedy finally spoke: "I'm not so sure."

Kennedy asked the doctors to come back to Washington and meet with him and Clark and Edelman to discuss their findings and further options. Once they arrived, Kennedy listened intently, Coles noticed. At almost the same time, Dr. Raymond Wheeler, a pediatrician from North Carolina, passed Coles a note that said about Kennedy, "Those eyes, they don't let go of you!"

Wheeler soon learned why Kennedy was watching him so intently. Kennedy, by this time a Washington veteran, realized that Wheeler's southern accent and soft-spoken manner would play well on television news shows, and, during the hearings, his testimony would be given more weight by southern lawmakers who were quick to bristle at perceived insults or denigration of their region or home states by an outsider.

Kennedy knew that he would have a better chance of helping the children he had seen in the South if he kept these powerful men off of the defensive. However, as he continued to listen, it was his turn to bristle at the doctors' tale of how one official had scolded them for antagonizing some of those southern conservative lawmakers. "You don't have to take that. This is the beginning, not the end. You don't have to be discouraged," he said.

After a few telephone calls, Kennedy and Clark had scheduled a new round of hearings for the middle of July. Kennedy wanted to bring the doctors' findings to the public, and he spent time coaching them on how to maximize

Congressman Jamie Whitten represented much of the Mississippi Delta in Washington and, as chairman of a subcommittee, resisted efforts to get food to the Delta. Credit: Jamie L. Whitten Collection, Archives & Special Collections, University of Mississippi.

their political impact. Coles and Senn considered it an education. "We doctors learned how a determined leader who knew his way around the executive branch of our government as well as Congress, and who had the ear of newspaper writers and television reporters, did his work," Coles writes.

Kennedy filtered the doctors' findings and opinions through his considerable political and media experience. In one instance, he questioned Coles about how fat some of the children looked in the photo exhibits he had prepared. Coles was surprised that Kennedy didn't know how the children could be overweight yet undernourished and began to explain the effects of a poor diet. Kennedy was blunt. The children weren't on his mind at that point. He was, instead, considering what "ordinary, middle-class people would think."

Kennedy went on to tell Coles that the poor had few advocates in Congress, but that the people who were happy to exploit them were "well-represented." Language was important, he emphasized. One person's welfare was another person's subsidy, he told Coles. "A smile crossed his face as we contemplated the basic irony of wealthy, conservative planters in Mississippi denouncing 'handouts' to the poor, while accepting them as lifesaving for themselves—a kind of socialism for the rich, free enterprise for the poor." Kennedy knew better than the doctors the obstacles they faced, but he remained optimistic. "We'll get through this struggle, and I expect that if we do, some children will eat better than before," he told them.

However, Mississippi officials were not about to let the criticism of their state go by without response. Senator John Stennis, joined by the state's other senator, James O. Eastland, who, Peter Edelman noted, smoked a big cigar as he listened in the July heat, were invited to sit with the subcommittee. The Mississippi senators were especially incensed by the doctors' implications that the state's leadership was pursing an intentional policy of denying aid to the displaced farm workers in the Delta so they would leave the region for northern cities.

Dr. Raymond Wheeler, the North Carolina native whom Kennedy had recommended to speak for the group, responded, telling the subcommittee that the state was a "kind of prison" for poor blacks. The isolated people there were "a great group of uneducated, semi-starving people from whom all but token support has been withdrawn." It was a national disaster, he said.

The Mississippi senators weren't having it. "Gross libel and slander," Stennis pronounced. Such assertions were "totally untrue. Nothing could be further from the facts," argued Eastland. They produced state health officials to rebut the doctors' claims. They complained that the one-day April hearing in Jackson had only featured aggrieved, handpicked witnesses and that the subcommittee had overlooked state health reports that presented "positive information."

When Dr. A. L. Gray, the executive officer of the Mississippi State Board of Health, began to testify at the request of Stennis and Eastland, Kennedy, who had cut his teeth questioning witnesses like Jimmy Hoffa, was waiting for him.

Gray nervously joked as he took his seat that he hoped Kennedy would be "merciful." Kennedy ignored this comment and went straight to the point, asking Gray if the conditions described by Coles and the other doctors existed in the Delta.

"I am sure they do throughout the United States, in isolated situations," Gray said.

Calling what he had seen in the doctor's state "a serious situation," Kennedy asked Gray what was needed to help the "more important issue of many of these young children on the edge of starvation."

"In most instances, jobs would help, "Gray answered.

"Are there jobs available?" Kennedy asked.

Gray conceded that there were some jobs, but most required "a good, basic education . . . and most of them do not have it."

As he questioned Gray, Kennedy grew more and more impatient, firing questions at him as the Mississippi official hedged and dodged.

"What are we going to do about it?" Kennedy asked. "We not only have the grownups who can't find jobs because of mechanization of the farms, and whatever else has taken place, but also the children can't find jobs. What are we going to do to deal with that?" Kennedy asked, adding that the committee wasn't looking for scapegoats.

Gray volunteered that state officials were happy to have eight new doctors in the Delta region, but as for anything else to help the "rather peculiar situation" found in the Delta at that time, he just wasn't sure. "I am not an economist, and I cannot answer that question. I think that's a big reason why we have the U.S. Senate. You asked an awfully big question," he said to Kennedy.

After a little more sparring, Stennis finally intervened, asking Kennedy to clarify his question.

"I thought I made it clear," Kennedy said. He repeated his question: Did Gray take issue with the findings of the doctors who had visited Mississippi in May?

"Absolutely," Gray said.

"In what way?" Kennedy asked.

"I take it this way, because they have not identified anything except that 'we went into a county, stayed three days, and came out with this answer,'" Gray said.

"I suppose," Kennedy asked, "that they saw people on the edge of starvation?"

"I am sure they saw something that they evaluated in that way," Gray responded.

At that point, Kennedy had had enough.

"I am not a doctor," he said, his patience wearing thin. "I went there, as I have gone to Latin America, and East Africa, and Asia. I suppose I spent days or weeks in each of those areas. I saw that type of situation in Mississippi. I don't have to have a doctor to accompany me to tell me that that child is sick and suffering. I asked the child when he had something to eat, and he said he did not have any lunch . . ."

Gray interrupted: "Can you tell me how many children you saw?"

"I saw dozens of children," Kennedy shot back.

"I don't think this committee is aiming at the State of Mississippi," he continued. "Nobody has any animosity toward the people in that state, but we found a situation there," one that had been independently confirmed by both a team of doctors and news reports, he said.

"There was no grand plot to say 'we found a situation bordering on starvation in the Delta in Mississippi.' We actually found the conditions as they exist there," he said. What, Kennedy asked Gray again, should they do about it?

"That is a question of many facets," Gray responded.

Before Kennedy could respond, Senator Joseph Clark, the chairman of the subcommittee, jumped in, asking all the men from Mississippi, including Stennis and Eastland, if they would welcome shipments of "good, nutritive food," to the Delta.

"Certainly," Gray said, "if they need more food, and they can't get it otherwise, by working for it, they ought to have it, rather than probably sending so much of it to some other country." The doctor quickly added that he was, of course, only speaking for himself.

Then Stennis jumped in, reminding Clark and the committee that he was on record as "against hunger, malnutrition, and disease."

"I never doubted that you stood firm on that, Senator," Clark said, dryly.

Stennis added that he only wanted to make sure the aid would go to the "right places, in the right ways."

Eastland concurred, adding, "Of course the hungry should be fed, but I deny that there is mass malnutrition in the Mississippi Delta," he said.

Kennedy resumed his questioning of Gray.

"I gather that we have decided we want to feed the hungry" he said. "But we don't know how we are going to feed them. What else can we do?" he asked Gray.

"There are many problems in Mississippi that can't be solved by money," Gray answered. The doctor then drifted into details about reciprocal state medical certification procedures.

"Again, I don't think that is the problem," Kennedy said. Didn't Gray agree, Kennedy asked, that someone who doesn't have enough to eat would be frustrated to listen to the two of them arguing over certification?

"A child is going to die in the meantime," Kennedy said.

Unmoved, Gray continued to talk about the state's public health programs. Finally, Kennedy pulled out photographs of hungry children in the Delta.

"Would you mind taking a look at these pictures, doctor?" he asked.

"I have seen situations like that," Gray conceded.

"Does it have any effect on you as to what you think we should do about it?" Kennedy asked.

"Yes, I think we should feed them," Gray said, but then added quickly that he wasn't qualified to tell the local, state, and federal government what to do about the problem.

"Do you have any suggestions as an American citizen as to what we should do?" Kennedy queried, with perhaps a touch of sarcasm.

Gray got lost in a tangle of words about incorrect reporting of the state's immunization programs, and Kennedy cut in. He and Clark, the Field Foundation doctors, and news reporters had all found the same kind of dire situation in Mississippi, he reiterated.

"A lot of it affects not just grownups, who can perhaps make their own decisions in life, but it affects the lives of many, many children and forever. You as a doctor in the state of Mississippi and me as a member of the Senate of the United States, we have a special responsibility for these people who can't care for themselves. . . . I think we have to do better in Harlem, in Bedford-Stuyvesant, in Massachusetts, Illinois and every other place."

"This is an acute and emergency problem, and I think as you see it, if you have any compassion at all, you would want to do something about it," Kennedy said.

Now Gray was incensed. "Are you indicating that I do not have compassion after I spent 37 years . . ."

Kennedy interrupted him. "I am talking about people," he said. Winding down, Kennedy said, "I turn it over to you and Senator Stennis." But he couldn't stay quiet. Stennis and Gray began again to talk about medical licensing regulations, and Kennedy cut in to make one last point.

"I don't think this child," he said, referring to the photograph, "cares whether a doctor goes through all that license procedure or not. I think the child would like some help now," he said.

The denials of mass malnutrition by Mississippi officials in the hearing carried no weight with Dr. Raymond Wheeler either. Emphasizing his love for the South and the people, black and white, who lived there, he invited the senators to walk the "vast farmlands of the Delta" with him. "I will show them the children of whom we have spoken. I will show them their bright eyes and innocent faces, their shriveled arms and swollen bellies, their hunger, their sickness and pain, and the misery of their parents. Their story must be believed, not only for their sakes, but for the sake of all America," he said, looking right at Stennis and Eastland as the room grew silent. After a moment, the two Mississippi senators said they had no further questions.

◆ ◆ ◆

On the second day of hearings, the outsized influence of another Mississippian was felt, but not seen. Secretary of Agriculture Orville Freeman's testimony devolved into a shouting match with Senator Jacob Javits, a moderate

Republican from New York. His department was not mired in bureaucracy, Freeman insisted.

"I resent the repeated use of bureaucracy like we are sitting on our backsides doing nothing. I won't have it," he said. Freeman rejected the call of Javits, who had been in Jackson for the April hearing, for a state of emergency in Mississippi, saying it was "very intemperate, violent and emotional."

Javits refused to apologize for his emotion. "Perhaps a little more passion and a little less bureaucracy would help," he said.

Freeman insisted that the law would not let him send food to the Delta without local authority and refused to acknowledge pressure from Whitten. When asked whom he was afraid of, Freeman shot back that he wasn't afraid of anyone.

However, Jamie Whitten would later sound proud of his efforts to block what would have been the quickest way to get federal aid to the Delta, telling a reporter, "I *helped* the Secretary by making two points with him," Whitten recalled. "I told him he had to charge people what they were accustomed to paying for food stamps because that's what the law says . . . And I pointed out to him that the law forbids selling food stamps and distributing commodities in the same counties."

When national syndicated columnist Drew Pearson wrote that Whitten was blocking food aid to hungry people in the Delta, Whitten took to the floor of Congress to defend himself in a speech his office called, "Let's Keep the Record Straight."

Whitten argued that Congress, on his recommendation, had provided $140 million for food stamps in that year's budget. Freeman, Whitten said, still had $59 million "in his hands, not mine." Whitten went on to tell his colleagues that he did not believe there was "such a general situation in [his] State, but, if as the Senators claimed, there were families in such condition," the answer was welfare.

"I immediately called the public welfare director in my state and gave her full information on each family and asked that she have her people check the situation of these families and make proper provision for them. This she is doing," he said.

Charges that he was blocking funds dismayed Whitten, the congressman said.

"No one likes to be accused of hurting people. I dislike such charges, especially since from my District Attorney days to date I have tried to be fair to all people, regardless of race and regardless of the section of country in which they live," he said.

Journalist Nick Kotz, who examined in detail Whitten's role in shaping America's food aid policy in his book *Let Them Eat Promises: The Politics of*

Hunger in America, argues that Whitten, like other southern politicians of the time "could not afford to see the truth of the Negro's suffering because to feel that truth would have shattered a whole way of life. Jamie Whitten truly believes in his own fairness, his idea of good works, and the imagined affection he receives from Negroes back home. For 59 years, he has anesthetized his soul to the human misery and indignity only a few yards away from his home, and has refused to believe that the responsibility for that indignity lies on his white shoulders."

◆ ◆ ◆

Two weeks later, Senator James Eastland's nephew, Hiram, who was seventeen years old and visiting Washington from Mississippi, asked to meet Robert Kennedy. Surprised, Eastland asked why. The young man, who had grown up in the Delta, explained that the poverty of his playmates had always troubled him. He told his uncle that he had seen the coverage of Kennedy's visit there in April and was interested in his efforts to help. Robert Kennedy, however, was unavailable, so Eastland took his nephew to meet Senator Edward Kennedy. On the way, they ran into him in the Senate cloakroom.

"Hey Jim," Edward Kennedy boomed, "[d]o you want me to speak for you or against you on the floor of the Senate today?"

As he shook Kennedy's hand, Eastland said, "Hell, Teddy, [y]ou know I want you to speak against me. Every time you do, I pick up 100,000 votes in Mississippi." He introduced his nephew, and after a few minutes of conversation, Kennedy laughed and headed toward the door.

Eastland, who hated to miss a chance to embarrass two people at the same time, his nephew said, called out, "Teddy, you weren't Hiram's first choice today. He really wanted to meet Bobby."

Ted Kennedy threw up his hands, saying, "Aw hell! I get that all the time!" and walked out.

◆ ◆ ◆

As the efforts to mobilize the government to help the people of the Delta dragged on, Robert Kennedy was still grappling with what he had seen in Mississippi. At one point during the hearings, Kennedy invited one of the doctors from the Field Foundation visit, Dr. Robert Coles, to walk with him outside the Capitol. Kennedy and Coles, Peter Edelman recalled, had developed a special rapport, the kind of relationship that may be distant in time and space, but remains close in spirit. In their first meeting, after a hearing on another mater in the fall of 1966, the senator and the doctor remained in the empty meeting room long after it was over. They fell into a deep, thoughtful conversation about children, Edelman said, discussing the contrast between the faces of black children with white children in well-to-do families and how the faces of black children changed as they began to "develop some consciousness of the cruelty of the world," Edelman said. "They absolutely grooved on each other. It was just one of those very emotional kinds of happenings. And the conversation, it was as though—there were not that many people in the room—but for a while it was just the two of them. The other people just became irrelevant to them," he said. This time, in the summer of 1967, Coles observed that as they walked outside the Capitol Kennedy was "stirred emotionally" by the children he had seen in Mississippi.

"This is terrible, that in a country as powerful and wealthy as this, that such children go on and live these lives," Coles recalled Kennedy saying as he ruefully shook his head.

After a pause, he said to Coles, "I wonder how the hell you can stand this." Then Kennedy put his hand on the doctor's shoulder.

"Thank you for letting some of us know about it. More people should know."

Coles should keep speaking and writing about children in poverty, Kennedy told him. More attention to the issue would help move Congress. Kennedy was doing what he could to help, he said, but there were limits to what a single senator could accomplish. "You know I'm one [senator] of dozens and dozens, and sometimes to get something done in this town, it has to come from one or two people over in that big building there called the White House," Kennedy told Coles, gesturing toward Pennsylvania Avenue.

One year and one day after he heard Marian Wright testify about the hunger crisis in Mississippi, Robert Kennedy announced his candidacy for president in the same room where she testified and where his brother launched his presidential campaign. Credit: AP Photo.

Chapter 10

I'd Feel Better if I Were Doing What I Think Ought to Be Done

The atmosphere in the Senate Caucus Room on March 16, 1968, was dynamic. Television lights outshone the crystal chandelier, and excited chatter bounced off the granite columns and Italianate marble. Reporters packed the seats. Kennedy family members lined the front row.

It was exactly one year and a day since Kennedy had left the chill of his brother's graveside on the Ides of March in 1967. After the reinterment ceremony that morning, Marian Wright had urged him and the other senators to help the suffering people of the Mississippi Delta. Now Kennedy was back in the same room in the Old Senate Office Building. But this time, there was no panel of senators, no fidgeting witnesses waiting to speak. Instead, reporters and supporters crowded into the room. Ethel Kennedy had the children neatly dressed and lined up nearby. Kennedy stepped up to the podium. "I am today announcing my candidacy for the presidency of the United States," he said, his clipped Boston accent ringing through the same room where his brother had announced his own presidential ambitions in 1960.

In his remarks, Kennedy called for a change in the "the disastrous, divisive policies" of the nation, including ending the bloodshed in the nation's cities, as well as "closing the gap between black and white, rich and poor, between old and young" in America. And although the focus of the press at the time was on Kennedy's position on the war in Vietnam, what he had seen in Mississippi had clearly affected his decision to run as well. "As a member of the Cabinet and the Senate I have seen the inexcusable and ugly deprivation which causes children to starve in Mississippi, black citizens to riot in Watts; young Indians to commit suicide on their reservations because they've lacked all hope and feel they have no future, and proud and able-bodied families to wait out their lives in empty idleness in eastern Kentucky," he said.

It may be hard to comprehend in today's political landscape, where candidates plan their campaigns years in advance, but when he toured Mississippi in 1967, it was not at all clear that Robert Kennedy would be on the ballot in 1968. Although the press regularly suggested that Kennedy harbored presidential ambitions, he had grown more uncomfortable with waiting as the months unfolded after the trip to the Delta. He began weighing his chances if he ran earlier than most seasoned political hands thought prudent.

The tremendous cost to the nation in both lives and revenue with the raging war in Vietnam; the inner-city riots in the summer of 1967; and Johnson's weakness as a candidate, demonstrated by Eugene McCarthy in the New Hampshire primary in early 1968, all played a role in his choice to run. But there is convincing evidence that his experience in Mississippi served as an important catalyst as well.

Kennedy's former aide and longtime friend John Seigenthaler, along with Kennedy's brother, Ted, and much of the Democratic establishment wanted RFK to wait until 1972 to run. They thought it was too soon and too hard to beat a sitting president from the same party. But Seigenthaler began to sense that Kennedy was weighing an earlier bid. Not long after the visit to Mississippi, Seigenthaler talked with Kennedy's senatorial aide, Peter Edelman. Kennedy, Edelman told him, was still disturbed by what he had seen in the Delta.

"If you talk to him, he needs help through this," Seigenthaler recalled Edelman telling him. Kennedy and Seigenthaler stayed in touch regularly, almost weekly, and the topic soon came up.

"So when I talked to him about it, he [Kennedy] said, 'have you been there?'" and I had, in Benton County, Tennessee, which was an extension of the Delta," Seigenthaler said. During that conversation, the two men shared their impressions of the "life, just the grinding life" of those communities.

"The point of it all for him," Seigenthaler recalled, "the thing that pierced the most and hurt the deepest, were the children. He would say, 'what in the name of God is this country going to do? Where are they [the children] going to go? What can make a difference?' It was clear that the state of Mississippi had no interest in providing education or nourishment that would change the lives of those children in any meaningful way."

Although Seigenthaler presented pragmatic arguments to Kennedy about why he should wait to run for president, he would later say he also believed that the intensity of the experience in the Delta, which he thought was regularly reinforced by Kennedy's aides who wanted him to run, weighed heavily in Kennedy's mind as he considered the 1968 race.

Seigenthaler said,

> He [Kennedy] would be the first to say if he were sitting here where I am to-day, that the visit to the Delta was unlike any visit to any other slum or any other area he had visited. Seeing those beautiful children trapped in searing hunger, seeing hungry children in the middle of the day and understanding that they were going to grow up to be something, and we had not done a damn thing to break the cycle of poverty or the intersection between race and poverty. I think that was the message he brought back from the Delta. Where were these kids going to be in 20 years?

Robert Kennedy's brother and fellow senator, Ted, also believed that the Mississippi trip affected his decision to run. "No one can fully understand Bobby's candidacy without recalling his engagement with rural hunger and poverty; his emotional interlude with a near-comatose, starving child that he held in his lap inside a shack in the Mississippi Delta, and his vow as he arose that 'I'm going back to Washington to do something about this,'" Ted Kennedy later wrote in his autobiography.

Years later, Ted Kennedy also told a reporter from Mississippi that the trip had a deep impact on Robert Kennedy. Freelance magazine writer Chip Mabry contacted Senator Ted Kennedy's office in 2003 for a comment about a story he was writing about RFK's 1967 trip for *Delta Magazine*. To Mabry's surprise, Kennedy took the call immediately. He told Mabry that when he saw the subject of his inquiry, he knew he wanted to talk to the reporter.

In his interview with Mabry, Kennedy called the impact on his brother "monumental." It was also, Kennedy told Mabry, an important point in the process of Robert Kennedy's movement from a basic commitment to public service because of Joe and Rose Kennedy's expectations and toward a passion for it in his own right. Senator Ted Kennedy also told Mabry that he didn't think the trip to the Delta and what it had meant to Robert Kennedy got enough attention.

"My brother's trip to the Mississippi Delta was a powerful and emotional experience for him," Kennedy said in the article. "Seeing the squalor of the living conditions and the listless eyes of the malnourished children was enormously painful. It made him want to come back to Washington and do whatever he could to help."

❖ ❖ ❖

When Robert Kennedy left Annie White's home in Cleveland, Mississippi, in April 1967 it was by no means clear that his efforts to help her children and others like them would include a run for the presidency in 1968. However, during the year that followed, Kennedy grew to understand much more deeply the magnitude of hunger and poverty across America. In the later months of the year, Kennedy and the subcommittee visited Indian reservations, the hills of Kentucky, and poor migrant farming communities in Texas and California. In each instance, Kennedy went beyond official testimony about policies and programs. Instead, as he had in Mississippi, he personally sought out poor families, learning as he went about both the magnitude and complexity of hunger and poverty remaining in America and the limitations of the contemporary efforts to alleviate it.

Although Kennedy remained convinced of the value of involving the poor in the decision and administration of poverty programs designed to help them, during the summer of 1967, Congress, under pressure from big-city mayors and southern conservatives alike, stripped the community action portion from the War on Poverty legislation. Federal money now had to flow through local governments, the very leaders that Kennedy knew from experience were often insensitive, if not downright hostile, to the needs of the very poor in their midst.

However, Kennedy was not holding out for a perfect solution. A short time after the hearings where Dr. Raymond Wheeler spoke so passionately about the hungry children in Mississippi, John Stennis's office called Kennedy's aide Peter Edelman as they were traveling in New York. Stennis offered $10 million in appropriations in emergency relief. Edelman was insulted at what he believed was a paltry amount in the face of the great need in the area. "I remember going back to him [Kennedy] and saying that it was such a copout. He said to me, 'We will take it, and say it is just a beginning, and that we are glad they are doing this. Nobody is going to think we are selling out.'"

Issues of race and poverty remained in the headlines through the summer of 1967. On the same July day that Orville Freeman, the secretary of agriculture, sparred with Senator Jacob Javits during his testimony, African American neighborhoods in Newark, New Jersey, erupted in riots. During the next five days, the city saw twenty-six people dead, hundreds of people injured, and property damage in the millions. Riots in other cities, including parts of Harlem and Detroit raged throughout the summer. As he watched, Kennedy was shocked by Johnson's cold, unsympathetic approach to the issue. When the president called in tanks and paratroopers to pacify Detroit, Kennedy said, "The president is not going to do anything more. That's it. He's through with domestic problems, with the cities. . . . He's not going to do anything. And he's the only man who can."

Kennedy had his own plans for addressing inner-city poverty, ideas that had grown out of his experience working with the Bedford-Stuyvesant project. That summer he introduced two wide-ranging bills on housing and employment, which, among other things, provided tax incentives for businesses and corporations to invest in communities. Deeply researched and highly detailed, the bills were consistent with Kennedy's vision of a cooperative approach, involving public, charitable, and corporate solutions. They also included an opportunity for the poor to influence and administer the programs in their communities.

However, despite Kennedy's efforts to promote his proposed legislation through speeches to business leaders around the country, Congress only scheduled three days of hearings on the housing bill and took no action on Kennedy's proposals.

Kennedy was also concerned about attacks on other programs that helped the poor. As historian Edward Schmitt says in his examination of Kennedy and the War on Poverty, *President of the Other America,* "In spite of his critiques of the welfare system, he believed the social safety net had to be strengthened, and he was determined to fight proposed House limits on the welfare program which he called 'a grim joke' and 'reminiscent of medieval poor law philosophy.'" He was particularly incensed that in more than two thousand pages of testimony on one of the bills, only ten of them had any testimony from people who actually received welfare. "By the fall of 1967, the War on Poverty had become at best a holding action, and Kennedy was one of the few national political leaders still calling for an advance," according to Schmitt.

◆ ◆ ◆

Back in March 1967, a month prior to his visit to Mississippi, Kennedy had stirred controversy with a proposal for ending US involvement in Vietnam. Despite rampant, ongoing press speculation, he had declined a request in the fall of 1967 by antiwar advocates to challenge Johnson for the presidency, a position he maintained for the rest of that year. However, as Kennedy devoted much of his workday energy toward trying to get aid to the hunger-stricken families in Mississippi, improving inner cities, and targeting programs to help the rural poor and migrant workers, the war raged on. Thousands more soldiers had died in the year since Kennedy had released his three-point plan to end the war, while the fighting continued to escalate.

All that fall and winter, Kennedy wrestled with the idea of running for president. College students, who had long been passionate supporters, began to challenge him on the issue of Vietnam. One sign on a campus he visited read "Bobby Kennedy: Hawk, Dove or Chicken?" Students, reporters, and other supporters asked how he could argue that Johnson's policies, both foreign and domestic, were disastrous and even immoral, yet refuse to act against them, a line of questioning that was wrenching for Kennedy, who so often spoke about the need to act with courage in the face of moral responsibility.

However, Kennedy fretted about challenging a sitting president, one who could manipulate events to influence the election. He worried about the adverse effects of a divisive primary. It might leave the Democratic Party weak going into the general election, setting up a win for a right-wing candidate like Richard Nixon. It could hurt the party in down-ticket senate and gubernatorial races. Moreover, the press had long focused on the mutual antipathy between Kennedy and Johnson, and Kennedy was reluctant for his candidacy to be cast as a personal attack against Johnson. "People would say that I was splitting the party out of ambition and envy. No one would believe that I was doing it because of how I felt about Vietnam and poor people," he told some friends who were urging him to run.

As Kennedy hesitated, antiwar advocates had turned to recruit Senator Eugene McCarthy of Minnesota, who soon began a campaign to challenge Johnson on the Vietnam issue and was gaining popularity on college campuses. Kennedy had little faith in McCarthy's effectiveness, or indeed, even his competency, to master the dangerous and complex challenges facing the nation that year.

America's involvement in Vietnam lay at the nexus of the issues Kennedy was most passionate about. When Kennedy surveyed the national landscape, he saw more and more young men, especially ones from poor families, dying in Vietnam. He saw deceit, incompetence, and immorality in President Johnson and the Pentagon's execution of the war. With what he believed was their flawed leadership, he saw no end in sight to an expensive war, one that was draining away money that hungry children like those he had seen in Mississippi so desperately needed. He saw a deep racial divide rending the nation. He heard angry rhetoric from black power advocates growing more militant. He saw a need for still more progress on civil rights at a time when administration officials hesitated to anger the southern conservatives in Congress who controlled the war's funding. He saw the cities restless and combustible. He saw his natural allies, college students full of potential and altruistic impulses, turning away, disillusioned and angry. And, of the two candidates vying for the Democratic nomination, Lyndon Johnson had wrought much of this disastrous terrain, and Eugene McCarthy, in Kennedy's view, could not lead the nation successfully through it. Yet Kennedy still held back.

As 1968 opened, American troops in Vietnam suffered a series of major setbacks as the Viet Cong and North Vietnamese Army launched the Tet Offensive at the end of January. The massive attack caught American forces and their allies off guard and caused them to temporarily lose control of key cities, including, for a brief time, even the US Embassy in Saigon. The uprising and attacks shocked Kennedy and the nation and stood in sharp contrast to recent assurances by US military officials that the war was going well. The Tet Offensive and the Johnson administration's response, which was to call for an additional two hundred thousand troops, in the words of Kennedy biographer Arthur Schlesinger, "changed everything."

Kennedy was incensed and spoke out in his most passionate condemnation of the war to date, generating a backlash of criticism, with some, even a few of his usual allies, casting him as a traitor. From then on, the unfolding catastrophe, as he saw it, of Vietnam dominated his deliberations and lent exigency to his decision about entering the race. Decades later, his widow, Ethel, would estimate that the carnage in Vietnam was 90 percent of his decision. Yet he had not forgotten the crying needs of poor children.

Although the Department of Agriculture had eventually made some minor modifications in food stamps policy allowing some of the poorest families to get loans to buy the stamps, even after eleven months, the "emergency" food aid that Congress had eventually authorized for the forty to sixty thousand needy residents of the Delta had yet to actually reach Mississippi. (In fact, it was not until April 1968, a full year after his visit, that any of it reached the state.) Furthermore, Lyndon Johnson's administration, distracted and on the defensive because of the war, barely acknowledged a surprisingly frank report on the impact of racial discrimination on the state of the nation's cities. And, as Kennedy had discovered in the months since his trip to the Delta, American families on Indian reservations, in the hills of Appalachia, in the farmlands of California, and elsewhere were still hungry, still waiting.

For weeks Kennedy discussed the pros and cons of running for the White House with friends and family. At one point, John Seigenthaler again went over why his friend should not run in 1968. "I recognize the logic of everything you say," Kennedy responded. "But I'd feel better if I were doing what I think ought to be done and saying what I know should be said." By early March, Cesar Chavez, the charismatic leader of migrant farm workers in California, was in a labor conflict and had been on a hunger strike for a month. Chavez would not break the fast, he said, unless Robert Kennedy came to California and broke bread with him. Peter Edelman took the message to

Kennedy, who agreed immediately. He was already going to be in Iowa, for the Jefferson-Jackson Dinner on March 9. They could just continue on to California the next day, Kennedy said. Seigenthaler joined them in Des Moines, and another friend, Ed Guthman, met the group in Los Angeles. Why, Edelman wondered, were Seigenthaler and Guthman there? He soon found out. On the plane to Delano, Kennedy told them he had decided to run, Edelman recalled. It was a bombshell. He had repeatedly said to them and others that he would not run. Edelman maintains that it is important to note the timing of Kennedy's revelation—two days before the New Hampshire primary had demonstrated President Johnson's weakening position.

Some journalists and historians have placed Kennedy's decision to run after the primary results came in, Edelman notes, implying incorrectly that Kennedy jumped in only after he knew the waters were hospitable. In fact, his private resolve must have come even sooner. Biographer Larry Tye notes that as early as March 4, Kennedy had asked a political ally in California to quietly make sure his name was on the ballot by the March 6 deadline for the state's primary, setting Kennedy on a path toward a thrilling, yet tragically final, victory.

Chapter 11

Bring the Poor People to Washington

I t was the end of the journey. Draped in an American flag, Robert Kennedy's casket was on its way to Arlington National Cemetery for burial under a darkening sky. On June 8, 1968, he was bound for the same hillside where, just fifteen months earlier, he had shared an umbrella with Lyndon Johnson at the consecration of John Kennedy's grave. On that day back in March 1967, he had departed from Arlington for the first hearing in which he learned about hungry and desperate families in Mississippi, the beginning of a journey that profoundly shaped his vision for the nation as he sought its highest office. By this night's end, however, Robert Kennedy's body, also torn and bloodied by an assassin's bullets, would lie under that same Virginia soil that was his brother's final resting place.

Three days earlier, Kennedy was shot just moments after concluding his victory speech following the California primary. Sirhan Sirhan, a twenty-four-year-old Palestinian immigrant who later said he was angry over Kennedy's support for Israel, approached the forty-two-year-old candidate as he walked through the kitchen at the Ambassador Hotel and shot him. Three bullets struck Kennedy; the fatal one ripping into the right side of his head. He died twenty-six hours later.

As Kennedy lay dying in California, back in Jackson, Mississippi, state officials reacted to the attack on Kennedy with muted alarm. Although they expressed their sympathy for the Kennedy family, their comments focused primarily on the threat against authority that the shooting represented.

Robert Kennedy's fourteen-year-old son, Robert Kennedy Jr. (first on the right), serves as a pallbearer at his funeral in Arlington National Cemetery in June 1968.Credit: The Associated Press.

Governor John Bell Williams, who had replaced Paul B. Johnson in January 1968 after defeating Ross Barnett and William Winter in the 1967 Democratic primary and Republican Ruebel Phillips in November, was out of the state. In Williams's place, Lieutenant Governor Charles L. Sullivan, looking uncomfortable, spoke to a WLBT reporter.

"It is a well-known fact that I personally have not been a supporter of Senator Kennedy, but that has nothing to do with my feeling of outrage and dismay, and, as a matter of fact, a sense of sickness that in this country that a presidential aspirant, a member of the United States Senate would be shot by a would-be assassin in a crowd of people at the very time that he is engaged in seeking the presidency of the U.S." Sullivan added that he was sure "every single Mississippian shares my very sincere and deep regret."

An unidentified older lawmaker said nothing about Kennedy directly beyond calling what had happened "deplorable." The shooting, he went on to say, had further convinced him that the nation needed a stronger focus on law enforcement.

"I believe it is necessary to put law enforcement back in the hands of our police departments throughout the United States," he said.

The nation could not continue with "law enforcement being harassed and ridiculed." "The nation's salvation," he opined, was "to restore the respect that the law enforcement agencies through the U.S. so rightly deserves."

Another, younger, legislator said the attack on Kennedy was "distressing," and he too emphasized that it highlighted the need for an increase in the local and state police powers to afford "national leaders every protection."

In contrast, a reporter questioned an African American man on the street that morning during Kennedy's final hours. He was shocked and saddened, especially with Kennedy's shooting coming so soon after Martin Luther King's death.

"Where does it stop?" he asked.

After Kennedy's last breaths had his left his body, Mississippian Charles Evers sat on the steps of the Ambassador Hotel, watching as the sun rose. Its rays pushed away the night's darkness, but did not penetrate his despair.

"God, they kill our leaders and they kill our friends," he told a reporter.

◆ ◆ ◆

Robert Kennedy's shocked and grieving family flew his body to New York City for a funeral Mass in St. Patrick's Cathedral on June 8. That morning, tearful crowds gathered outside. Loved ones, friends, and colleagues mourned as his brother Teddy eulogized him. "My brother need not be idealized, or enlarged in death beyond what he was in life, to be remembered simply as a good and decent man, who saw wrong and tried to right it, saw suffering and tried to heal it, saw war and tried to stop it."

When the train arrived at Union Station in Washington, DC, President Johnson was there waiting. Slowed by the mourning crowds of people who had gathered along the railroad route holding signs, standing at attention, or weeping, the train arrived much later than anticipated; it finally rolled in just after 9 p.m. Fourteen-year-old Robert Kennedy Jr. climbed into one of a line of cars waiting to carry him and his family to the cemetery. It had been an exhausting day, yet the young man still had a pallbearer's somber task awaiting him after this final leg of the day's sorrowful journey.

As the dark limousines followed the hearse through the humid Washington night, the boy watched as familiar monuments came into view. A soft rain was falling. Here, too, crowds lined the streets five deep. From the sidewalk, a spontaneous cheer went up and just as quickly fell silent as the entourage passed his father's Senate office building. The car paused before the Lincoln Memorial. Through the rain-splattered window young Kennedy glimpsed the huts and tents of Resurrection City, where nearly three thousand people, including some from the Mississippi Delta, had been camped out near the

Reflecting Pool for weeks. They were part of the Poor People's Campaign, a live-in protest designed by civil rights leaders to pressure Congress and President Johnson to act on issues of economic justice and aid to the nation's neediest people.

Like elsewhere along the route, a crowd waited at Resurrection City, but these people were not well-dressed office workers. Instead, they wore overalls, denim, t-shirts, and bandanas, Robert Kennedy Jr. remembered in a 2014 interview. Their solemn reverence remains one of his strongest memories of that sad day.

"They all came to the sidewalk while we drove by, and they stood there silently. They held their hats against their chests, and they had their heads bowed as we went by and took Daddy up the hill to bury him next to his brother at Arlington."

Then, as the hearse moved on through the moonlit night toward the cemetery, the crowd began to sing Kennedy's favorite hymn, the "Battle Hymn of the Republic," Marian Wright Edelman recalled. "It was one of the most moving moments of my life," she said.

The presence of Resurrection City in the nation's capital, where it brought the needs and issues facing the hungry from rural areas to confront the nation's leaders, was due, in part, to Robert Kennedy and his visit to Mississippi. As Kennedy focused on getting help to the Delta during the spring and summer of 1967, Marian Wright and Peter Edelman worked closely together. As the season heated up, their relationship deepened into a serious romance. By the end of that summer, they were in love. Edelman has written that Kennedy was happy for them and supportive of their relationship, even though interracial couples were still quite unusual. "Kennedy was very taken with her, and supportive of our romance. He was especially there for me when my father's initial reaction to the interracial relationship was less than enthusiastic. The three of us spent considerable time together over the next year, until his death," Edelman writes. In fact, when they met, Wright and Edelman's marriage was still illegal in 1967 in Virginia, where Kennedy lived. But there was a case making its way through the courts that they hoped might bring a change.

During one of her visits to Washington that summer, Wright stopped by Hickory Hill with Edelman to say goodbye to Kennedy. Out by the pool, Kennedy chatted with her for a few moments. Wright knew that children in Mississippi were still hungry and, like Kennedy, was frustrated at the pace of the efforts in Washington to help them. When Wright mentioned that she was stopping by Atlanta to see Martin Luther King on her way back to Mississippi, Kennedy had a message for King.

Bring the poor people to Washington, he told her. After all the bureaucratic wrestling, it was important that the American people see them so they could understand their struggles. Their visibility would put pressure on politicians, including Johnson, to act. Congress wouldn't act until it became too painful or embarrassing not to take action, he told her.

When Wright arrived in Atlanta, she found King discouraged and struggling with how to proceed. He faced a difficult task. He was seeking a path to the future that would on the civil rights movement's legislative success help end the war in Vietnam, offer solutions to the violence in the cities, and help the rural poor. He and his associates had been weighing a march or demonstration by poor people in Washington for months, but his aides were divided about whether and how to proceed. Standing in King's modest study, Wright gave him Kennedy's message.

"He treated me as if I were an angel delivering a message. He immediately understood that it was right," she later told an interviewer. King's ensuing operation brought three thousand men, women, and children from pockets of poverty across America to wait for meaningful reform. Wright left Mississippi for Washington to become counsel for the Poor People's Campaign, a move that brought her closer to Edelman as well.

However, after the deaths of King and Kennedy, demoralizing conflict soon marked the end of the Poor People's Campaign. The Johnson administration instead focused on passing a controversial tax bill and refused to add changes in food aid policy that would have expanded the food stamp program and provided aid to more poor school children. Then, twelve days after Robert Kennedy's coffin passed by, a thousand policemen took over the remnants of Resurrection City and tore it down. They used tear gas to clear protestors angry over the passage of Johnson's tax bill from the street near the Department of Agriculture.

As discussed earlier, Kennedy's push in the summer of 1967 had ultimately prompted a few changes in the food stamp program, removing the cost for the poorest families, for example, and triggered more private aid to the region. However, the "emergency" food assistance authorized by Congress only reached the Delta in April of 1968, a full year after Kennedy's visit. Significantly, for a complex set of reasons, including the mounting demands of the Vietnam War and his own fear of and dislike of Kennedy, Johnson never got behind the changes for which Kennedy and his allies had advocated.

After Kennedy's death, his allies in the Senate, such as Joseph Clark, Jacob Javits, and George McGovern, continued to push for food aid reform and formed a select senate committee to examine the issue. Javits memorialized Kennedy in a tribute on the floor of the US Senate several weeks after the shooting. Kennedy, Javits said, had "the deepest concern for the underdog of anyone I had ever met." The Republican senator went on to praise Kennedy's idea to include several counties in southern New York in the poverty programs for Appalachia and his work in the city at Bedford-Stuyvesant. Kennedy's deep Catholic faith meant that when any proposals were made to solve the problems of poor Americans, "they could never be patronized but should be given the opportunity to stand up and help themselves as individuals of dignity," Javits said, as he urged his fellow senators to approve more emergency funding for malnutrition in the Delta and elsewhere, some of which was still under debate at the time.

In his eulogy, Javits also observed that it was the trip to Mississippi that touched Kennedy more deeply than any other. His reaction to what he saw in the Delta "left Senator Kennedy practically shaking with indignation," Javits said. From that point on, Kennedy "never ceased to declaim against what he considered to be one of the worst inequities that his work in the Senate had uncovered."

In his statement in the Senate memorial, Senator James O. Eastland of Mississippi praised Kennedy as a "striving, seeking Senator, an American who did not mind being in the forefront." His absence from the Senate would be felt for years to come, Eastland said.

"I have been closely associated with Bob Kennedy during phases of his service to our country on both an official and personal basis. Our relationship will remain in my memory, and I will think of him as a completely candid and courageous advocate of his views and opinions.

Although he and I disagreed strongly on various issues, we maintained a mutual respect which means much to me at this tragic time." Eastland closed by calling Kennedy "a gallant member of a gallant family."

After Kennedy's death, however, the other candidates in the 1968 race for the presidency—Eugene McCarthy, Hubert Humphrey, and Richard Nixon—gave little attention to poverty issues. As a result, the future success of efforts of the loose coalition of antipoverty advocates seemed uncertain and perhaps lost.

But it was the incoming president, Republican Richard Nixon, who surprised advocates when he began to bring up the issue in his speeches. Nixon was prompted in part by statistics from a devastating federal nutrition survey, one that Kennedy and Clark had fought for soon after returning from Mississippi. Surprisingly, it was the first comprehensive survey of hunger in the nation, and when it finally was complete, it showed that pockets of Americans in every region suffered from the kind of malnourishment found in undeveloped nations.

Ironically, the hungry people in Mississippi whom Kennedy saw, however, were excluded from the survey. That's because in August of 1967, Congressman Jamie Whitten, applying subtle but powerful backchannel pressure on federal officials, ensured that his state was left off the list schedule, reportedly saying, "We're not going to have another smear campaign against Mississippi, are we?"

Whitten had remained on the defensive through the spring of 1968. In April of that year, a Citizen's Board of Inquiry into Hunger and Malnutrition came out with *Hunger U.S.A.*, another report that found a chronic problem of hunger and malnutrition in almost every part of the nation. This report said that food stamp programs were inadequate for the 10 million Americans they estimated were going hungry on a regular basis.

Other forces came into play in the efforts to help hungry Americans around the same time. Kennedy's 1967 trip had spawned further media coverage (such as CBS' stunning 1968 documentary *Hunger in America*, where a malnourished newborn died on camera) of the issue. Nick Kotz's prize-winning series on the politics of hunger ran in newspapers across the nation. The book *Still Hungry in America,* by photojournalist Al Clayton with text by Dr. Robert Coles, movingly portrays the struggles of hungry children and adults.

In response to this attention to Mississippi's hungry families, on May 2, 1968, Whitten took to the floor of the US House of Representatives in a speech called "Enjoining Adverse and Untrue Publicity from Being Distributed by News Media," to read a letter from an unnamed resident of Marks, Mississippi, who claimed to have seen the CBS camera crews providing ragged clothing for African Americans to wear on camera. They also asked the black families to move their cars away from their houses and take down their television antennas, the letter's author said. Whitten continued to quote from the letter: "They wrote up about a Negro baby not having any milk, and yet they are giving away food stamps to all those who are needy."

A year later, Nick Kotz, the Washington correspondent for the *Des Moines Register*, reported that Whitten sent FBI agents in the spring of 1968 to follow reporters and investigators for the Citizen's Board and question the families they interviewed, a terrifying prospect for African Americans in a place as violently oppressive as Mississippi could be in the 1960s. "The FBI agents assigned to the House Appropriations Committee did not seek to investigate conditions of hunger or poverty," Kotz writes in his 1969 book about the issue, "but systematically began to question countless persons connected in any way with the Board of Inquiry or the CBS documentary." The agents spent hundreds of man-hours on the investigation, Kotz reported.

◆ ◆ ◆

A month after Kennedy's death in 1968, the Senate created the Senate Select Committee on Nutrition and Human Needs, with Senator George McGovern, a Democrat from South Dakota and Senator Bob Dole of Kansas as the ranking Republican member.

"Perhaps more than any other single force, . . . [the committee] brought credibility to the issue as it heard testimony from all walks of life that presented problems, described needs, and proposed solutions," wrote child nutrition scholar Josephine Martin in 1999.

Although, as a select committee, it could not report legislation to the floor of the Senate, it often followed Kennedy and Joseph Clark's model of traveling to see poverty and hunger firsthand, bringing with them media attention. With bipartisan support, the panel's work influenced several pieces of legislation that had a significant impact on the nation's food aid policies and programs, including expansions in the food stamp programs; school lunch program; the Special Supplemental Program for Women, Infants and Children (or WIC); and national nutrition guidelines.

Until it was subsumed into the Senate's Agriculture and Forestry Committee, McGovern's committee played several important roles, according to political scientist Peter K. Eisenger. "During that time, its role shifted from that of a primarily educative body dedicated to calling attention to the existence of domestic hunger to that of the major institutional shaper of food assistance policy. In this role, the select committee emerged as an oversight vehicle and as the most visible advocate for the hungry." However, it never completely overcame the weaknesses of its institutional limitations.

Advocates for the hungry also won some surprising support from the White House. In early May of 1969, President Richard Nixon buttressed the work of advocates with an address to Congress recommending a program to end hunger in America. Later that month, a delegation from the Poor People's Campaign, led by Ralph Abernathy, Jesse Jackson, and Marian Wright, traveled to the White House to urge Nixon to dramatically expand aid for the poor.

Nixon responded with a proposal in August for the elimination of many federal benefit programs in favor of direct cash assistance to the poor, an idea which died quickly after the leaders on the left charged that it was inadequate and those on the right criticized it as unfair. In December of 1969, Nixon called the White House Conference on Food, Nutrition and Health and spoke passionately about ending hunger in America.

Although a week after Kennedy's assassination, Orville Freeman had appeared before the House Agriculture Committee to urge $100 million increase in the food stamp program, it was not until President Richard Nixon signed the Agriculture and Consumer Protection Act in 1973 that food stamps were expanded to every county in every state.

However, it was still be ten years after Kennedy's trip to Mississippi before the purchase requirement for food stamps would be completely eliminated with the Food Stamp Act of 1977.

The aides and advocates who had worked beside Kennedy for these poverty programs set aside their grief and carried on as well. As the funeral train rolled on to Washington, Marian Wright and Peter Edelman were still committed to helping poor children, and now, they no longer hid their growing commitment to each other.

The grieving young couple were to be wed in a little more than a month. Planning a wedding is rarely a revolutionary act, but until just one year earlier, it had been illegal in Virginia since 1662 for black and white people to marry each other. The case that changed all that began a decade earlier, when a sheriff had even burst into the bedroom of an interracial couple in Central Point, Virginia. When Mildred and Richard Loving protested that they were married and pointed to their marriage certificate, the officer said, "that's no good here," as he arrested them and charged them with a state felony.

Later, Mildred Loving grew tired of the terms of their sentencing, which meant she couldn't visit her family in Virginia with her husband. She wrote to Robert Kennedy, who was then attorney general, who wrote back suggesting they contact the American Civil Liberties Union.

◆ ◆ ◆

The bride wore flowers in her hair. The groom wore a broad smile and, in a sure sign of the times, a white Nehru jacket.

Among the smiles there were tears, of course; almost every wedding elicits a few. But this early evening wedding in McLean, Virginia, was just five weeks after Robert Kennedy had drawn his last ragged breath, so perhaps more than the usual tears christened this couple's happy day as two hundred of their friends and family watched.

Marian Wright and Peter Edelman joined their hands and their lives on July 14, 1968, in a simple ceremony that honored both of their faith traditions. The relationship had started with the surprise of an intense late-night conversation in Jackson a year earlier. It had strengthened as they fought together to help children like the one they had watched Robert Kennedy hold in the Mississippi Delta. It deepened over the ensuing months while Wright took on the challenge of counsel to the Poor People's Campaign in Washington and Edelman weathered the thrills and challenges of Kennedy's presidential campaign.

As the campaign in the California primary wound down just a month or so before the wedding, Edelman had selected a glittering bracelet at the jewelry store in the Ambassador Hotel, a birthday gift for Wright. As the returns came the night of the election, for a moment, the future they imagined must have unfurled, bright and exciting, before them.

Then shots echoed through the kitchen of the Ambassador Hotel and into the history books. The candidate fell. His life ended in the early morning hours of June 6, 1968, Marian Wright's twenty-ninth birthday. She never wore the bracelet.

On a grassy slope in Adam Walinsky's backyard, the chaplain at Yale and fellow civil rights activist William Sloan Coffin Jr. stood ready to marry them. Peter Edelman had once clerked for former Supreme Court Justice Arthur Goldberg, and he too waited to offer a reading, standing by an arch covered with snapdragons, ferns, and chrysanthemums that glowed palely in the late afternoon shadows.

Wearing a tiara with white roses and ribbons streaming behind, Wright's caramel skin was a radiant contrast to her knee-length dress of airy, white dotted-swiss. At thirty years old, Edelman looked handsome and confident in his white, high-collared jacket and black pants.

The *New York Times* noted that the bride and groom spoke their vows to each other "firmly" and then read aloud lines to each other from John Donne's poem "The Good Morrow":

> I wonder, by my troth,
> what thou and I did,
> 'til we lov'd . . .

In the stillness that followed, the gathering shadows deepened. Yet the birds still sang their twilight songs, and the laughter of a child playing in the distance carried through the warm air, echoing like a benediction over the union.

◆ ◆ ◆

Marian and Peter Edelman have gone on to raise three sons, Joshua, Jonah, and Ezra, and have several grandchildren. They have spent most of their professional lives since 1967 advocating for the poor. When the Poor People's Campaign dissolved in 1968, Wright Edelman formed a public interest law firm, the Washington Research Project. In 1973, she created the Children's Defense

Peter and Marian Wright Edelman married in July 1968 and continue to work on issues of poverty and children's health and welfare. Credit: Doug Mills/*The New York Times*/Redux.

Fund, a research and advocacy organization. From that platform as founder and president, she has advocated for children's issues on the national stage for more than forty years, work that would eventually earn her many honors, including a Presidential Medal of Freedom from President Bill Clinton. During the course of her career she has worked to pass more than thirty laws aimed at helping children and families, including the State Children's Health Insurance Program that gave millions of poor children health care coverage with its passage in 1997. Wright Edelman has also written eight books about the needs of children and families and those who work with them.

Over the years, both in interviews and in her writing, she has recalled the lesson of active compassion that Robert Kennedy taught her when he knelt on a dirty floor in Mississippi and held Annie White's hungry boy. "I remember watching him in near tears because I kept saying to myself,—I had this, this complicated feeling—I was moved by it and wondering whether I would have gotten down on that dirty floor. But, I'm deeply respectful that he did. He could do almost anything after that, and I trusted him from that time on, just as a human being," she recalled.

Looking back from 2017, Martin Luther King and Kennedy's deaths were profound losses, but Marian Wright Edelman said she made a conscious choice to continue her work on behalf of children. "You get up and you don't think about 'what might have been.' You pick up and figure out what you are going to do next. And the whole question then was how do we end poverty? And that's still my obsession. How do we end child poverty in this nation? How do we deal with the hunger?" she said.

Wright Edelman said that Kennedy wouldn't be pleased that American children were still hungry after 50 years, but he would acknowledge the progress that has been made.

"We still have problems that are significant. There are a number of people who still have no income, and food stamps are the only thing that's keeping those four million people from starvation. But we have an amazing amount of infrastructure that has been created around nutrition and healthcare. If you look at the legislation that has been passed, the impact is quite extraordinary."

Peter Edelman, after practicing law and working in higher education, went on to join another Kennedy campaign, this time Edward Kennedy's unsuccessful primary campaign for the presidency in 1980. Later, he served as a top official in the Clinton administration, but he resigned in protest. When Bill Clinton signed a welfare reform bill in 1996, Edelman thought it did little to address the problems that existed with the nation's welfare system, damaged the nation's safety net, and unfairly penalized poor mothers.

He is the Carmack Waterhouse Professor of Law and Public Policy at the Georgetown University School of Law and the faculty director of the school's Center on Poverty and Inequality. He is also the author of three books about poverty and public policy.

In one of them, *Searching for America's Heart: RFK and the Renewal of Hope*, he reflected upon his transformative time with Kennedy.

> Like many who experienced so much so quickly in the sixties, I was not the same person at age thirty that I had been at twenty-five. I had been shaped by witnessing injustice in the company of a man who constantly sought it out and tried to right it. His passion to make a difference left a permanent mark. If there was a specific time when the mark became indelible, it occurred a year before he was murdered, when, in Mississippi. . . . I saw children starving in this rich country and at the same time met my wife-to-be.

Chapter 12

It Let Us Know that There Was Somebody Who Cared

I n the Mississippi Delta of the twenty-first century, the soil remains rich and fertile, although it is saturated every year with more chemical herbicides and pesticides. The roads still stretch long and straight between seemingly endless fields, although more of them are paved than in 1967. The rhythm of the seasons remains timeless, however. The same species of birds, seeking the sun's warmth, follow the same flyway as they migrate along the muddy river that made this region and shaped the fortunes of the humans who lived near it, for better or worse. Each year, the earth is broken, seeds go in, crops sprout, flower, mature, and are harvested.

Even though much of the Delta's essential nature has stayed the same, there have been some fundamental changes since Kennedy came through in 1967. Federal food aid reaches a much larger percentage of poor Delta families now.

In 2013, 90,000 mothers and children in Mississippi received food, milk, and baby formula in the Supplemental Nutrition Program for Women, Infants and Children (WIC) program. About 64 percent of the state's children qualify for free or reduced lunch, and all of Mississippi's public schools now provide free or reduced-price lunches (and often breakfast) for more than 318,000 children, unlike in 1967, when local officials often failed to take advantage of or manipulated school lunch programs for political ends.

In June 2015, 628,633 people in Mississippi received benefits of about four dollars a day from the Special Supplemental Nutritional Assistance Program (SNAP). For some, it serves to supplement their diet of some, but for

A timeless scene from the Mississippi Delta in the twenty-first century. Credit: Maude Schuyler Clay

thousands more, it is their only source of food. In each of the three counties that Robert Kennedy visited, more than one-third of the population receives SNAP benefits: 37 percent in Washington County, approximately 32 percent in Bolivar County, and 38 percent in Coahoma County.

However, despite the state's high percentage of poor households, Mississippi's state regulations make it more difficult than other states to qualify and receive SNAP benefits.

In Mississippi, applicants must appear for an in-person interview, which is often difficult for families without reliable transportation. Mississippi also makes it harder on families who receive WIC. As of 2014, it was the only state that did not use the electronic benefit transfer system. Instead, the mothers and children who receive WIC benefits must pick them up from a county distribution center.

It must also be noted that changes that the federal and state governments implemented after the creation of Temporary Aid to Dependent Families (TANF), which replaced the federally run cash assistance program has dramatically reduced the number of poor families in Mississippi who receive aid but has done little to reduce the number of people who actually need aid. In Mississippi, only 14.5 percent of the money the state gets from the federal government for welfare actually goes to families in in the form of payments. Only 11,623 people in Mississippi were receiving TANF benefits in October 2016, but there were approximately 650,000 people living below the federal poverty line.

To Peter Edelman, the damage that the 1996 changes in the welfare system grows more apparent each year.

> What Robert Kennedy began in Mississippi led to a remarkable and successful national program that fights hunger and has made a major difference for millions upon millions of our people. But in too many parts of the country we don't have enough jobs to go around and too many of the jobs we do have pay barely enough to live on. On top of that, the safety net for the lowest-income people has sustained a huge gash in TANF. Mississippi has just 11,000 people on TANF, compared to the 600,000 who get SNAP. Even SNAP and TANF combined provide only 40 percent of the [amount of the] poverty line, and just 5 percent of the state's children living in poor families get TANF.

◆ ◆ ◆

As Robert Kennedy anticipated, seismic changes in voting patterns have remade the political landscape. Mississippi now has the most African American elected officials in the nation, with 530 in 2006. One of them, US Representative Bennie Thompson (who was a college senior in the audience when Kennedy spoke to students at Tougaloo College) now represents much of the Delta region that used to be in Jamie Whitten's old district.

From early in his tenure as attorney general, Kennedy believed that guaranteeing voting rights and bringing African Americans into the active electorate, would give them the power through self-governance to improve their circumstances. At the beginning of his brother's administration, Kennedy said, "the long-range solution for Negroes is voting rights. I think all other rights for which they are fighting will flow from that. Political power comes from votes and rights come from political power." He also told Martin Luther King Jr. in those early days that if he could successfully register enough African Americans to vote, "Jim Eastland would change his mind."

In 2016, the three counties that Kennedy visited, Washington, Bolivar and Coahoma, all have black majority populations and elect officials of both races. Although the reasons are complex and beyond the scope of this work, it is safe to say that this expanded political power has brought improvements, but has yet to translate into economic power for many of its poorest residents.

◆ ◆ ◆

The economy in the Delta has changed too since 1967. Through the 1970s into the 1990s, the region's economy did diversify beyond agriculture to include more industry such as textile plants, catfish operations, and chicken processing plants. Senator James O. Eastland, who stayed in office until 1978, had responded to his young nephew's question about what to do for the poor, mostly African American residents of his district with "Basic manufacturing. That's what we've got have. Basic manufacturing." He saw little chance of educating forty-year-old displaced farm workers and thought that bringing in low-skill jobs would be the most rapid way of lifting them and their families out of poverty, according to Hiram Eastland.

However, the land in the Delta was and is still valuable for growing cash crops even if cotton production has dropped in recent years. In Mississippi farmers grew 1,000,600 acres of cotton in 2001, but by 2016, the state had only 450,000 acres of cotton in production. As Sven Beckert points out in his book *The Empire of Cotton*, American cotton no longer dominates the market. "Twenty five thousand highly capitalized cotton farmers remain in the United States, mostly in Arizona and Texas. The cotton they grow is so uncompetitive on the world market that they receive enormous federal subsidies to continue to farm it, subsidies that in some years equal the GDP of the country of Benin." Crops such as soybeans and corn have replaced much of the acreage once devoted to cotton in the Delta. And modern farming techniques continue to require fewer and fewer workers.

◆ ◆ ◆

Despite these efforts, the Delta's children are still at risk. Poverty rates there are still more than twice those of the rest of the nation. The high school dropout rate in Mississippi's Delta counties is 43 percent. An astonishing 70 percent of births in the region are to single mothers. And, although infant mortality rates have improved in recent years, at 8.2 deaths per 1,000 births in 2014, they are still among the highest in the nation.

Even today, fifty years after Kennedy's visit, Mississippi's Second Congressional District, which encompasses most of the Delta, has the second highest rate of food insecurity, at 28.7 percent, of any district in the United States. In that district, 208,530 people do not have access to enough food to feed all the family members at some point during each month, or they have to choose between paying bills or buying food. Holmes County, a portion of which is in the Delta, has the highest rate of food insecurity in the nation. About 33 percent of its population qualifies as food insecure.

In the Mississippi counties that Kennedy visited, nearly half or more of the children under eighteen still live in poverty. In Washington County, where he talked with Catherine Wilson and her family, 46 percent of the children are poor. In Cleveland's Bolivar County, where Kennedy tried to coax a response from Annie White's son and Charlie Dillard ached with hunger, 53 percent of the residents under eighteen live in poverty. And in Coahoma County, where Brenda Luckett rode her bike and Aaron Henry and Andrew Carr struggled to create a biracial coalition to expand the opportunities for Clarksdale's poor families, 44 percent still live at or below the poverty line.

In many ways, poverty in the Delta looks different today than in 1967. At that time, it was not unusual for poor children to wear tattered clothes or miss school because their families couldn't even provide enough clothes or shoes. Visitors to their homes would see few or no toys at all. But today, the Delta, like the rest of America, is awash in cheap goods from overseas. This means that, although there are certainly families for whom clothing their children is a struggle, thrift stores and hand-me-downs are more plentiful. Cheap toys are as close as the nearest dollar store.

The suffering is at times harder to see for these reasons, but it is there, nonetheless. There are many families for whom the federal and state safety nets, limited as they are, provide most of the meals their children eat. Without them, they would undoubtedly be as hungry as the children Robert Kennedy encountered in the Delta fifty years ago.

Poor families in the Delta today still live lives marked by struggle and want. However, in contrast to the stark hunger and children with sores and bloated bellies that Kennedy found in 1967, a visitor today finds that too many of them suffer from a peculiarly modern paradox. They are poorly nourished yet obese. A 2012 study found that 47 percent of children living in the Delta counties of Mississippi were overweight, and 28 percent of that number qualified as obese. Many of these children are feeding on the cheapest but nutritionally empty processed food, which provides few benefits and dramatically increases risks of serious illnesses such as diabetes, high blood pressure, and heart disease as they age, casting yet another shadow over their future.

Food insecurity plays a surprising role in rising obesity rates. Children who do not always have enough to eat tend to overeat when food is plentiful. The effects of periodic overeating are magnified: when the body has unpredictable access to food, it also begins to store fat reserves. Families in food-insecure households are also often coping with additional stress from health care crises, housing problems, higher rates of crime in their neighborhoods, and financial pressures from bills and debts. These stressors take a toll on the bodies and minds of these children and their parents that can lead to further unhealthy eating patterns and weight gain.

Most of today's Delta rural communities are small and shrinking further. The roads are often in poor condition, and taxis and other forms of public transportation are almost nonexistent. If they don't have gardens, the area's residents must travel miles through the vast, fertile fields of cotton, soybeans, and rice in order to shop for fruits and vegetables. To get there, many of them must arrange to borrow a car, or, even more problematic for those on a tight budget, pay someone to take them. In these so-called "food deserts," access to affordable, healthy food is limited, but sugary, fat-laden food is as close as the nearest convenience store. According to one study, more than 70 percent of families in Mississippi who received SNAP benefits live more than thirty miles from the nearest supermarket.

◆ ◆ ◆

For Catherine Wilson, it is nine miles to the nearest grocery store from her home in rural Washington County, a long way for someone like her, who doesn't have a car. Wilson, now in her sixties, lives alone in the crumbling remnants of Freedom Village, the settlement that ultimately grew out of Freedom City, where Kennedy met her and her family in 1967.

For a few years after Kennedy's visit, the Delta Ministry's vision of a cooperative, egalitarian community looked as if it would grow and thrive. Grant money from federal and charitable sources flowed in. The group planned to build fifty individual houses like Wilson's three-bedroom cinderblock house, but only a few, about fourteen, were ever completed.

The former displaced plantation workers came together to grow soybeans, wheat, rabbits, and hogs. They built a craft studio to make and sell ceramics. They had a neighborhood laundromat and playground. For a time, the settlement even had a Head Start center and offered job training and literacy classes.

However, no significant private business or manufacturing operation ever invested in Freedom City. The soil on the land they purchased was heavy and hard to work. It flooded often. Crops failed, some families left, others fell into disputes over the details of how to run the cooperative. In 1978, the Mississippi Delta Blues and Heritage Festival started to hold an annual music festival at Freedom Village, which generated about $10,000 a year, but it moved its operation in 1987.

Through all of Freedom Village's changes and trials, Catherine and her mother, along with some of her siblings and their families, remained, holding to the vision that unfolded before them in a Freedom School during the

Catherine Wilson still lives near Greenville, Mississippi, in Freedom Village, which thrived for a time after Robert Kennedy visited but is now in disrepair. Credit: Alysia Burton Steele.

summer of 1964. Since that summer, when she first learned about the rights guaranteed to her in the US Constitution, she had faced threats from the Ku Klux Klan, jail, failed crops, storms, hunger, uncertainty, and strife. She had been called "nigger" and punched as she integrated the nearby high school. However, the years of schooling that she missed took their toll, and she didn't graduate. She participated in several War on Poverty job-training programs, but, except for a short time in a janitorial job at a Christian school, Wilson never worked outside of Freedom Village. She never married and stayed to care for her mother until Ora Wilson died in 2014 at the age of ninety-seven. Now, living alone in her mother's house at Freedom Village, which still floods on occasion, Catherine is sanguine about her life thus far and has no plans to leave the land. "It seemed like to me that I was traveling on a journey, a journey where I was trying to get to my destiny," she said.

As she spoke, she gazed out the door of her home, toward where the swing set on the settlement's derelict playground leans askew. Less than a handful of the thirty houses the Delta Ministry originally built are still inhabited. Some are nothing but rubble, and another is a burned-out shell. Piled up trash litters the empty lots, and someone has moved a trailer in next door. The administration building is closed.

Though still standing, Wilson's home needs painting. The mortar has cracked between many of the cinderblocks, and the elements seep in. Her air conditioner is broken, and she's trying to save money to get it fixed. Her neat, well-kept front room is hot in the sweltering Delta summer, and she frets about getting the money to fill the propane tank before winter.

Like many others her age in the Delta, Wilson struggles with her weight and the accompanying health risks. She sometimes runs out of food before the end of the month, and her nephew Rufus steps in to help her out. Old enough for Medicare, she does have health care, but her teeth are not good, and she doesn't see as well as she used to. Despite her deprivations, Wilson still has her hopes for her little community. She refuses to give up on the vision that lured her family here fifty years ago.

"We're still trying to make Freedom City. Where there's a will, there's a way," she said.

◆ ◆ ◆

Twice, life took Charlie Dillard away from the Delta, where he was living with his grandparents when Kennedy came to their home on Cleveland's Chrisman Avenue. However, both times he found his way back. Today, he lives thirteen miles from Cleveland on the edge of tiny Winstonville, Mississippi.

Not long after Kennedy talked with him about what he had to eat that day, Dillard's mother, Pearlie Mae, returned to Cleveland for her children. She had found work near the southern tip of Florida picking tomatoes and other vegetables in Immokalee, the same area where CBS had filmed its landmark documentary, *Harvest of Shame,* on the plight of migrant workers in 1960.

In Immokalee, Charlie and his siblings helped their mother work in the fields. When they weren't working, they also attended school there, where Charlie fell in love with learning. An afterschool program for migrant workers' children helped him catch up, and Charlie excelled.

But after a few years, Pearlie Mae was on the move again. By this time, Charlie had a stepfather who had found work in the tobacco fields of North Carolina. Pearlie Mae followed him and soon sent for her children. Charlie, who was sixteen by that time, disliked North Carolina and was tired of caring for his eight younger siblings, so he returned to his grandparents' home on Chrisman Avenue. But there was a catch. Charlie could stay, his grandfather Joseph Dillard said, but he had to go to work. School was out of the question, he said, so Charlie went to work on a garbage truck for the city.

After a few years, like so many African Americans before him, he left the South in search of better pay and a better life. He heard of high-paying jobs

Reverend Charlie Dillard lives in Winstonville, Mississippi. The man who loved school as a boy worked at a variety of jobs in the Delta and earned his GED in 2005. Credit: Alysia Burton Steele.

in Portland, Oregon, from extended family members. But the job prospects in the late 1970s were not as promised. After only a few months, he returned to the Delta for good.

For more than a decade, he changed oil and delivered appliances at a tire and appliance store, and then spent twelve years sharpening knives at a chicken processing plant, rising to crew leader. In 2002, however, the plant, like so many others that employed low-skill labor, closed, throwing Charlie and 550 others out of work. Since then, his health has deteriorated, making it difficult to work, even if he could find it, and pushing him onto disability. At times, his legs ache and wake him up in the night, like the hunger pains did so long ago. His wife of thirty-five years, Shirley, a woman who wept when he told her about the hard, hungry days of his childhood, believes the pains are the result of those years of deprivation. These days he stays busy, for he answered a call to the ministry in 1985, and he pastors a small church nearby that he helped found. But, like many Delta towns, Winstonville is shrinking. Down to 189 residents, it has lost 40 percent of its population, which is 97 percent African American, since 2000.

Charlie and Shirley Dillard have raised four children, two boys and two girls, and he has a daughter from an earlier marriage. Their photos, along with pictures of smiling grandchildren, cover the walls of his comfortably appointed manufactured home. Charlie, the boy who loved school, grew into a father who emphasized education. The shelves in his living room hold books and religious texts. All of his children finished high school. One of his daughters is a teacher in nearby Mound Bayou. She has finished her master's degree and is working on a doctorate. A second daughter is pursuing a master's degree in optometry school. One of his sons served in Afghanistan and attended community college when he returned. Both of his sons own and drive their own eighteen-wheelers. But among the many young faces on the wall of their cheerfully decorated living room is one older one. In it, Charlie smiles wide wearing a cap and gown. On that day in 2005, he earned his GED diploma.

On a recent warm fall day, three of Charlie Dillard's grandchildren arrived for an after-school visit. Healthy, bright-eyed, and lively, they were dressed in the khakis and blue shirts of their public-school uniforms from nearby Mound Bayou. They greeted their grandfather affectionately and listened politely when he told them about meeting Robert Kennedy. As the children and Charlie watched a video clip of that day in 1967, he reflected on Kennedy's visit.

"Kennedy didn't look like he was trying to look down on us. He seemed sincere and concerned about our situation," he recalled. Charlie vividly remembers the summer day when he heard of Kennedy's assassination. He was hurt and surprised. "I never thought they would kill a white man who was running for office, just for trying to help people," he said.

"I couldn't believe it. It was really devastating."

◆ ◆ ◆

For Annie White, life in the Delta with her children improved after Kennedy's visit. "Meeting Robert Kennedy changed her life," her son Lorenzo White, who was a three-month-old baby in 1967, said. "She had been to the welfare office and never could get any, and the week after he came, they were knocking on her door." Boxes of canned food and necessities like soap, deodorant, and toothbrushes arrived every so often after Kennedy's visit, too, although the White children don't know who sent them.

Two years after Kennedy's visit, White and her six children were receiving seventy-nine dollars a month. Although her children still did not receive free lunches at school, she told a reporter at the time that she was able to use thirty-two dollars from her welfare payment to buy eighty dollars' worth of food stamps, which provided about two weeks' worth of groceries.

By that time, the home she was living in when Kennedy visited had been demolished, and she had moved to another house on Ethel Street, one with

When Robert Kennedy visited in 1967, he was moved by the plight of a toddler in Cleveland, Mississippi. David White now lives in Mesquite, Texas, and has five sons of his own. Credit: Will H. Jacks.

electricity and a toilet. The rent on this new home took twenty-four dollars per month, and utilities claimed another ten to fifteen dollars per month. With the food stamps, they shopped more often at the local Sunflower grocery store, and David White remembered walking home carrying the groceries in the heat and the rain. Even though the family began receiving aid, there were still hungry times, her children recalled. But there was a difference, they said, because Annie White had money for clothes and shoes for school and even an occasional toy.

As they grew older, her children found ways to help, too. They picked up bottles and redeemed them for pennies. Annie White loved to fish, and they dug worms for her and sold the extra to other fishermen. They went door-to-door selling peaches and other produce from local farmers for four dollars a basket, keeping one dollar for themselves. That's how David and his brothers earned enough to buy their first bicycles.

When Edna started high school, her family's poverty became more apparent and harder to bear. The teenager had to wear her few clothes again and again. She lined her shoes with cardboard to cover the holes in the soles. But her mother soon found a farmer who still needed day workers occasionally, and from then on, the children picked cotton each season to earn enough to buy some school clothes. Because of where they lived, some other African American children at school who lived in better houses called them "Alley Brats," David said. Though it was meant as an insult, he and the other children on the city's poorest street took it as a badge of honor. "We stuck together and were proud of it. It meant we knew how to survive," he said.

The toddler that Kennedy treated so tenderly as the child picked at rice on the floor no longer lives in the Delta. Now in his fifties, he owns a modest brick home a few blocks from the interstate in Mesquite, Texas. He is married and has five sons of his own and three grandchildren. Like his mother, he loves to cook and work in his garden.

Like so many young black men in the Delta, where the dropout rate is still as high as 40 percent in some districts, David White left high school in Cleveland without graduating. He never went back to school. At fifteen, he started mowing the grass for the local Western Sizzlin' Steakhouse. Soon, the owner hired him as a dishwasher. The money was good, more than he ever had to spend before, so he quit school and worked his way up at the restaurant, to cook, head cook, meat cutter, and then assistant manager.

In the early 1990s, Dallas, Texas, was booming. David's younger brother, Lorenzo, had moved there for work, and, after hearing about his success, David soon followed him. Within a week of arriving, he had two jobs, one at a Western Sizzlin', and one at a fast food restaurant. He worked for several more years at the steakhouse, then he worked for five years as a janitor for a hospital.

As the new millennium began, he was working on a lighting installation crew for a dollar store chain when an eighteen-wheeler slammed into his crew's van. He was seriously injured in the crash and had surgery on his back in 2005, which has made working more difficult since then. "It aches every day, but you get used to it," he said. He now works as an independent contractor delivering flowers for a florist in the Dallas area.

Although he has no memory of Kennedy's visit, some of his first memories are of how cold that house was where Kennedy held him in 1967. David White also remembers the sacrifices his mother made for him and his brothers and sisters during those years.

"We still talk about that now. She would say, 'y'all go ahead and eat first and I'll eat whatever is left.' I remember times she would just have a glass of milk and a piece of cornbread," he recalled. "We still talk about that to this day. I think she done the best she can with what she had." She would want people to know, David said, that "just because you start at the bottom, you don't have to end up there."

As her children grew to adulthood, they remained close, talking every week and visiting Mississippi often. Annie delighted in her grandchildren and helped to raise some of them. She loved babies, and if you gave her yours to hold, it would be hard get it back, David said with a laugh. One of those babies called her his "blue grandmother" because his maternal grandmother was white, David said. His family is part of the growing trend of interracial marriages in America, which have gone from 0.7 percent in 1970 to 3.9 percent of all marriages in 2008 (US Census).

In her later years when food was more plentiful, Annie petted her children by making them each their own sweet potato pie when they came home for a visit. "One pie wasn't enough," David White said.

Annie White died of cancer in 1996, but not before losing both her legs to diabetes, a scourge that plagues the Delta today. Before she grew ill, expansions in federal housing aid in the late 1970s allowed her and her children to finally move into a two-bedroom house with indoor plumbing and a nice yard that she filled with flowers. "Now we have some life," she told them.

◆ ◆ ◆

Brenda Luckett didn't need Kennedy's urging as he left Clarksdale to stay in school and get good grades. She already loved school, and her parents dreamed of college for her. She also already knew that not all of the children she met in the Delta had the same solid foundation of learning that her parents had provided for her. As early as kindergarten at Miss Minnie B.'s House, Brenda had wanted to be a teacher. While at her small kindergarten, she took extra care to work with one of her classmates who was mentally challenged, an act of kindness that hinted at her future career.

In 2016, Luckett retired from thirty-three years of teaching special education. The last twenty of those years she spent at George H. Oliver Elementary School in Clarksdale, the same school she was attending when Kennedy visited in 1967. However, her path to the career she loved was not always straight or easy.

Soon after Kennedy visited, her father got a coveted spot as a Pullman porter with the railroad, which meant the family had to move to Chicago. "We weren't really financially secure until he became a porter," she said. They lived in Illinois for three years. Chicago offered an escape from the racially discriminatory imperatives of the South, but Brenda wasn't happy. "To me, it was confining. There was too much concrete. There was violence. I was used to riding my bike anywhere all over Clarksdale and playing outside until the streetlights came on, but in Chicago, it was not safe to be out like that in our neighborhood," she recalled. The family eventually moved back to Clarksdale, but her father finally realized his dream in the 1970s by becoming the first

Brenda Luckett was thrilled to see Robert Kennedy in Clarksdale. She retired in 2014 after twenty-six years of teaching special education in her hometown. Credit: Alysia Burton Steele.

African American locomotive engineer on his segment of the *City of New Orleans'* route.

By the time Brenda entered high school, the student body at Clarksdale High School was integrated. They had new books and better materials than at her old school. It was the first time she had gone to school with white students, she said.

"The students—we got along wonderfully. We got to be friends and many of us still are," she said. There were some problems, however. Many of the black teachers were moved in as assistants to white teachers. Black principals and coaches weren't given equivalent responsibilities. However, many students of both races mourned the district's decision to cut all after-school social and extracurricular events, Luckett said. School officials and some parents were concerned that students would socialize too much, she said. African American and white students had separate dances, separate proms, and separate clubs.

A National Merit Scholar, Luckett excelled at school and applied to only two colleges: Howard University in Washington, DC, and the University of Mississippi. She was quickly accepted at both places; however, she knew her parents would have to struggle to send her to Howard. In contrast, the University of Mississippi, the school she and her parents had watched James Meredith integrate in the face of violence, offered her a generous scholarship.

At Ole Miss, Luckett majored in communicative disorders and finished in the early 1980s, disproving the public prediction of a professor in one of her first classes that African Americans would have a hard time becoming speech pathologists. Luckett's chosen field usually required a master's degree, so she started graduate school. Unfortunately, her mother fell ill and then died, and she couldn't afford to continue. She got a special license for speech therapy. After two years in the Delta town of Marks, she moved on to serve as a prison guard at Mississippi's notorious penitentiary at Parchman. After a few years there and then as a guard in Pascagoula, a friend told her about a teaching job in Mound Bayou. In 1989, Brenda had a baby daughter (named Edna for her mother), and in 1990, nearby Delta State University offered a program that paid for students to seek a master's degree in special education because it was a critical-needs area. She finished the degree there and began teaching at her old elementary school in Clarksdale in 1994.

Brenda still lives in the house her father helped build on Peacock Street. She stays active in the community when she's not visiting her two grandsons in Oxford. She loves the Delta, but she's discouraged that there are still so many poor children in the region and that what she calls "the plantation mentality" on the part of both races is still so prevalent in the area.

She has not forgotten Kennedy's visit or her horror when he was assassinated so soon after Martin Luther King. "It [Kennedy's visit] connected us to a faraway land. It let us know that there was somebody who cared about or even recognized us and our experience," Luckett said. She believes that Kennedy's visit to Clarksdale, even as short as it was, motivated more people to register to vote. When he was killed, many of the people who had seen him in Clarksdale saw a kind of inevitability about his death.

"We felt like Kennedy was purged. He should have gotten out. It's like we knew they were going to kill him for helping black people; that's the way a lot of people felt at the time. He was like family to us."

Children and their parents greet Robert Kennedy in 1967 as he visits an adult education program at Sacred Heart School, a Catholic school for African American children in Greenville, Mississippi. Credit: Jim Lucas Estate.

Chapter 13

We Don't Speak of Statistics, Numbers. We Speak of Human Beings

Even though the unfolding catastrophe of the Vietnam War and Lyndon Johnson's weakness as a candidate were the main issues that catapulted Robert Kennedy into the 1968 presidential race, poverty remained a significant part of his focus. As he traveled around the nation in the months following his visit to the state, he found that there were far too many other malnourished, hungry children in America like those he had seen in Mississippi. For Kennedy, this was unacceptable, and he said repeatedly that America can and should do better. In fact, he was still talking about rural poverty and starving children like those he had seen in the Delta five minutes before his assassin gunned him down.

Author Larry Tye's 2016 biography traced Kennedy's journey to his iconic status as standard-bearer for the underclasses and outcasts from his early roles as aide to McCarthy, then as a hard-nosed campaign manager, and finally as his brother's chief protector in the cabinet. Tye agrees that the Mississippi trip was both an "epiphany regarding the depth of poverty in America and proof of his ability to focus a laserlike spotlight on a hidden issue like starvation."

Much of Kennedy's transformation, however, grew out of his struggle to transcend the profound personal losses he experienced during his forty-two years of life. "The odyssey he had been through—the painful deaths of three siblings, the loss of his father's guiding hand, crises over the Cuban missiles and campus race riots—brought to the surface his sense of irony and empathy," Tye writes. Kennedy's journey was an incremental one, and it ran counter to conventional wisdom, which expects individuals to harden as they age and gain more power and prominence, according to Tye. Instead, for Robert Kennedy, "sanctimony and starchiness increasingly yielded to his introspection and idealism."

When Kennedy died, the issue of food aid reform did not die with him, but his death did deprive the nation's hungry children of a politically skilled, charismatic ally. Although these days Kennedy is frequently identified with Far Left politics, in fact his positions were more centrist and mainstream than is often remembered. Peter Edelman has written that "Robert Kennedy was uncomfortable when anyone called him a liberal—in fact, when anyone tried to put any label on him." However, he did believe "in national policy, national leadership, and national funding."

Far from operating as an ideologue, he was pragmatic enough to accept Mississippi senator John Stennis's offer of $10 million for emergency food aid after the Field Foundation doctors' testimony, even though it was far too little to be very effective. Kennedy, moreover, was skillful and sensitive enough to remain on good terms with his Republican counterpart representing New York, Jacob Javits, to find common ground on poverty issues, both rural and urban. In his tribute to Kennedy after his death, Javits said: "To put it in very blunt terms, he had a deep concern for the people whom our society . . . had disenfranchised in terms of opportunity and in terms of the legacy to which we feel all Americans are entitled. He was not the only man in public life to have this feeling in his heart; but, in my judgment, it burned in him more brightly than in any other man I have ever known.

Javits went on to say, "He had great humor and wit. He did not take himself all that seriously. But when his mind directed itself to this problem, he throbbed with its significance, like an Old Testament prophet."

Before the hearings in July, Kennedy had talked with the doctors who the Field Foundation had sent to Mississippi. He cautioned them to consider the impact of their words on their listeners and to not forget the political context of their report. Dr. Robert Coles recounts Kennedy's admonition to him: "Politics, he remembered, is not only, alas, 'the pursuit of the just,'" through speeches made, votes cast, laws enacted. Politics, he pointed out with patience but not patronizingly, is constant compromises made, and 'above all, survival is important.'"

Make no mistake, though, Kennedy was no saint. He could be arrogant, rigid, and headstrong. He was certainly opportunistic and wasn't above playing politics. He nursed grudges and collected enemies. At times, he was too protective of his brother and his brother's image after his death.

His virulent dislike of Lyndon Johnson, which could be almost irrational in its intensity, kept him from working with perhaps the one person who could have been his most effective ally on poverty. The author of *President of the Other America,* historian Edward Schmitt, offers a compelling summation of the issue: "If political cooperation was at the heart of Kennedy's vision of community, his own actions sometimes betrayed that ideal, with significant consequences. He recognized politics to be a blood sport, and his personal disdain for Lyndon Johnson, while substantive on a number of matters, manifestly contradicted his ideal of cooperation."

However, unlike so much of modern political rhetoric, Kennedy deliberately focused his critiques on issues, ideas, and policies rather than leveling personal attacks on his opponents. He never publicly accused officials in the states where he saw hunger of starving children, even when they were resistant and defensive. Despite his horror at what he had seen in Mississippi and elsewhere, he was careful to emphasize that the problems were *American* problems that required a national commitment.

His campaign for the presidency, with its focus on ending the war and the needs of the poor, both rural and urban, had drawn together an unprecedented coalition, one that united white working-class Catholics, African Americans, Latinos, many white and black college students, and upper-middle-class liberals. However, his assassination, coming only nine weeks after the murder of Martin Luther King, fragmented this alliance. His death, and the subsequent violence at the Democratic National Convention left the cohort of his young supporters in his camp especially disillusioned.

Kennedy's former aides say that if he were alive today, he would appreciate the progress and developments in poverty programs which provide thousands of children to receive free breakfast and lunch programs and the no-cost food stamps. He was not a purist, and would acknowledge progress that made a problem better, even when if it didn't solve the problem.

However, the numbers of children in single-parent households in the Delta and other parts of the country shocked and grieved him, former aide Adam Walinsky said. And Kennedy would be singularly dismayed at how many hungry children remain in the Delta and elsewhere in America fifty years after his efforts to eradicate the problem. He would also be saddened by how little attention leaders pay to the issue today, especially in states like Mississippi, and how vigilant advocates must be to protect the gains for which they fought so hard.

As those battles unfold, Kennedy would almost certainly recognize the echoes of the same arguments that Mississippi leaders such as Senators John Stennis and James O. Eastland and Representative Jamie Whitten made in 1967. Whether it is the move in Congress in 2013 by House Republicans, including all but one of the Mississippi delegation, to cut food stamps during a recession; or state officials' refusal in 2016 to seek a simple waiver of federal food benefit regulations that cut SNAP benefits to fifty-six thousand people—the officials making these decisions often cite the same reasons as in 1967–protecting taxpayers, fears of breeding dependence, bristling at federal interference.

Kennedy would also recognize a similar pattern in Mississippi's reluctance to pass enabling laws to access federal money that helps the poor. In 1967, the state passed up millions of available dollars that would have given welfare aid to children with an unemployed father. Health care was out of reach for many of the two hundred thousand eligible residents in 1967 because Mississippi did not adopt Medicaid until 1970.

In 2014, Mississippi's governor and lawmakers continued the tradition of resisting aid. The state declined to expand Medicaid as part of Obamacare, which was designed to cover people too poor to qualify for subsidies on the insurance marketplaces. This left 138,000 low-income Mississippians with no insurance options at all.

In 1967, editorial writers and officials in the state argued that caring for the poor should be the voluntary responsibility of churches and charities. It should not be a function of government and certainly not lead to budget-breaking entitlements. Back then, as there are today, there were many Mississippians and organizations who gave generously. Businessman Clarke Reed of Greenville said the problem of poverty in the Delta was overwhelming. Most of the people of the Delta inherited the situation they were in, and they were struggling through an agricultural revolution. He remembered that his family had food "going out the door" all the time in the 1950 and 1960s. They never turned anyone away, he said, and didn't know of anyone who did. "We thought the answer is to get work for them. But I remember there was never a night, . . . somebody called the house every night for something. And when I was a kid, always somebody at the back door eating. So we were not hard-hearted people," he said. And, in fact, Mississippi regularly rates at or near the top in national charitable giving surveys.

However, it is unlikely that at any point in Mississippi's history charitable giving has ever matched the level of need. Even today, anyone who gave a neighboring family a pound of bacon per week would have good reason to believe that they were truly generous. But anyone who has children also knows that they want and need to eat frequently, and if you have several children to feed three or more times a day, that pound of bacon will not last long.

Charity, while certainly a virtue, has its own pitfalls. It can create an uneven balance of power between the giver and the recipient. Dr. Robert Coles recounts a lament from a woman in the Delta community of Savage, Mississippi, during the 1960s. "Every morning the first thing I think about is what can I do to feed the kids. I don't have no money coming in," she said. She went on to explain that the man for whom her husband worked would give them "some things and they won't give you others." The boss let them live in the house on his place but told them not to "get any smart-alecky ideas" about voting, or they would be put out. He also gave them money sometimes, "[T]here'll be ten dollars one week, and maybe five the next, and he gave us $20 for Christmas, I'll say that for him," she said. The boss's wife occasionally gave them grits "and once or twice in the year some good bacon. She tells me we get along fine down here, and I says yes to her. What else could I be saying, I ask you? But it's no good. The kids aren't eating enough, and you'd have to be wrong in the head, pure crazy, to say they are."

In 2016, Mississippi leaders still, upon occasion, react angrily to efforts to highlight the needs of the state's poor. Data released by the census from 2015 showed Mississippi's poverty rate, 22 percent, was the highest in the nation and that the state was one of only four whose poverty rate had increased. The state's median income, at $40,593, had increased slightly from 2014, but was still the lowest in the country. When a reporter for the nonprofit, nonpartisan online news organization *Mississippi Today* contacted Governor Phil Bryant's office for a response, his spokesperson's reply had echoes of the response of state leaders and editors like Cliff Langford in it: Why are you only looking at the bad things about Mississippi? This is partisan. Washington and the press are always picking on poor old Mississippi.

The reporter, Adam Ganucheau, wrote: "When asked for a comment, Clay Chandler, Gov. Phil Bryant's director of communications, sent this email response: 'I will insist that you run this in its entirety. Attribute to Gov. Bryant:

> It is interesting how these statistics only seem important to the media now that,Republicans have some political power. Unemployment has been reduced from 9.5 percent to 6 percent. Teen pregnancy is down 26 percent and 92 percent of third graders passed their reading test in 2016. Mississippi is recognized as the most creative state in the nation for public education by the Education Commission of the States. But Mississippi Today and other media outlets gleefully focus on the negative statistics, often produced by the Obama Administration, in an ob-

vious attempt to discredit any gains Mississippi has made. My suggestion would be to remove the bipartisan label from your heading and print your desires."

◆ ◆ ◆

Robert Kennedy's efforts to help children like Catherine Wilson, Charlie Dillard, David White, and Brenda Luckett were, in a way, a continuation of his civil rights work. His visit to the Delta opened his eyes to the real and painful consequences of generations of exploitation and oppression in a place like Mississippi, and once he saw it there, he began to see it elsewhere in America, in the hills of Kentucky and the lettuce fields of California. It is always far easier for leaders like Kennedy to think in abstract terms like slavery, sharecropping, segregation, disenfranchisement and poverty and deplore them, and even work to correct them, but from afar.

But in the Mississippi Delta, perhaps Kennedy glimpsed the very real human pain and struggle that were, in part, sad consequences of America's great original sin. For there are consequences when a nation enslaves a people. There are consequences when, even after that slavery ends, a nation allows the powerful to continue to use those people and their children as they would animals or machines and then discard them when they are no longer useful. There are consequences when a Department of Justice turns a blind eye as generations of people are stripped of their rights as citizens because of the color of their skin. There are consequences when a nation is slow to address the violent intimidation and murder of men and women who simply asked to exercise rights that could have been used to improve their lot. There are consequences when banks redline neighborhoods, forcing too many people of color into dilapidated rural shacks, slums, and ghettos. Perhaps what Kennedy saw so clearly that day was that when America refuses to see and address these wrongs and others like them, it is more than just a political calculation. It is a choice that leaves children to cry softly in the night while mothers pray, and listless babies to grasp for bits of rice on a dirty floor.

On April 4, 1968, in speeches that would be overshadowed by his heartfelt response later that day to the assassination of Martin Luther King, Robert Kennedy spoke to college students at Ball State and Notre Dame as he began his campaigning for the Indiana primary. Puzzling some political observers with his choice of topic, "Feeding America's Hungry," Kennedy's speech offered little to appeal to the groups in the state that he needed to win over to do well in the primary.

Instead, he outlined his proposals for addressing the problem of hunger and framed the issue for the students as one of American ideals. On the surface, it seemed to be a nonpolitical choice. However, even though it was a topic that mattered deeply to Kennedy, there was, characteristically, a political motive behind it too, his aide and speechwriter Adam Walinksy said. Kennedy saw a way to distinguish himself from his opponent in the primary by focusing on poverty as a civil rights issue in front of college students. Senator Eugene McCarthy had entered the race months before Kennedy, and his vigorous opposition to the war in Vietnam made him popular with college students and young voters. Kennedy needed a way to peel some of them away from McCarthy, Walinsky said.

Appealing to the idealism of the youth vote was one way to accomplish this. Politically beneficial as this strategy may have been, it was not, however, fundamentally hypocritical on Kennedy's part. Finding a solution to the problems of hunger within the context of civil rights meshed with Kennedy's own vision of America, a vision that Kennedy's experiences had sharply, sometimes painfully, honed over the past seven years of his life. So, when he arrived at Notre Dame, he told the five thousand students who packed the auditorium, many of them fellow Catholics, that if the United States could not "feed the children of our nation, there is very little we will be able to succeed in doing to live up to the principles which our founders set out nearly 200 years ago." He concluded with a plea for the students to take a direct, personal interest in using the political process to shape the nation's future: "How are we going to end poverty and deprivation? We will do so by channeling the concern of the individual citizens into that sense of personal responsibility. This is our nation. It is for us to turn this nation toward a path of honor."

At Ball State, he spoke passionately about their responsibility to fellow citizens, many of who were living lives of desperation. "These men and women and children that we hear about that I'm talking about here, they're not statistics, they are human beings whom I have seen." They had, he said, "a right to live a life of dignity and purpose just as much as you and I have."

As he talked with the students, he spoke about his trip to Mississippi. "Here in America there are children so underfed and undernourished that many of them are crippled for life in mind and body before the age of three . . . children who are starving to death—not malnutrition—actually starving to death. I've seen them with extended stomachs, with faces covered with sores of starvation."

He went on to elaborate on poverty elsewhere—in the cities and on Indian reservations—but came back to his experience in Mississippi and repeated for the third time that he could personally bear witness to their suffering, for he had seen them himself. "We don't speak of statistics, numbers. We speak of human beings."

Beyond this emphasis on the humanity of the poor, Kennedy saw the issue in patriotic terms. The nation's greatness depended, in large measure, on its commitment to extending the hope for a life of "dignity and purpose," not just to the powerful or the privileged, but to the very least of its citizens. "If we cannot prevent our fellow citizens from starving, we must ask ourselves what kind of country we really are," he said. "We must ask ourselves what we really stand for. We must act, and we must act now."

ACKNOWLEDGMENTS

Mississippi author Eudora Welty once wrote that she was startled and disappointed to learn as a child that books "had been written by people, that books were not natural wonders, coming of themselves like grass." Books have always held an enchantment for me as well, but, now, at the end of writing one, the realization that they do not "come of themselves" does not bring a sense of disillusionment. Instead, I am filled with a sense of wonder and joy at the collaborative nature of their creation. I know now that even though it is the author's name that goes on the cover, books only happen with the support, hard work, and encouragement of many, many good people.

I owe my first debt of gratitude to my parents, C. Alex and Barbara Williams Meacham, who showed me early on that there was magic in books and made sure I knew I could add a little to that magic one day with a book of my own. Beyond that, however, my parents taught me through their words and deeds that the lives, problems, and *stories* of poor people matter just as much as those belonging to people of power and privilege. Watching my father and mother live and work as a lawyer and teacher in a small southern town, I absorbed the lessons of respect, attention, compassion, and humor I find essential to making a connection with storytellers, regardless of their background.

Many other members of my family gave their love and support to me in this endeavor. My brother, Sam Meacham, also read portions of the book and provided intelligent and useful feedback. In addition to reading carefully and listening with kindness to too many discouraged phone calls, my sister, Kate Meacham, along with her husband, Davis Jones, always said yes when I needed a babysitter. My aunt, Ernestine Huff, read chapters and made excellent suggestions. My cousin Jon Meacham set an inspiring example, provided early encouragement, and shared contact information for two sources essential to the story. Charlotte Huff, Clint Huff, Johnny and Amy Winkle, Jason and Felicia Winkle, and their families were also supportive and helpful in countless ways.

◆ ◆ ◆

This book would not exist without journalist, author, and master storyteller, Curtis Wilkie. Curtis's eloquent recollections of Robert Kennedy's visit to Mississippi in his memoir started me on this road, and his thorough and compelling reporting from 1967 smoothed my path. He also provided unfailing support, encouragement, and very real help with advice and many sources, contacts, and critiques. It is our friendship, however, that I value most of all.

In addition to Curtis, several other journalists who were in the Delta or wrote about hunger in 1967 generously shared their memories, helped guide my research, and read various drafts of the book, including Wilson F. "Bill" Minor, Hodding Carter III, Nick Kotz, and George Lapides. In addition, the irreplaceable Bill Rose was always willing to help, listen, or read. This work is far better than it could have ever been without him.

This book would be dry and incomplete indeed without the painful yet beautiful stories from the children whom Robert Kennedy met in 1967. Catherine Wilson, Charlie Dillard, Brenda Luckett, and Annie White's children— Edna White Brisby, and Willie, Michael, David, and Lorenzo White—all lived the struggles recorded here. They told their families' stories with honesty, grace, and dignity. I am thankful for their friendship and will be forever in their debt. As I worked on this book, I was deeply conscious of the fact that I am a white author who is often telling the stories of people of color. As such, I am an imperfect vessel at best, and ill equipped to convey the totality of their experiences. I appreciate their (and the reader's) patience with any inadequacies on my part in that regard.

I must also extend my deepest personal thanks to Peter and Marian Wright Edelman. Peter generously shared his memories of Kennedy and the trip to Mississippi, and he was always available to answer a question, clarify a fact, or offer encouragement. Marian Wright Edelman, in many ways the heroine of this book, shared her memories and insights with me, participated in a panel discussion of Kennedy's visit in 2012, and has set an example of speaking up for the needs and rights of children for more than fifty years that never fails to inspire me.

In addition, I interviewed more than fifty people for this book, and I am thankful for the help of each one. It is a gift when someone shares their time and stories with me. I can only hope I did them justice.

◆ ◆ ◆

As you can see, the photos and images in the book are an essential part of understanding the story, and I owe more than I can repay to the photographers and their heirs. Early on, Jane Hearn shared her late husband Jim Lucas's contact sheets from his hundreds of fabulous photographs of Kennedy's visit, which enabled me to follow the trip frame-by-frame almost as if I were watching a movie. Through her generosity, not only did I gain valuable insight into Kennedy's time in Mississippi, but I gained a wonderful friend as well.

David and Melinda Guravich were kind enough to act upon my strange hunch and search through their closets to find the stunning photos created by David's father, Dan Guravich, and shared Dan's contact sheets with me. Red Morgan was a pleasure to work with and made the Lucas and Guravich photos all look very good.

Troy Catchings also dug through collections of old negatives and entrusted me with his photos from Clarksdale. My friend Alysia Burton Steele, author of *Delta Jewels,* brought her expert eye and creative sensitivity to the beautiful portraits of three of the adults who met Kennedy as children. Plus, she's an awesome person to take along on a trip through the Delta.

I am also lucky that Will H. Jacks jumped in on short notice to contribute two fine photographs. The artist William Dunlap thoughtfully shared his story along with the lovely, carefully rendered portrait of Kennedy he sketched during the Jackson hearing. I've long admired the work of Delta photographer extraordinaire Maude Schuyler Clay, and I am thankful she let me use one of her Delta dog photographs. And we are lucky that Ed Meek donated the photographs he so astutely captured of Ole Miss during the 1960s.

◆ ◆ ◆

I would be remiss if I did not acknowledge that much of this book rests upon a foundation of thorough and thoughtful work by many excellent scholars, including Taylor Branch (whose description of Kennedy's reaction to the visit to Mississippi prompted the title of the book), James C. Cobb, Charles Eagles, and Mark Newman, as well as earlier Kennedy biographers Arthur J. Schlesinger Jr. and Evan Thomas. Nick Kotz's *Let Them Eat Promises* tracked the behind-the-scenes congressional negotiations and highlighted the forces that blocked food aid reform following Kennedy's trip to the Delta. His top-notch journalism was indispensable. Edward Schmitt's meticulously researched *President of the Other America* focused on Kennedy's evolution on poverty issues and put the trip to Mississippi in the context of Kennedy's other work in impoverished areas. Ed also provided important encouragement, analysis, and the careful reading of several chapters.

Larry Tye, author of 2016's *Bobby Kennedy: The Making of a Liberal Icon*, is an exhaustive researcher whose writing makes for fascinating reading. His biography of Kennedy provides a much more thorough understanding of the man and his motivations. Beyond that, however, I will always be grateful to Larry for his help to me on this project. He generously shared information, gave excellent advice, and answered questions with intelligence and good humor.

Charles Reagan Wilson, a gentleman and scholar, never laughed at my pitiable first attempts and never seemed to tire of helping me in a wide range of ways. His contribution was also essential to this book's fruition.

My friends on the faculty and staff at the Ed and Becky Meek School of Journalism and New Media have offered consistent support and advice, despite listening to me drone on about this project for nine long years. Special thanks are due to John Baker, Mark Dolan, Nancy Dupont, Samir Husni, Cynthia Joyce, Ed Meek, Charlie Mitchell, Charles Overby, Jennifer Sadler, Debora Wenger, and Kathleen Wickham. I also am happy to note that for more than twenty-five years, Will Norton has been in my corner, providing wisdom and encouragement (along with the occasional push) whenever I needed it. Also, my brave, intelligent students teach me something new almost every day. Their sweet faith in me never failed to spur me on.

Many researchers provided valuable assistance on this project, including Stephen Plotkin and Abigail Maglione at the John F. Kennedy Presidential Library and Museum; Leigh McWhite and Jennifer Ford at the University of Mississippi Special Collections, Cecilia Tisdale at the Mississippi Department of Archives and History, Minnie Watson at Tougaloo College, Debra McIntosh at Millsaps College, Researchers at CBS, ABC, and Bill Moyers.com tracked down video footage and made it available for review. Here in Oxford, Michelle Bright, Daniel Fudge, Hannah Hurdle, and Anna McCollum were tremendously helpful.

Old friends and new made this process a pleasure with their kind words and support. Mike Carr helped immensely with his Delta contacts and insights. The indispensable Hiram Eastland has the gift of encouragement, knows a million stories, and just about as many people. This book is better because he shared both his stories and his people with me. Angela Moore Atkins mapped a way forward when I was stuck. Bill Bayne read and critiqued my first efforts. Richard and Lisa Howorth shared their deep knowledge of the book world with me and never failed to offer kind words. I am also grateful to Jojo Fell and Bertha Toles, who helped me out, cheered me on, and gave me excellent advice on building trust with sources. Lolly and Bill Bailey are truly some of the "golden people," and I love them like family.

The editors and staff of University Press of Mississippi have been wonderful to work with, including Emily Bandy, Craig Gill, Camille Hale, and Shane Gong.

Others deserving of thanks who have helped me along the way include Jack Bass and Nathalie Dupree, Peter and Kari Boyer, Shannon Cohn, Scott Coopwood, Dan and Janet Edens Conover, Dr. Richard DeShazo, Shirley Dillard, Rufus Donald, John T. Edge, the Forgette family, Oleta Fitzgerald, George Gibson, Vivian Davis Giles, Ellen Kellum, Susan Glisson, Deborah Grosvenor, Synovia Jackson, Bill Luckett, Jerry Mitchell, Tom Oliphant, Lisa and Billy Percy, Tom Pittman, Reverend Sammie Rash, Golden Sharpe, Larry Simmons, Jennifer Stollman, Rebecca Turner, Larry Wells, Annie Wince, and many, many more.

My husband, John Winkle, has supported me in countless ways throughout this process and, most importantly, always believed in this book and in me. Soon after starting this work, I got pregnant with our son, Will. Watching him grow into a fine, healthy boy, I understood in a much more profound way the heartbreak of parents who have no food to give their hungry child. While Will has, I am thankful to say, never known a time when we were without enough to eat, he has also never known a time when I wasn't working on this book. He's taken my distraction and occasional absences with good grace and often provided sweet encouragement. As he grows, I hope he will understand how to notice with compassion when people are suffering and realize, like Robert F. Kennedy, that we must do the best we can to help them.

SOURCE NOTES

Preface

xii   **"A nation that"**: Charles Marsh, *The Beloved Community*, 129.

xii   **"reached up to him"**: Wilson F. "Bill" Minor, author interview, December 2006.

Prologue

xv   **Robert Kennedy stood**: RFK1963. "RFK Part 2 Last Speech Ambassador Hotel." Filmed [June 4–5, 1968]. YouTube video, 09:56. Posted [September 5, 2006], https://www.youtube.com/watch?v=ae7HoaWFWNY.

xv   **"The country wants to move"**: Ibid.

xv   **"what we are going to do"**: Ibid.

xvi   **As his wife**: Michael Cohen, *American Maelstrom*, 140.

Chapter 1. "Now This Problem Has to Be Faced"

3   **A member of**: Robert B. Semple, Jr. "Johnson at Grave with Kennedys," *New York Times,* March 16, 1967.

3   **A force of 250 soldiers**: Ibid., "Bodies of Kennedy, Children Are Moved to Permanent Grave," *New York Times (NY)*, March 15, 1967.

4   **"Be at peace, dear Jack**: "Robert Semple, Jr., Johnson at Grave with Kennedys," *New York Times (NY)*, March 16, 1967.

4   **"marked by 'tension'"**: Ibid.

4   **At 9:30 on**: U.S. Senate. Committee on Labor and Public Welfare. Subcommittee on Employment. *Examination of the War on Poverty: Hearings before the United States Senate Committee on Labor and Public Welfare, Subcommittee on Employment, Manpower, and Poverty, Ninetieth Congress, first session.* Hearing, March 15, 1967. Washington: U.S. Government Printing Office. 1967.

5   **"Other presidents had asked:** "Carl M. Brauer, "Kennedy, Johnson, and the War on
        Poverty," *The Journal of American History* 69, No. 1 (1982): 99.

5   **"Listen, goddammit"**: Jeff Shesol, *Mutual Contempt: Lyndon Johnson, Robert Ken-
        nedy and the Feud that Defined a Decade*, 5.

5   **He grew up**: Ibid., 5

5   **As Johnson grew**: Ibid., 4. LBJ Presidential Library, *Discover LBJ*, http://www.lbjlib.
        utexas.edu/johnson/archives.hom/biographys.hom/lbj_bio.asp, accessed Febru-
        ary 22, 2014.

5   **"Thirty-eight years"**: Lyndon Johnson. "Remarks at the Welhausen Elementary
        School, Cotulla, Texas," November 7, 1966.

6   **"If you do good"**: Brauer, 115.

6   **"It's right here"**: Ibid.

6   **Historian Carl Brauer**: Ibid.

6   **"I'm no budget slasher"**: Ibid.

7   **"If you looked"**: Ibid., 113–15.

7   **"This budget"**: Lyndon B. Johnson, State of the Union Address, January 8, 1964,
        The American Presidency Project, http://www.presidency.ucsb.edu/ws/index
        .php?pid=26787.

7   **"architect of the War on Poverty"**: Robert D. McFadden, "R. Sargent Shriver, Peace
        Corps Leader, Dies at 95," *New York Times*, January 19, 2011, 20.

7   **Furthermore, though the public**: Shesol, 166.

7   **Kennedy knew well**: Brauer, 99.

7   **circled "poverty" six times**: Edward Schmitt, *President of the Other America*, 96.

8   **Johnson eventually built**: Ibid., 103.

8   **"walls of silent conspiracy"**: Ibid.

8   **"Have you ever talked"**: Ibid., 102.

8   **"This is fundamental"**: Ibid.

9   **He showed little evidence**: Evan Thomas, *Robert Kennedy: His Life, 2000*, 05.

9   **Kennedy cast about**: Thomas, 293–94.

9   **Kennedy had only been**: Thomas, 306.

9   **Historian Edward Schmitt**: Schmitt, 120.

9   **He spoke sympathetically**: Schmitt, 120.

9   **Kennedy had little**: Schesinger, 815.

9   **Kennedy and Johnson both realized**: Thomas, 317.

10   **That summer, he called**: Peter Edelman, *So Rich, So Poor*, 109.

10   **"full participation in"**: Schmitt, 124.

10   **Although welfare had**: http://socialwelfare.library.vcu.edu/public-welfare/
        aid-to-dependent-children-the-legal-history/.

10–11 **"You white politicians"**: Thomas, 319.

11   **"I don't have to"**: Ibid.

11   **What emerged was**: Edelman, *So Rich, So Poor*, 109.

11   **"the best of community"**: Ibid., 110.

12   **This approach also**: Jeff Shesol, *Mutual Contempt: Lyndon Johnson and Robert Kennedy and the Feud That Defined a Decade,* 167–71.

12   **Wright knew firsthand**: Marian Wright Edelman, Interview for Makers: The Largest Video Collection of Women's Stories, http://www.makers.com/marian-wright-edelman, accessed March 10, 2016.

12   **Dressed in**: Description of what she is wearing is from a Getty Images photograph taken on March 15, 1967.

12   **Wright's journey**: The summary of Wright's life is a synthesis taken primarily from her memoir about mentors, Marian Wright Edelman, *Lanterns: A Memoir of Mentors,* Harper: Perennial, 2000, as well as interviews and other biographical information.

12   **"unfair assaults"**: Wright Edelman, *Lanterns,* xiv.

12   **"All the external"**: Wright Edelman, *Makers* interview.

12–13 **"One of the lessons"**: Ibid.

13   **"There was never"**: Ibid.

13   **"Don't let anything"**: As quoted in Thought Co., *Marian Wright Edelman, Founder, Children's Defense Fund,* http://womenshistory.about.com/od/marianwrightedelman/p/m_w_edelman.htm, accessed March 21, 2017.

13–14 **"a tea-pouring"**: Wright Edelman, *Lanterns,* 24.

14   **"I realize that"**: Ibid.

14   **"What people do"**: Ibid., 62–64.

14   **"As I walked"**: Ibid., 71.

14   **Wright was at**: *Examination of the War on Poverty: Hearings before the United States Senate Committee on Labor and Public Welfare, Subcommittee on Employment, Manpower, and Poverty, Ninetieth Congress, first session.* Hearing, March 15, 1967, Washington: U.S. Government Printing Office, 1967, 157.

15   **She was there**: Wright Edelman, *Makers* online video.

15   **"I don't know"**: Ibid.

15   **"People who had"**: Ibid.

15   **"After two"**: Hearings, U.S. Senate Subcommittee on Unemployment, Manpower, and Poverty, March 15, 1967, 157.

15   **Wright's time**: The experiences described here are primarily from her memoir, *Lanterns: A Memoir of Mentor,* her interview in the *Makers'* video, and the transcript of her interview for the *Eyes on the Prize* documentary.

16   **Wright operated**: Wilson F. "Bill" Minor, author interview, December 2006.

16   **She was one**: Kenneth D. Nordin. "Mississippian sees Negro lawyer need," *The Christian Science Monitor,* May 10, 1966.

16   **The Mississippi Sovereignty Commission**: "Sovereignty Commission Online." Mississippi Department of Archives and History. Summary of searches for: Marian Wright, Marian E. Wright, accessed September 19, 2016, http://www.mdah.ms.gov/arrec/digital_archives/sovcom/.

16   **"Never have I felt"**: Wright Edelman, *Lanterns,* 71.

16   **"Now, what are we"**: The quotes from Marian Wright and Senator Joseph Clark in
          this chapter are as quoted in the transcript of the hearings of the U.S. Senate Sub-
          committee on Unemployment, Manpower, and Poverty, March 15, 1967, 164–65.
18   **Under the new**: Crystal Sanders, *A Chance for Change*, 43.

Chapter 2. "We Were to Try Harder than Anyone Else"

The biographical details of Robert Kennedy's life in this chapter are a synthesis of the oft-
cited events and factors that shaped him in his childhood, his youth, and his early career.
Several thorough biographies and numerous articles recount the same basic outline of
events in his life prior to his trip to Mississippi in 1967. Arthur Schlesinger Jr.'s 1977 biography; Evan Thomas's 2000 analysis of his life and the influences on his psychological development; *Brother Protector*, by James Hilty examines his relationship to JFK; *The Bystander* by
Nick Bryant highlights JFK and RFK's complicated legacy for civil rights; and most recently,
Larry Tye's 2016 *Bobby Kennedy: The Making of a Liberal Icon*, which examined his evolution
from Cold Warrior to liberal standard bearer, shed new light on this oft-overlooked part of
Kennedy's experience. I also drew upon David Nasaw's book, *Patriarch*, which provides an
extensive examination of Joseph P. Kennedy's life and his relationship with his sons.

21   **It was almost time**: Arthur Schlesinger Jr., *Robert Kennedy and His Times*, 23.
22   **"It showed either"**: Evan Thomas, *Robert Kennedy: His Life*, 35.
22   **"What I remember"**: Ibid., 31.
22   **"I was the seventh"**: Schlesinger, 23.
22   **"the most thoughtful"**: Ibid., 22.
23   **While it almost certainly**: Thomas, 21.
23   **"In contrast"**: Schesinger, 20–21.
23   **"nothing came easy"**: Edward R. Schmitt, *President of the Other America*, 10.
23   **"We were to try"**: Schlesinger, 15.
24   **However, while Kennedy's**: James Hilty, *Brother Protector*, 23.
24   **"What we did"**: Robert F. Kennedy, Edwin O. Guthman and Jeffrey Shulman, *Robert
          Kennedy, in His Own Words*, 66.
24   **Although Bobby had**: Thomas, 59.
25   **Biographer Arthur Schlesinger**: Schlesinger, 99.
25   **John Kennedy was**: Thomas, 64.
25   **"Bobby's the tough one"**: Schlesinger, 99.
25   **Robert Kennedy emerged**: Thomas, 62–63.
25   **As John F. Kennedy**: Ibid., 64–65.
25   **the concept that**: Halberstam, *The Fifties*, 56.
26   **Although Robert Kennedy's**: Larry Tye, *Bobby Kennedy*, 25.
26   **"Like his father"**: Ibid.
26   **a "serious internal"**: Schlesinger, 110.
26   **During his late twenties**: Thomas, 67.

27   **"the worst ever"**: Ibid., 75–76.

27   **"one of the deepest"**: Thomas, 85; Tye, 67.

27   **"there were times"**: Robert Kennedy, *The Enemy Within*, 74.

27   **During this time**: Tye, 78.

28   **It was during his**: The description of Kennedy and Seigenthaler's first and subsequent meetings is taken from the author's interview of John Seigenthaler on July 30, 2013. It has also been recounted elsewhere.

28   **"About six weeks"**: John Seigenthaler author interview.

28   **Later, the two**: Ibid.

28   **By the end of**: Warren Rogers, *When I Think of Bobby*, 8, 111.

29   **Ethel's support**: Tye, 64–65.

29   **"central to her upbringing"**: Kerry Kennedy, "Interview with Kerry Kennedy," *Boston.com*, September 8, 2008, http://archive.boston.com/news/local/massachusetts/articles/2008/09/07/interview_with_kerry_kennedy/?page=full.

29   **According to Kathleen**: Kathleen Kennedy Townsend, *Failing America's Faithful*, 41.

30   **As historian**: Schmitt, 74–75.

30   **Kathleen Kennedy Townsend**: Kennedy Townsend, 56.

30   **"When the priest"**: Tye, 102.

31   **"chasing bad men"**: Schlesinger, 238–39.

31   **"every ounce"**: Hilty, 189.

31   **"I don't know"**: Schlesinger, 231.

31   **In mid-December**: John Seigenthaler author interview.

31   **"men of ability"**: W.H. Lawrence, "Dillon Appointed Secretary of Treasury, Kennedy's Brother is Attorney General," *New York Times*, Dec. 17, 1960, 14. (The descriptions of the day in this portion are from the photographs accompanying the article.)

31   **"Bobby we'll make"**: Schlesinger, 240.

32   **"I won't say"**: Schlesinger, 289.

32   **"I think if there"**: Philip Goduti, *Robert Kennedy and the Shaping of Civil Rights 1960–1964*, 175.

Chapter 3. "It's to Hell with Bobby K"

33   **"Communist!"**: Joseph Loftus, "Poverty Hearing Set in Mississippi: Police Brace for Crowd," *New York Times*, April 11, 1967.

33   **"on behalf of"**: Andrew Reese Jr., "Bobby, Two Other Senators Land in Jackson; Stennis Lead-Off Poverty Quiz Witness Today," *Northeast Mississippi Daily Journal*, April 10, 1967.

34   **Just the year**: Gene Roberts, "Dr. King Proposes Annual Incomes," *New York Times*, August 9, 1966.

35   **John Kennedy represented**: Robert Dalleck, *An Unfinished Life*, 215–16. Michael O'Brien, *John F. Kennedy: A Biography*, 371.

35   **John Kennedy was**: Dalleck, 225; Nicholas Bryant, *The Bystander,* 58, 66

35–36   **At the 1956**: William Winter, author interview, July 8, 2016.

36   **"In doing so"**: James N. Gregory, "The Second Great Migration, 19.

36   **Gregory writes that**: Ibid., 19–20.

37   **This softening was**: Bryant, 55–56.

37   **In the last-minute**: Ibid., 58.

37   **"In those days"**: Wilson F. "Bill" Minor, author interview, June 10, 2016. The quotes in
         this chapter from *Times-Picayune* reporter Wilson F. "Bill" Minor are from a series
         of interviews, December 6, 2006, March 14, 2008, July 28, 2014, via telephone, and
         August 16, 2016, via telephone.

37   **Delegate William Winter**: Winter, author interview, July 8, 2016.

37   **"He was young"**: Ibid.

37–38   **"They were the"**: Ibid.

38   **"He'd say"**: Ibid.

38   **"As much as"**: Ibid.

38   **However, the state's**: Wilson F. "Bill" Minor, author interview, June 10, 2016.

38   **"Fresh faced"**: William Winter, author interview.

38   **"There was a"**: Ibid.

38   **"There was still"**: Ibid.

38   **After Mississippi voted**: Bryant, 58–59.

38   **Governor J. P. Coleman**: Ibid., 60 (from Bryant's *The Bystander*).

38   **In 1963, however**: Charles Eagles, *The Price of Defiance,* 435.

39   **Wirt Yerger Jr.**: Gene Wirth, "Senator Kennedy Hits GOP Complacency," *The Clar-
         ion-Ledger,* October 18, 1957.

39   **Kennedy risked losing**: William Winter, author interview, July, 8, 2016; Jay Milner,
         "Kennedy Pushed into Statement on Segregation by Time, GOP," *The Delta Dem-
         ocrat-Times,* October 20, 1967.

39   **"akin to sleeping"**: Bryant, 86.

39   **As he opened**: Papers of John F. Kennedy. Pre-Presidential Papers. Senate Files.
         Speeches and the Press. Speech Files, 1953–1960. Young Democrats dinner, Jack-
         son, Mississippi, 17 October 1957. JFKSEN-0898-017. John F. Kennedy Presidential
         Library and Museum.

40   **"times of tensions"**: Ibid.

40   **"I have no hesitancy"**: Ibid.

40   **"I now invite"**: Bryant, 85.

40   **"What unites us"**: Ibid.

40   **Winter still**: William Winter, author interview, July 8, 2016.

40   **Even the state**: Gene Wirth, "Senator Kennedy Hits GOP Complacency," *The Clarion-
         Ledger,* October, 18, 1957, 1; Arthur Krock, "In the Nation: Mississippi Ovation with
         Far-Reaching Echo," *New York Times*, October 31, 1957; Gene Wirth, "Magnolia
         Mirror," *The Clarion Ledger,* October 19, 1957.

41   **The editorial writers**: "Our New Political Leonidas," *The Clarion-Ledger,* October, 18,
         1957.

41   **Not everyone in**: Gene Wirth, "Kennedy Falls Short of Expectations, *The Clarion-Ledger,* October 20, 1957.

41   **By 1960 John**: Bryant,145.

41   **Although supportive of**: Arthur Schlesinger Jr., *Robert Kennedy: His Life and Times,* 224–26.

41   **Consequently, the Mississippi**: William Winter, author interview, July 8, 2016.

42   **They embraced a**: Minor, Wilson "Bill" F. "Eyes on Mississippi," *Clarksdale Press-Register,* December 8, 2000.

42   **"mingle socially with"**: J. Lee Annis, *Big Jim: The Godfather of Mississippi, 73.*

42   **"save the children"**: "Gov. Barnett Urges Vote for Children, *The Clarion Ledger,* November 8, 1960.

43   **"by a stroke"**: *Freedom of Communications: Final Report of the Committee on Commerce, United States Senate . . . , Part III: The Joint Appearances of Senator John F. Kennedy and Vice President Richard M. Nixon and Other 1960 Campaign Presentations. 87th Congress, 1st Session, Senate Report No. 994, Part 3.* Washington: U.S. Government Printing Office, 1961.

43   **"oppose any foe"**: Kennedy, John F. Innaugural Address, January 20, 1961.

43   **"the best doctors"**: Charles Evers, *Have No Fear,* 158.

43   **"I won't say"**: Schlesinger, 298.

43   **Arthur Schlesinger**: Ibid.

43   **"At this point in his life"**: Ibid.

44   **"Tell them to"**: Bryant, 264.

44   **"pain in the ass"**: Ibid.

45   **"Jim Eastland could"**: Schlesinger, 244.

45   **Over the years**: Curtis Wilkie, *The Fall of the House of Zeus,* 9.

45   **By the 1960s**: Jack Bass and De Vries, *The Transformation of Southern Politics,*188.

45   **Eastland, who was**: Marjorie Hunter, "James O. Eastland is Dead at 81, Leading Senate Foe of Integration," *New York Times,* February 20, 1986; Nick Kotz, *Let Them Eat Promises,* 118; Chester Morgan, Mississippi History Now. Website of the Mississippi Historical Association. http://mshistorynow.mdah.state.ms.us/articles/367/james-o
-eastland, accessed June 7, 2016.

45   **However, despite**: Hiram Eastland Jr., author interview, March 21, 2014.

46   **Eastland was almost**: Chester Morgan, Mississippi History Now. Website of the Mississippi Historical Association, http://mshistorynow.mdah.state.ms.us/articles/367/james-o-eastland, accessed June 7, 2016.

46   **Also, Eastland and**: Robert F. Kennedy, Edwin O. Guthman, and Jeffrey Shulman, *Robert Kennedy, in His Own Words: The Unpublished Recollections of the Kennedy Years,* 77.

46   **"Irish weakness for rogues"**: Schesinger, 244.

46   **When Edward Kennedy**: Edward M. Kennedy, *True Compass: A Memoir,* 193–95.

46   **"Eastland subtly telegraphed"**: Kennedy, Guthman, and Shulman, 78.

46   **"The whole thrust"**: Ibid.

47   **"And he always . . .":** Ibid.

47   **However, Eastland was:** Nevin Sledge, author interview, January 31, 2014.

47   **"We kept telling":** Ibid.

47   **John Seigenthaler, one:** David. Halberstam, *The Children*, 288.

47   **Years later, Kennedy:** Hiram Eastland Jr., author interview, March 14, 2016.

47   **After his efforts:** David Niven, *The Politics of Injustice: The Kennedys, the Freedom Rides, and the Electoral Consequences of a Moral Compromise*, 101.

47   **Barnett, the son:** Eagles, 281–82.; William Winter, author interview, July 8, 2016. David Sansing, Mississippi History Now, Website of the Mississippi Historical Association, http://mshistorynow.mdah.state.ms.us/index.php?s=extra&id=150, accessed August 12, 2016.

48   **"curiosity seekers and":** Official Statement by Attorney General Robert Kennedy, May 24, 1961, https://www.justice.gov/sites/default/files/ag/legacy/2011/01/20/05-24-1961b.pdf.

48   **After all his:** James Hilty, *Robert Kennedy: Brother Protector*, 328.

48   **According to historian:** Nicholas Andrew Bryant, *The Bystander: John F. Kennedy and the Struggle for Black Equality*, 282.

49   **"I had been":** James Meredith and William Doyle, *A Mission from God: A Memoir and Challenge for America*, 57.

49   **"I knew that":** Ibid.

49   **Cold War politics:** Eagles, 231.

49   **"on the spot":** Ibid.

49   **"The ruling was":** Bryant, 332.

49   **Kennedy certainly spoke:** Annis, 183–85.

49   **The Justice Department's:** Eagles, 275.

50   **Kennedy negotiated with:** Bryant, 335.

50   **"regarded Gov. Barnett":** Schlesinger, 331.

50   **Barnett and Kennedy:** Kennedy, Guthman, and Shulman, 160.

50   **"He laughed about":** John Seigenthaler, author interview, July 30, 2013.

50   **After several aborted:** Curtis Wilkie, *Dixie: A Personal Odyssey through the Events That Shaped the Modern South,* 105.

51   **"like a big Nazi":** Ibid., 104.

51   **"As the thousands":** Ibid., 105.

51   **"Son: Your great":** Ibid., 104.

51   **On Sunday, September:** Hilty, 334.

52   **Robert Kennedy later:** Ibid., 345–46.

52   **However, Kennedy:** Evan Thomas, *Robert Kennedy: His Life,* 209.

52   **"torn between an":** Hilty, 345.

52   **At this point:** Charles W. Eagles, "The Fight for Men's Minds: The Aftermath of the Ole Miss Riot of 1962," *The Journal of Mississippi History.*

52   **"only by breaking":** Eagles, *Defiance* 219.

52   **"the dastardly acts":** Dittmer, *Local People,*142.

53   **"mean a triumphant":** Eagles, *Defiance* 289.

53 **"From Occupied Mississippi"**: *Bumper stickers from the period, collected by Walter Lord*, Ole Miss, John F. Kennedy Presidential Library & Museum.

53 **"I don't know"**: Kennedy, Guthman, and Shulman, 75.

53 **"So much needed"**: Ibid.

53 **"Yes, in fact"**: Ibid.

53–54 **The shooting of**: Robert Kennedy Jr. "Recorded Address to Medgar Evers Scholarship Banquet," June 2013.

54 **Horrified by the**: Ibid.

54 **By November**: John Seigenthaler, author interview. July 30, 2013.

54 **"His elegant, well-read"**: Schlesinger, 856; Kathleen Kennedy Townsend, *Ethel,* HBO.

54 **"I think he"**: Kathleen Kennedy Townsend, *Ethel,* HBO.

54 **Although Kennedy's grief**: Kennedy Guthman, and Shulman, xvi.

55 **In Mississippi, the**: Myrlie Evers, 80, Reuben Smith, author interview, December 2007.

55 **"I knew when"**: Constance Curry, *Silver Rights*, 167.

55 **Mississippi's African American**: Bill Minor, Brenda Luckett, Curtis Wilkie, William Winter, author interviews.

56 **But, as had**: Marian Wright, oral history transcript, Jean Stein Oral History Collection, box 1, 3.

56 **According to Schlesinger**: Schlesinger, 670.

57 **"Well, boys, you've"**: *Howard Ball, "COFO's Mississippi 'Freedom Summer' Project," Murder in Mississippi, 62.*

57 **Between 1882 and 1964**: Monroe Work Collection, "Lynchings, Whites and Negroes, 1882–1968," Tuskegee University Archives and Repository, http://192.203.127.197/archive/bitstream/handle/123456789/511/Lyching%201882%201968. pdf?sequence=1&isAllowed=y, accessed on March 12, 2017.

58 **Cox was born**: Gordon A. Martin, *Count Them One by One: Black Mississippians Fighting for the Right to Vote*, 54.

58 **Eastland had been**: Hilty, 391.

58 **However, the fledgling**: Martin, 54.

58 **Moreover, Cox was**: Hilty, 391.

58 **"He wasn't," he**: Schlesinger, 321.

58 **Cox quickly became**: Hilty, 391.

59 **"Bobby said he"**: Evers, *Have No Fear*, 138.

59 **"where American buries"**: Ibid., 142.

59 **"All through the"**: Ibid., 141.

59 **After meeting with**: Ibid., 142.

59 **Robert Kennedy continued**: Ibid., 143.

59 **"Our strongest link"**: Ibid., 158.

60 **"I don't give"**: Ibid., 174.

60 **As the race**: Ibid., 172, 176.

60 **"You're lucky to"**: Ibid., 176.

60 **"Bobby Kennedy means"**: Ibid.

60   **After Robert Kennedy's death**: Peter B. Edelman Oral History Interview—RFK #6,
          February 21, 1970.

60   **"It was like"**: Ibid., 204–13.

61   **But Kennedy was**: Ibid.

61   **"lay the groundwork"**: John Seigenthaler, author interview, July 30, 2013.

61–62 **Once he accepted**: Peter B. Edelman Oral History Interview—RFK #6, February 21,
          1970.

62   **The university's chancellor**: Joshua Morse, "Oral History Interview of Dean Joshua
          Morse by Kate Medley, *Opening New Doors/Forging New Paths,* September 29,
          2007, 16, http://www.umopeningdoors.org/transcripts/dean-joshua-morse.pdf.

62   **The invitation scandalized**: Schlesinger, 813.

62   **Who invited this**: George M. Street Collection. Archives & Special Collections, J. D.
          Williams Library, The University of Mississippi.

62   **"How can you"**: Ibid.

62   **"sense of acceptance"**: Ibid.

62   **"As a 72-year-"**: Ibid.

62   **"They could not"**: Vera Pierce, Vera Pierce to J. D. Williams, Vicksburg, Miss., 1966. ⋅
          George M. Street Collection. Archives & Special Collections, J. D. Williams
          Library, The University of Mississippi.

62   **"What is wrong"**: George M. Street Collection. Archives & Special Collections, J. D.
          Williams Library, The University of Mississippi.

62–63 **"an apostle of"**: *Klan Ledger,* George M. Street Collection. Archives & Special Collec-
          tions, J. D. Williams Library, The University of Mississippi.

63   **With an eye to**: Morse, Oral History Interview, *Opening New Doors*, 16.

63   **We drove our**: Ibid.

63   **"And Kennedy says"**: Ibid.

63   **"Whoa! Whoa! What,"**: Ibid.

63   **"putting a fox"**: Lapedis, George, *Memphis Press-Scimitar,* March 19. 1966.

63–64 **"You have no"**: Robert F. Kennedy, speech to University of Mississippi Law School
          Forum, Oxford, Mississippi, March 18, 1966.

64   **"Your generation—this"**: Ibid.

64   **Kennedy's remarks horrified**: W. F. "Bill" Minor, "Eyes on Mississippi: Barnett Uses
          RFK Visit to Revive Ole Miss Issue," *The Times-Picayune,* April 16, 1967.

64   **"An interesting state"**: Willie Morris, *New York Days*, 227.

64   **"private, half-disguised"**: Ibid.

64   **Around the same**: Morris, *New York Days*, 229.

64   **"an easy job"**: Schlesinger, 814.

Chapter 4. "They Are Starving"

68   **In the days**: *Clarion-Ledger,* "Stennis Renews Attack on Activities of CDGM," April,
          10, 1967, 1.

68   **And even some**: Polly Greenberg, *The Devil Has Slippery Shoes,*17.

69   **Most of the**: Kotz, *Let Them Eat Promises,*14–15.

69   **For their parents**: Crystal R. Sanders, *Chance for Change,* 58.

69   **Program directors sought**: Ibid., 60.

69   **The centers had**: Erika Duncan, "ENCOUNTERS: Long After '65, Still Fighting to Overcome," *New York Times,* September 10, 1995, http://www.nytimes.com/ 1995/09/10/nyregion/encounters-long-after-65-still-fighting-to-overcome.html ?pagewanted=all.

69   **"They wanted receipts"**: Ibid.

69   **Stennis and other**: Crystal Sanders, *A Chance for Change,* 150.

69   **There was also**: Judith Sealander, *The Failed Century of the Child,* 243.

69   **The federal dollars**: Hodding Carter, Interview gathered as part of *America's War on Poverty,* Produced by Blackside, Inc., Housed at the Washington University Film and Media Archive, Henry Hampton Collection, March 21, 1994.

69   **"What was really"**: Ibid.

69   **Violence, however, as**: Ibid.

70   **What the whole**: Ibid.

70   **Many of CDGM's**: In an interview for the *Eyes on the Prize* documentary, Hodding Carter maintained that he accepted the position on MAP because OEO officials told him it was the only chance to preserve any Head Start programs in the state rather than in a move to undermine CDGM.

70   **However**: Sanders, 159.

70   **But in the end**: Gene Roberts, "Antipoverty Aid Stirs Ire in South" *New York Times,* March 6, 1967.

71   **Giant interlocking rings**: William Dunlap, author interview, August 27, 2016. Jim Lucas, photograph contact sheets, April 10, 1967; "Remembering the Heidelberg," *Mississippi Preservation,* https://misspreservation.com/2009/09/17/ remembering-the-heidelberg/.

71   **Prior to entering**: Jacques Steinberg, "George Murphy, Singer and Actor Who Became Senator, Dies at 89," May 5, 1992.

71   **After the group's**: Jim Lucas Photographic Contact Sheets, April 10, 1967; Joseph A. Loftus, "Poverty Hearing Set in Mississippi," *New York Times,* April 10, 1967.

71   **Clark and Senator Jacob**: Ibid.

72   **"Scanning the crowd"**: William Dunlap, author interview, August 27, 2016.

72   **"It was as"**: Ibid.

72   **Unlike many of**: Ibid.

72   **"neither a witch hunt"**: U.S. Senate. Committee on Labor and Public Welfare. Subcommittee on Employment. *Examination of the War on Poverty: Hearings before the United States Senate Committee on Labor and Public Welfare, Subcommittee on Employment, Manpower, and Poverty, Ninetieth Congress, first session.* Hearing, April 10, 1967. Washington: U.S. Government Printing Office. 1967, 521.

72   **Despite his courtly**: Rosenbaum, David, "John C. Stennis, 93, Long-time Chairman of Powerful Committees in the Senate, Dies," April 24, 1995, http://www.nytimes.

com/1995/04/24/obituaries/john-c-stennis-93-longtime-chairman-of-powerful
-committees-in-the-senate-dies.html.

73–74 **However, unlike his**: The description of Stennis's testimony and his exchange with
Robert Kennedy in this and the following paragraphs are taken from the transcript of U.S. Senate. Committee on Labor and Public Welfare. Subcommittee
on Employment. *Examination of the War on Poverty: Hearings before the United
States Senate Committee on Labor and Public Welfare, Subcommittee on Employment, Manpower, and Poverty, Ninetieth Congress, second session.* Hearing, April
10, 1967. Washington: U.S. Government Printing Office. 1967, 522–39.

74   **Stennis didn't snap**: Ibid.

75   **Perhaps the biggest**: Robert Ezelle, testimony before *Examination of the War on Poverty: Hearings before the United States Senate Committee on Labor and Public Welfare, Subcommittee on Employment, Manpower, and Poverty, Ninetieth Congress,
second session.* Hearing, April 10, 1967, 539.

75   **Out of the state's**: Ibid., 539, 553.

76   **"What are their"**: Britton, Dr. A. B., ibid., 553.

76   **"Take, for example"**: ibid., 557.

76   **The man in**: Wright, Marian. Testimony before *Examination of the War on Poverty:
Hearings before the U.S. Senate Subcommittee on Unemployment, Manpower, and
Poverty, Ninetieth Congress, second session.* Hearing, March 15, 1967, 159.

76   **"It is a tragic"**: Dr. A. B. Britton, 561.

76   **"That is the"**: Ibid., 572.

76–77 **"I think this"**: Ken Dean, ibid., 577.

77   **"To be successful"**: Robert F. Kennedy, ibid.

77   **"So it is"**: ibid., 577–78.

77   **"Would you say"**: Kennedy, like a: ibid., 578.

77   **Not only does**: Ibid., 581–82.

79   **"It's the only"**: Ibid., 592–93.

79   **"We have children"**: Ibid., 585.

79   **"Is there hunger . . ."**: Ibid., 592.

79   **"What happens to"**: Ibid.

79   **"They starve,"**: Blackwell: Ibid.

79   **"Is there some"**: Ibid.

79   **"Well, some folks"**: Ibid.

79   **"We need some . . ."**: Ibid., 593.

79   **"Is the hunger"**: Ibid.

79   **"It's spreading"**: Ibid., 593, 594.

80   **On a lark**: Ron Greer, author interview, February 24, 2014, and July 7, 2014.

80   **A banner reading**: W. F. "Bill" Minor, "Miss. Politics Silences RFK," *Times-Picayune,*
April 12, 1967.

80   **The school newspaper**: Mary Jane Marshall, "Senator Kennedy Asks, Answers Questions in Informal Appearance," *The Purple and White,* April 13, 1967.

80   **"hanging around"**: Robert Kennedy, *Transcription of Robert F. Kennedy's Speech to Millsaps Audience, April 10, 1967,* transcribed by Ted Houghtaling, Millsaps College Archives, box J9, folder 10.

81   **"The future of"**: Ibid.

81   **"their time and"**: Ibid.

81   **"Oh God," he**: Ibid.

81   **"I understand," Kennedy**: Ibid.

81   **Kennedy answered a**: Robert Burns, "Sen. Kennedy Is Deluged with Questions at Millsaps," *Jackson Daily News,* April 11, 1967, 20.

82   **"I don't think"**: Robert Kennedy, *Transcription of Robert F. Kennedy's Speech to Millsaps Audience, April 10, 1967,*transcribed by Ted Houghtaling, Millsaps College Archives, box J9, folder 10.

82   **Kennedy ended his**: Ron Greer, author interview, February 24, 2014, and July 7, 2014.

82   **She quickly ticked**: The summary of Marian Wright's testimony in this and the following paragraphs, including her interaction with Senator Joseph Clark and Senator Jacob Javits, are all taken from the hearing transcript. Ibid., 642–51.

83   **"run things for"**: Ibid., 642.

83   **"He is wrong"**: Ibid., 647.

83   **The audience, unused**: Taylor Branch, *At Caanan's Edge,* 598.

84   **"We feel we"**: Marian Wright, testimony *Examination of the War on Poverty: Hearings before the United States Senate Committee on Labor and Public Welfare, Subcommittee on Employment, Manpower, and Poverty, Ninetieth Congress, second session.* Hearing, April 10, 1967, 648.

84   **"I thought I"**: Marian Wright Edelman, Interview for Makers: The Largest Video Collection of Women's Stories, http://www.makers.com/marian-wright-edelman, accessed March 10, 2016.

84   **One of them**: Wright Edelman, *Lanterns,* 106–107.

84   **When Peter Edelman**: Edelman, *Searching for America's Heart,* 49.

85   **In contrast, Edelman's**: Ibid., 2–3.

85   **He was close**: Ibid.

85   **"an instinctive but"**: Ibid.

85   **For Edelman, such**: Ibid., The information in this paragraph and the following paragraphs about Edelman's career are from pages 30–33.

86   **"Are you going"**: Ibid., 33.

86   **As Kennedy's aide**: Ibid., 41–42.

86   **"Some have suggested"**: Ibid., 42.

86   **"RFK always saw"**: Ibid., 34.

86   **Upon arrival, Edelman**: Wright Edelman, *Lanterns,* 107.

86   **"you have to eat"**: Peter Edelman, author interview, July, 2008.

87   **"It was a"**: Edelman, *Searching for America's Heart,* 49.

87   **This young woman**: Ibid., 49. Adam Walinksy, author interview, July 1, 2015.

87   **For her part**: Wright Edelman, *Lanterns,* 106–7.

87   **When Kennedy's turn**: The description of Marian Wright's testimony and Senator Robert Kennedy's questions are drawn from the transcript of *Examination of the War on Poverty: Hearings before the United States Senate Committee on Labor and Public Welfare, Subcommittee on Employment, Manpower, and Poverty, Ninetieth Congress, second session.* Hearing, April 10, 1967, 651–56.

88   **Hendrick was at**: Becky Hendrick, author interview, July 2016.An Unwilling Partnership with the Great Society Part I: Head Start and the Beginning of Change in the White Medical Community, Richard D. deShazo, Wilson F. (Bill) Minor, Robert Smith, Leigh Baldwin Skipworth, *The American Journal of the Medical Sciences* 352, 1, 109–19.

88   **Crowds were milling**: Wilson F. "Bill" Minor, author interview, August 29, 2016.

88   **Hendrick knew something**: DeShazo, et al., 116.

89   **As the hearing ended**: Hendrick, author interview. Wilson F. "Bill" Minor, author interview.

89   **Ed King**: Ed King, author interview, March 13, 2017.

89   **Known to her**: Constance Slaughter Harvey, author interview, February 17, 2017.

89   **"Once I got"**: Ibid.

90   **"I think that"**: Ibid.

90   **The Slaughter family**: Ibid.

90   **"He was kind"**: Ibid.

90   **As Kennedy left**: Charlotte Slaughter Moman, author interview, September 11, 2016.

91   **"does not advocate"**: Gene Roberts, "New Leaders and New Course for 'Snick,'" *New York Times,* May 22, 1966, 208.

91   **An eloquent, well**: Ibid.

91   **Carmichael stood in**: Ibid.

91   **"[E]very courthouse ought"**: Gene Roberts, "Marchers Stage Mississippi Rally," *New York Times*, June 18, 1966, 20.

91   **This is the**: Gene Roberts and Hank Klibanoff, *The Race Beat*, 399.

92   **By the time**: Gene Roberts, "Rights March Disunity," *New York Times,* June 28, 1966, 23.

92   **Carmichael's rhetoric**: Roberts and Klibanoff, *The Race Beat,* 400.

92   **In the Delta, white**: Wilkie, *Dixie*, 2001.

92   **The scheduling of**: Bill Carey, "A Vanderbilt Guest Starts a Riot," *Nashville Post*, http://www.nashvillepost.com/business/education/article/20400112/a-vanderbilt-guest-starts-a-riot, accessed February 14, 2017.

92   **the next day**: Ibid.

92   **Two days later**: Stokely Carmichael, Speech at Tougaloo College, Jackson, Mississippi, "We Ain't Going," April 11, 1967, http://www.speeches-usa.com/Transcripts/stokeley_carmichael-weaint.html. Stokely Carmichael, "We Aint Going," YouTube video clip. Posted by Educational Video Group, Uploaded October 13, 2009, https://www.youtube.com/watch?v=HKP5_qyGs8c.

92   **"Well, we could"**: Stokely Carmichael, Speech at Tougaloo College, Jackson, Mississippi, "We Ain't Going," April 11, 1967, http://www.speeches-usa.com/Transcripts/

stokeley_carmichael-weaint.html. Stokely Carmichael, "We Aint Going," YouTube video clip. Posted by Educational Video Group, Uploaded October 13, 2009, https://www.youtube.com/watch?v=HKP5_qyGs8c.

93   **Although Carmichael appeared**: Mississippi State Sovereignty Commission, "Mississippi State Sovereignty Commission Photograph," circa April 11, 1967, SCRID# 9–37–0–2–40–1-1ph, Series 2515: Mississippi State Sovereignty Commission Records Online, 1994–2006, Mississippi Department of Archives and History, April 20, 2006, http://www.mdah.ms.gov/arrec/digital_archives/sovcom/photo .php?display=item&oid=518 (2017/02/14), Mississippi State Sovereignty Commission, April 13, 1967, SCR ID # 1–92–0–45–1-1-1,Series 2515: Mississippi State Sovereignty Commission Records Online, 1994–2006, Mississippi Department of Archives and History, Memorandum, Erle Johnson to Herman Glassier, http:// www.mdah.ms.gov/arrec/digital_archives/sovcom/result.php?image=images/ png/cd02/007618.png&.

93   **That same day**: "Carmichael Treasonous, Says Solon," *The Clarion-Ledger*, April 13, 1967.

94   **"I thought Patt"**: Winifred Green, author interview, February 19, 2014.

94   **Green was a fifth**: "Winifred Green, Obituary," *The Clarion-Ledger*, February 10, 2016.

94   **When her mother**: Winfred Green, author interview, February 19, 2014.

95   **Deep red, lacquered**: Ibid.

95   **"well, I'm sitting"**: Ibid.

95   **"When he said"**: Ibid.

95–96 **Later that evening**: "Guest list with yeses and nos,": Derian papers, Mississippi State University. Oscar Carr. Oral History Interview, May 6, 1969. John F. Kennedy Oral History Collection, John F. Kennedy Library, 14.

96   **As the party**: Wilson F. "Bill" Minor, author interview, January 8, 2008.

Chapter 5. "Wherever One Looks in This Land, Whatever One Sees, That Is the Work of Man"

97   **The airplane carrying**: Mississippi Itinerary and Witness List, JFK Library, box 88, Poverty Subcommittee on Employment, April 9–April 11, 1967. Jim Lucas photo contact sheets, April 11, 1967.

97   **As the DC3 headed**: Ibid., ABC News footage, April 11, 1967, www.abcnewsvideo-source.com.

97   **On Monday night**: George Lapides, author interview, August 5, 2007.

98   **The next morning**: Ibid.

100   **Until the last**: For the best and most thorough overview of the Delta's history, see James C. Cobb's fascinating work, *The Most Southern Place on Earth: The Mississippi Delta and the Roots of Regional Identity*, 1992. For the role of cotton farming in America's race relations, see financial historian Gene Dattel's work, *Cotton and Race and the Making of America: The Human Costs of Economic Power*, 2009.

100   **"Taken as a"**: "Report on Cotton Production in the State of Mississippi," *Tenth Census of the United States of America* 5 (June 1, 1880): 246.

101   **"failed 'to take'"**: Cobb, *The Most Southern Place on Earth*, 7.

101   **This "empire of"**: Sven Beckert, *Empire of Cotton: A Global History*, xxi.

101   **"Countries fought wars"**: Ibid.

101   **"The empire of cotton"**: Ibid.

102   **They "brought order"**: Cohn, quoted in Leon Howell, *Freedom City: The Substance of Things Hoped For*, 15.

102   **"the prospect of"**: John Willis, *Forgotten Time: The Yazoo Mississippi Delta After the Civil War*, 2.

102   **"encourage black initiative"**: Ibid., 3.

102   **Newcomers, many of**: Nan Woodruff, *American Congo*, 21.

102   **"Indeed, by 1900"**: Ibid., 22.

103   **However, cotton farming**: Ibid.

103–4   **As Woodruff emphasizes**: Ibid., 3.

104   **"between 1900 and"**: Paul W. White, "The History and Development of the Mississippi Delta Economy," *Business Perspectives*, University of Memphis, 20, no. 1 (Summer/Fall, June 22, 2009).

104   **"organized along corporate"**: Woodruff, 2.

104   **But even if**: Isabel Wilkerson, *The Warmth of Other Suns: The Epic Story of America's Great Migration*, 167.

104   **It is a story**: Cobb, 277–84.

105   **These worsening conditions**: U.S. Census Bureau, Data Visualization Gallery, "The Great Migration shown through changes in African-Americans share of population in major US cities, 1910–1940 and 1940–1970," https://en.wikipedia.org/wiki/Great_Migration_(African_American)#/media/File:GreatMigration1910to1970 -UrbanPopulation.png, accessed March 14, 2017.

105   **"Most of them"**: John M. Barry, *Rising Tide: The Great Mississippi Flood and How It Changed America*, 307.

105   **"the most serious"**: Ibid., 313.

105   **A prime example**: Cobb, 187.

106   **"the most influential"**: Ibid, 186.

107   **The changes reduced**: Walter Rugaber, "In the Delta, Poverty Is a Way of Life," *New York Times*, July 31, 1967.

107   **In 1964, for**: Hodding Carter III, "The Negro Exodus from the Delta Continues," *New York Times Magazine*, March 10, 1968. Billy Percy, author interview, March 13, 2017.

107   **Research on new**: Billy Percy, author interview, March 13, 2017.

107   **Billy Percy remembers**: Walter Rugaber, "In the Delta, Poverty Is a Way of Life," *New York Times*, July 31, 1967.

107   **In addition, by**: Percy, author interview, March 13, 2017.

107   **By the mid-1960s**: Ibid.

108   **A July 1967**: Walter Rugaber, "In the Delta, Poverty Is a Way of Life," *New York Times*, July 31, 1967.

108   **Despite the concern**: Percy, author interview, March 13, 2017.

108   **With diminishing work**: Hodding Carter III, "The Negro Exodus from the Delta Continues," *New York Times Magazine,* March 10, 1968.

108   **Between 1960 and**: Walter Rugaber, "In the Delta, Poverty Is a Way of Life," *New York Times*, July 31, 1967.

108   **Consequently, as Ken**: U.S. Senate. Committee on Labor and Public Welfare. Subcommittee on Employment. *Examination of the War on Poverty: Hearings before the United States Senate Committee on Labor and Public Welfare, Subcommittee on Employment, Manpower, and Poverty, Ninetieth Congress, first session.* Hearing, April 10, 1967. Washington: U.S. Government Printing Office. 1967, 575.

Chapter 6. "I Just Couldn't Make a Living"

111   **As the sedan**: The descriptions of Kennedy's arrival are taken from the unpublished contact sheets of a series of photographs taken by freelance photographer Jim Lucas on April 11, 1967, as well as viewing archival footage from CBS News Archives, *CBS Evening News*, "Daniel Schorr on RFK in Mississippi," April 12, 1967.

111   **When Robert Kennedy**: Catherine Wilson, author interview, November 5, 2015. The description of Catherine Wilson's life experiences come from interviews with her and her mother, Ora D. Wilson, April 9, 2014 and with Wilson alone on November 5, 2015.

112   **That morning**: John Car, "With RFK in the Delta," *American Heritage,* April/May 2002, Americanheritage.com.; Joseph A. Loftus, "Clark and Kennedy Visit the Poor of Mississippi," *New York Times*, April 12, 1967.

113   **"We're protecting Mississippi"**: Les Finnegan to Senator Joseph Clark, Bill Smith, et al., "Arrangements for Hearings, Dinners, and Delta Trip," JFK Library, Poverty Subcommittee on Employment, Manpower and Labor, Folder: Mississippi Itinerary and Witness List, box 88.

113   **"Bobby Kennedy Will"**: Joseph. A. Loftus, *New York Times*, April 12, 1967.

113   **When Kennedy disembarked**: Curtis Wilkie, *The Press-Register*, April 11, 1967.

113   **The city's chief**: Ibid.; George Lapides, "RFK, Sen. Clark Tour Delta Areas," *Press-Scimitar* April 11, 1967; Pat Dunne, author interview, July 7, 2008; Jim Lucas Photos.

113   **Decades later, with**: Hodding Carter III, author interview, March 22, 2016.

114   **By 1967, Carter's**: Carter was spirited in his defense of his positions when they were unpopular. For example, after the U.S. Supreme Court's decision in *Brown v. Board of Education* 1954, the paper's owner and editor at the time, Hodding Carter II, wrote an article critical of the White Citizens Council, a network of secretive white supremacist groups that emerged from the nearby Delta town of Greenwood to resist integration. When the Mississippi House of Representatives passed a resolution condemning Carter and calling him a liar, Carter responded with characteristic vigor by writing that if he were a liar, he'd be well qualified to

serve in that legislative body, and invited them to "go to hell, collectively or singly, and wait there until I back down." When he got threatening phone calls, according to his son, he would yell into the telephone: "Come and get me, you country-assed son of a bitch!" and wait in the front yard with a firearm and whiskey. Hodding Carter III, author interview, and Gordon Chaplin, "The Mouthpiece that Roared," *Washington Post Magazine*, https://www.washingtonpost.com/archive/lifestyle/magazine/1980/06/22/the-mouthpiece-that-roared/508b4c1d-0767–4f54 –9795–913f64397c88/?utm_term=.6ce9f2e7bb5d.

114   **"He said to"**: Hodding Carter III, author interview, March 22, 2016.

114   **Greenville's leadership also**: Newman, 85.

114   **This meant that**: Ibid.

115   **As Robert Kennedy**: Betty Jo Brent Boyd, author interview, April 11, 2014.

115   **With a polished**: Ibid. For the best in-depth exploration of the Delta Ministry and its work in Mississippi, see Mark Newman, *Divine Agitators: The Delta Ministry and Civil Rights in Mississippi* 2004, 33, 88. For a first-person account of working with the Delta Ministry, see Bruce Hilton's *The Delta Ministry*, 1969.

115   **Ruth Brent knew**: Betty Jo Brent Boyd, author interview, April 11, 2014.

115   **When word got**: Ibid.

115   **The callers to**: Ibid.

116   **"So he settled"**: Thelma Barnes, author interview, July 24, 2008.

116   **Outside the hotel**: Curtis Wilkie, author interview, February 17, 2017.

116   **In another part**: Clarke Reed, author interview, April 9, 2014.

116   **Since the early**: Ibid.

117   **With this goal**: Jan Sartor, "Reagan Charm Wins Round in White-Glove Battle," *The Commercial Appeal,* April 11, 1967.

117   **"It's God's country"**: Ibid.

117   **"A lot of people"**: Peter Edelman, author interview, June 4, 2008.

117   **"Number one, they"**: Hodding Carter, interview.

117   **"Carefully cultivated"**: Ibid. Pat Dunne, author interview, July 24, 2008.

119   **It was against**: Newman, 85.

119   **Greenville's surface civility**: Thelma Barnes, author interview; Betty Jo Brent Boyd, author interview; Hilton, *The Delta Ministry,* 39–67.

119   **As the passage of**: Newman, 84–85.

119   **After supporting and**: Hilton, 84–85; Newman 105.

120   **The winter of**: Hilton, 77.

120   **One federal program**: Cobb, 255.

120   **Hilton recalled**: Hilton, 78–79.

120   **Thousands of people**: Ibid., 77–85.

120   **Two days later**: Newman, 104.

121   **"It was snowing"**: Gene Roberts, "Air Force Ejects Negroes Occupying at Mississippi Base," *The New York Times*, February 2, 1966, 1.

121   **"People are hungry"**: Ibid.

121   **"They said that"**: Catherine Wilson, author interview.

121   **The initial idea**: Newman, 128–29.

122   **Although the organization**: Ibid.

122   **But there were problems**: Ibid.

122   **However, the residents**: Angus McEarchan, "Hardship and Heartbreak in Freedom City: For the First Time I Feel Like I'm Gaining," *National Observer,* December 26, 1966.

122   **"We're the funniest"**: Ibid.

122   **By the time**: Catherine Wilson, author interview, November 5, 2015; Bill Rose, author interview, January 20, 2012; Newman, 134.

123   **Catherine's brother Sammy**: Angus McEarchan, "Hardship and Heartbreak in Freedom City: For the First Time I Feel Like I'm Gaining," *National Observer,* December 26, 1966.

123   **"From the first"**: This quote, as well as those that follow are from Catherine Wilson, author interview.

124   **School improved**: Newman, 135.

124   **"surrounded by their"**: Hilton, 132.

124   **"the disaster got"**: Ibid., 132–33.

124   **When the storm**: Angus McEarchan, "Hardship and Heartbreak in Freedom City: For the First Time I Feel Like I'm Gaining," *National Observer,* December 26, 1966.

124   **When Kennedy walked**: Newman, 140.

125   **"Why did you"**: CBS News Archives, *CBS Evening News,* "Daniel Schorr on RFK in Mississippi," April 12, 1967; Bill Minor, "Senators View Miss. Poverty," *New Orleans Times-Picayune,* April 12, 1967.

125   **"I couldn't make"**: Ibid.

125   **At Freedom City**: Joseph A. Loftus, *New York Times,* April 12, 1967.

125   **Catherine Wilson's nephew**: Rufus Donald, author interview, July 7, 2016.

125   **"He was sort"**: Marian Wright, oral history transcript, Jean Stein Oral History Collection, box 1, 3.

125   **"I'm the star"**: Ibid.

126   **Always curious, Kennedy**: Ibid.

126   **"I said, 'John'"**: Ibid., 9–10.

127   **"All I could"**: Ibid.

127   **So many of**: Ibid., 14.

127   **Marian Wright, her**: Ibid., 14–15. In the interest of brevity, I have paraphrased the first half of the story of Cinderlilly from the full transcript of Marian Wright Edelman's 1969 oral history in the Stein Collection. I have, however, within my paraphrase, quoted directly the dialogue she included in her story. In later paragraphs, I pick up the story and quote it as Wright told it.

128   **"You're sure he's'"**: Ibid., 14–15.

128   **As Wright concluded**: Ibid.

128   **Kennedy remained quiet**: Ibid.

129   **Later in the day**: Wright Edelman, *Lanterns,* 107.

Chapter 7. "A Terrible Reflection on Our Society"

The descriptions in this chapter of Kennedy's visit to Cleveland and his interactions with the Dillard and White families are drawn from the author's interview of Charlie Dillard, Willie White, Michael White, and author interviews of news reporters who were there, including Hodding Carter III, Wilson F. "Bill" Minor, George Lapides, Bill Rose, and Curtis Wilkie. Two local pastors, Herman Johnson of Mound Bayou, Mississippi, and Sammie Rash of Cleveland, Mississippi, as well as Charles Evers of Jackson, Mississippi, contributed their memories as well. Frances Smith, a teacher in the Head Start program at Cleveland's United Baptist Church and her husband, Reuben Smith, also proved an interview.

The account presented in this chapter also draws upon reporter John Carr's description in "With RFK in the Delta" in *American Heritage* magazine, April/May 2002; photographer Dan Guravich's photos and contact sheets; ABC and CBS archival video footage; video footage and interviews in the *Eyes on the Prize* documentary; as well as contemporary newspaper accounts in the *Bolivar Commercial, Clarksdale Press-Register,* the *Greenville Delta Democrat-Times,* the *Memphis Press Scimitar,* the *New York Times,* and the *New Orleans Times-Picayune.*

Marian Wright Edelman recorded her observations of his time in the Delta in chapter 10 of her book, *Lanterns: A Memoir of Mentors*, and Peter Edelman provided two interviews to the author and has written about the visit in two of his books: *Searching for America's Heart: RFK and the Renewal of Hope* and *So Rich, So Poor: Why It's So Hard to End Poverty in America*. Charles Evers wrote about the trip in his book, *Have No Fear: The Charles Evers Story*, and Daniel Schorr's book, *Staying Tuned,* also provides an account of Kennedy in Mississippi, as does Nick Kotz's *Let Them Eat Promises.*

Some of these accounts do conflict from time to time. For instance, John Carr places Kennedy's encounter with the hostile newspaper editor outside of Greenville when it was thirty-five miles away, and Charles Evers remembered in a 2015 interview that they went to Issaquena County. In these instances, where information recounted in interviews decades after the fact conflicts with the news accounts, I have relied on the itinerary found in the RFK Senate Papers at the JFK Presidential Library and one I constructed using the news reports, video, and photographs from 1967, especially those reported by Curtis Wilkie, Bill Minor, George Lapides, and Daniel Schorr.

134   **As Kennedy came out**: The Associated Press, raw video footage, April 11, 1967.

134   **"What did you"**: *CBS Evening News,* "Daniel Schorr on RFK in Mississippi," April 12, 1967.

134   **"No," Rob said**: Ibid.

136   **Their teachers, including**: Frances Smith, Head Start director in Cleveland, Mississippi, author interview, December 17, 2006.

136   **Moore was a**: The summary of Amzie Moore's biographical background is a synthesis of information drawn from his oral history in Howell Raines, *My Soul Is Rested*, 233–37; the transcript of Moore's interview for the *Eyes on the Prize* documentary; and his biography in *American National Biography.*

137   **"Not a single bed"**: Raines, 233–34.

138   **Her parents, Charles**: Edna White Brisby, author interview, March 29, 2014. The information on Annie Wilkinson White's family is from interviews with her daughter Edna White Brisby and Willie White. When possible, I have matched them with documentary evidence.

138   **As the youngest**: "United States Census, 1930," database with images, FamilySearch, https://familysearch.org/ark:/61903/1:1:XMBH-Y6J: Annie Branch in entry for Charlie Branch, 1930. For some reason, (perhaps they were living with relatives with the name) the Wilkinson family is listed in the 1930 census with the last name of Branch. However, the first names and dates of birth of everyone in the family are match those of the family of Annie Wilkinson White.

138   **Although Charles and Pinkie**: "Mississippi Enumeration of Educable Children, 1850–1892; 1908–1957."

138   **In her early teens**: Edna White Brisby, author interview, March 29, 2014. The details of Annie White's life are drawn from interviews with her surviving children— Edna White Brisby, Willie, Michael, David and Lorenzo White—and contemporary news accounts.

141   **Annie White rented**: Ibid.

143   **"Hello, hi, hi"**: Nick Kotz, *Let Them Eat Promises*, 2.

143   **Marian Wright stood**: Marian Wright Edelman, conducted by Blackside, Inc. on December 21, 1988, *Eyes on the Prize II: America at the Racial Crossroads 1965 to 1985*. Washington University Libraries, Film and Media Archive, Henry Hampton Collection.

144   **Peter Edelman stood**: Peter Edelman, *Searching for America's Heart*, 52.

144   **He paused outside**: Unita Blackwell, *Barefootin': Life Lessons from the Road to Freedom*, 164.

145   **Just outside in**: *CBS Evening News*, "Daniel Schorr on RFK in Mississippi," April 12, 1967.

145   **Not everyone saw**: The following description of Kennedy and Langford's confrontation is taken from interviews by the author with journalists who were there, including Hodding Carter III, Bill Minor, Bill Rose, and Curtis Wilkie, as well as viewing frame-by-frame contact sheets from photographer Dan Guravich and archival footage from *CBS News* and the Associated Press.

145   **The editor had**: "Editor Dies in Bolivar," *Delta Democrat-Times*, October 24, 1972, 8., Mississippi State Sovereignty Commission, Mississippi State Sovereignty Commission Letter, Erle Johnston Jr. to Cliff Langford, November, 2, 1965, SCRID#99–100-0-243-1-1-1, Series 2515: Mississippi State Sovereignty Commission Records Online, 1994–2006, Mississippi Department of Archives and History, April 20, 2006, http://www.mdah.ms.gov/arrec/digital_archives/sovcom/result. php?image=images/png/cd10/079551.png&otherstuff=99|100|0|243|1|1|78526|.

147   **In addition to**: Nevin Sledge, author interview, January 31, 2014.

147   **The day Kennedy**: Hodding Carter III, author interview, April 29, 2014.

149   **Veteran CBS reporter**: Daniel Schorr, *Staying Tuned*, 200.

149   **"It was a"**: Ibid.

149   **With Kennedy in**: Ibid., 210.

150   **Hodding Carter III**: Hodding Carter III, author interview, March 22, 2016.

150   **"I can see"**: George Lapides, author interview, August 5, 2007.

150   **"shocked and hurt"**: Blackwell, 164.

150   **This was typical**: Adam Walinsky, author interview, July 1, 2015.

150   **Kennedy was intent**: Curtis Wilkie, "Wild Welcome Here Ends Kennedy-Clark Delta
       Tour," *Clarksdale Press-Register*, April 12, 1967.

150   **Passing through tiny**: Ibid., Peter Edelman Oral History Interview, RFK, #8, March
       13, 1974, John F. Kennedy Oral History Collection, John F. Kennedy Library, 18–19.

150   **Flustered at the**: Wilkie, "Wild Welcome," *Clarksdale Press-Register,* April 12, 1967.

151   **It was growing**: Ibid.

Chapter 8. "We Need to Make an Effort Together"

153   **"Ain't goin' let"**: Traditional Negro Spiritual adapted as a civil rights song.

153   **As the song**: The quotes and information about Kennedy's visit and the Luckett fam-
       ily are taken from the author's interview with Brenda Luckett on August 29, 2016.
       Further quotes and descriptions of the scene are taken from the news article and
       photographs. Wilkie, Curtis. "Wild Welcome Here Ends Kennedy-Clark Delta
       Tour," *Clarksdale Press-Register*, April 12, 1967.

159   **Emmett Till and**: Southern Poverty Law Center, "Civil Rights Martyrs," *Civil Rights
       Memorial*, https://www.splcenter.org/what-we-do/civil-rights-memorial/civil
       -rights-martyrs, accessed on September 30, 2016.

159   **"when you suddenly"**: Martin Luther King, *Letter from the Birmingham Jail*, April 12,
       1963, http://www.thekingcenter.org/archive/document/letter-birmingham-city
       -jail-0.

160   **Early in its history**: Nicholas Lemann, *The Promised Land: The Great Black Migra-
       tion and How It Changed America*, 315.

160   **However, the path**: The information about Coahoma Opportunities' evolution and
       programs is drawn from Nicholas Lemann's *Promised Land*, K.C. Morrison's
       Aaron Henry of Mississippi, and the author's interview with Andrew Carr.

161   **The poverty endemic**: Curtis Wilkie, *Dixie*, 115.

161   **It is no surprise**: The biographical information about Aaron Henry is a synthesis
       drawn from several sources, including Aaron Henry and Constance Curry, *Aaron
       Henry: The Fire Ever Burning*, 2000, 120–22; Minion K. C. Morrison, *Aaron Henry
       of Mississippi: Inside Agitator*, 2015; and Nicholas Lemann, *The Promised Land:
       The Great Black Migration and How It Changed*, 2011.

163   **Henry was no stranger**: The information about Henry's arrest and Robert Kennedy's
       intervention is taken from Aaron Henry and Constance Curry, *Aaron Henry: The
       Fire Ever Burning*, 120–22.

163   **"got busy"**: Ibid., 121.

164   **"We had no way"**: Ibid., 122.

164   **"Bobby Kennedy stayed"**: Ibid., 169.

164   **Like Henry, Andrew**: The biographical information about Andrew Carr is taken from the author's interview with him on April 22, 2014, as well as his oral history in the Civil Rights Digital Library. Andrew Carr, Interview by Homer Hill, Mississippi Oral History Program of the University of Southern Mississippi. March 14, 1994.

165   **In his position**: Hearings, U.S. Senate Subcommittee on Employment, Manpower, and Poverty, March 15, 1967, 51

166   **"Such a program"**: Ibid.

166   **"We're in a"**: Wilkie, "Wild Welcome, *Press Register,* April 12, 1967.

166   **"most helpful"**: Ibid.

166   **"The problems of"**: Ibid.

166   **"Stay in school"**: Ibid.

167   **"trying to touch"**: Wilson F. "Bill" Minor, author interview, December, 14, 2006.

167   **"At the airport"**: Unita Blackwell and JoAnne Prichard Morris, *Barefootin': Life Lessons from the Road to Freedom*, 164; Marian Wright Edelman, *Eyes on the Prize* documentary.

167   **Around 9**: Lisbeth Schorr, author interview, April 18, 2017.

167   **"It was maybe"**: Ibid.

167   **"There have been"**: Ibid.

167   **"It had clearly"**: Ibid.

Chapter 9. "You Don't Know What I Saw!"

169   **Dinner at Robert**: Ethel S. Kennedy, author interview, March 7, 2017.

169   **"It was a unusual"**: Ibid.

170   **Her husband was**: Ibid.

170   **"But as he"**: Kathleen Kennedy Townsend, *Failing America's Faithful: How Today's Churches Are Mixing God with Politics and Losing Their Way*; Kathleen Kennedy Townsend, author interview; Robert F. Kennedy Jr., author interview, Ethel S. Kennedy, *Ethel*, HBO.

170   **His visit to**: Ethel S. Kennedy, author interview, March 13, 2017.

170   **The atmosphere in**: Ethel Kennedy, author interview, March 13, 2017.

170   **In his daughter**: Kathleen Kennedy Townsend, author interview, November 11, 2011.

170   **Later, Kennedy Townsend**: Kathleen Kennedy Townsend, "The Delta in Our Home," *The New York Times,* June 4, 2008.

170   **"But on that"**: Ibid.

171   **Ethel Kennedy was not**: Ethel Kennedy, author interview, March 13, 2017.

171   **However, it wasn't**: Melody Miller, author interview, May 6, 2014.

171   **"Could you please"**: Ibid.

172   **"We were just"**: Amanda Burden, author interview, July 31, 2017.

172 **"When he would"**: Ibid.

172 **The young woman**: Evan Thomas, *Robert Kennedy: His Life,* 339.

172 **"You don't know"**: Ibid.

172 **The impact lingered**: Amanda Burden, author interview, July 31, 2017.

172 **"His passion for"**: Ibid.

172 **"And that, I"**: Ibid.

173 **On the morning**: "A Short History of SNAP (Supplemental Nutritional Assistance Program)," https://www.fns.usda.gov/snap/short-history-snap, accessed March 14, 2017.

173 **Consequently, Kennedy was**: Peter Edelman Oral History Interview, RFK, #8, March 13, 1974, John F. Kennedy Oral History Collection, John F. Kennedy Library, 21–23.

173 **Kennedy assured him**: Ibid., 20.

173 **As Edelman and Kennedy**: Peter Edelman Oral History Interview, RFK #1, July 15, 1969. John F. Kennedy Oral History Collection, John F. Kennedy Library.

173 **What Kennedy did**: Nick Kotz, *Let Them Eat Promises: The Politics of Hunger in America,* 79.

174 **While Freeman may**: Kotz, 83.

174 **Whitten was a**: Ibid., 82.

174 **As journalist Nick**: Ibid.

174 **For Jamie Whitten**: Ibid., 87.

174 **Whitten feared that**: Kay Mills, *This Little Light of Mine,* 256.

175 **And in 1964**: Ibid., 85.

175 **After meeting with**: Edelman, 54.

176 **While Freeman's aides**: U.S. Senate. Committee on Labor and Public Welfare. Subcommittee on Employment. *Examination of the War on Poverty: Hearings before the United States Senate Committee on Labor and Public Welfare, Subcommittee on Employment, Manpower, and Poverty, Ninetieth Congress, second session.* Hearing, April 10, 1967. Washington: U.S. Government Printing Office. 1967, 657.

176 **Johnson's aides were**: Peter Edelman Oral History Interview, RFK, #8, March 13, 1974, John F. Kennedy Oral History Collection, John F. Kennedy Library, 25, 30.

176 **"You tell them"**: Ibid.; Kotz, 64.

176 **Meanwhile, Kennedy's staff**: Peter Edelman Oral History Interview, RFK, #8, March 13, 1974, John F. Kennedy Oral History Collection, John F. Kennedy Library, 33. Kotz, 64–65.

176 **Retracing Kennedy**: Kotz, 63.

177 **Two weeks after**: Kennedy's testimony and exchange with other senators is taken from the official transcript of the hearing he attended. U.S. Senate. Committee on Agriculture and Forestry. Subcommittee on Agricultural Research and General Legislation. *Food Stamp Appropriations Authorization, Ninetieth Congress, first session.* Hearing, April 25, 1967. Washington: U.S. Government Printing Office. 1967, 6–14.

178 **The next day**: Robert F. Kennedy to Martin Luther King, April 28, 1967, http://www.thekingcenter.org/archive/document/letter-robert-f-kennedy-mlk-4.

179   **Andrew Young, who**: Andrew Young, American Experience, *JFK*, WGBH Educational Foundation, 2013.

179   **However, author Larry**: Larry Tye, *Bobby Kennedy: The Making of a Liberal Icon*, 125–29.

179   **Tye writes**: Ibid., 129.

180   **Once the Kennedys**: Arthur Meier Schlesinger Jr., *Robert Kennedy: His Times*, 310; James Hilty, *Brother Protector*, 328.

180   **"profound depression," his**: Taylor Branch, *Parting the Waters,* 672.

180   **"summoned the nation"**: Ibid.

180   **Alternatively King's**: Tye, 233.

180   **The most divisive**: Ibid., 233–34.

181   **When he got**: Robert F. Kennedy to Martin Luther King, April 28, 1967, http://www.thekingcenter.org/archive/document/letter-robert-f-kennedy-mlk-4.

181   **Other than a**: D. McDonald to Robert F. Kennedy, May 4, 1967, http://www.thekingcenter.org/archive/document/letter-robert-f-kennedy-dora-mcdonald. Tracking contact between Kennedy and King at this time is complicated by King's busy travel schedule; that meant he often made calls from the road that were not documented. Furthermore, Kennedy's senatorial correspondence from 1967 is not yet available for public research at the JFK Presidential Library archives.

181   **On the day**: Walter Rugaber, "Dr. King Declines Peace Candidacy," *The New York Times,* April 26, 1967.

181   **Meanwhile, the inevitable**: Kotz, 8.

181   **In Mississippi, the**: "Gnawing of Empty Brains," *Jackson Daily News*, April 13, 1967.

182   **The paper's vigorously**: "Covering the Crossroads with Jimmy Ward," *Jackson Daily News*, April 12, 1967.

182   **However, the reaction**: Oliver Emmerich, "Highlights in the Headlines," *McComb Enterprise Journal,* April 11, 1967.

182   **in Washington County**: "Candidates Answer Questions of Poverty," *Jackson Daily News*, April 13, 1967.

183   **Cliff Langford, the**: Cliff Langford, "Random Remarks by Ye Editor," *The Bolivar Commercial,* April 13, 1967.

183   **Later, on a**: Michael White, author interview, March 10, 2014.

183   **In the halls**: "Clark, Kennedy Visit Seen Effort to Thwart Stennis," *Jackson Daily News*, April 13, 1967.

183   **Governor Paul B. Johnson**: Wilson F. "Bill" Minor, author interview, January 9, 2008; Mike Smith, "USDA Unable to Find Proof to Back Up Hunger Charges," *Jackson Daily News*, April 14, 1967; "Poverty Visitors Criticized," *The Commercial Appeal*, April 14, 1967.

183   **Dr. Joseph Brenner, who**: This and the subsequent paragraphs are from Joseph Brenner, MD, author interview, April 9, 2015.

185   **The next day**: Ibid.

185   **When it was**: "Hungry Children. Special Report." Southern Regional Council, Atlanta, Georgia, 1967, 4.

185   **They examined nearly**: Ibid., 4, 7.

185   **"We saw children"**: Ibid., 5.

186   **"We do not"**: Ibid., 5–6.

186   **Even though Mississippi**: Paul B. Johnson to James O. Eastland, June 19, 1967, East-
        land Collection, file 3, subseries 4, box 35, folder 14 "MS Governor—Paul B. John-
        son Jr."

186   **The later report**: Wilson F. "Bill" Minor, Robert Smith, and Leigh Baldwin Skipworth,
        "An Unwilling Partnership with the Great Society Part I: Head Start and the
        Beginning of Change in the White Medical Community." *The American Journal of
        the Medical Sciences* 352, no. 1 (2016): 109–19.

186   **The anguish of**: Kotz, 86.

187   **"men hardly interested"**: Robert Coles, MD, *Lives of Moral Leadership: Men and
        Women Who Have Made a Difference*, 4–6.

187   **After several meetings**: Ibid.

187   **"We've done all"**: Ibid., 6.

187   **Kennedy asked the**: Ibid., 8.

187   **After a few**: Ibid.

187   **Kennedy knew that**: Kotz, 9.

187   **After a few**: Coles, *Lives,* 11.

188   **Kennedy filtered the**: Ibid., 12.

188   **Kennedy went on**: Ibid., 13.

189   **However, Mississippi officials**: Edelman, *Searching for America's Heart,* 55.

189   **Dr. Raymond Wheeler**: U.S. Senate. Committee on Labor and Public Welfare. Sub-
        committee on Employment. *Examination of the War on Poverty: Hearings before
        the United States Senate Committee on Labor and Public Welfare, Subcommittee
        on Employment, Manpower, and Poverty, Ninetieth Congress, first session.* Hearing
        July 11 and 12, 1967, 11.

189   **The Mississippi senators**: Kotz, 69.

189   **When Dr. A. L. Gray**: The exchange here and in the following paragraphs between
        Gray, Kennedy, Stennis, and Clark can be found in the transcript of the U.S. Sen-
        ate. Committee on Labor and Public Welfare. Subcommittee on Employment.
        *Examination of the War on Poverty: Hearings before the United States Senate Com-
        mittee on Labor and Public Welfare, Subcommittee on Employment, Manpower,
        and Poverty, Ninetieth Congress, first session.* Hearing July 11 and 12, 1967, 85–93.

192   **The denials**: Kotz, 69–70.

192   **On the second**: Nan Robertson, "Javits and Freeman Trade Shouts at Hunger
        Inquiry," *The New York Times,* July 13, 1967.

193   **"I resent the"**: Ibid.

193   **Javits refused to**: Ibid.

193   **Freeman insisted that**: Kotz, 86–87.

193   **However, Jamie Whitten**: Ibid., 89.

193   **When national syndicated**: Jamie L. Whitten Collection, Archives and Special Col-
        lections, J. D. Williams Library, University of Mississippi, Series 1, "Congressional

Record," subseries 1: "Excerpts," box 2, folder 11, May 1967, *Let's Keep the Record Straight.*

193   **Whitten argued that**: Ibid.

193   **"I immediately called"**: Ibid.

193   **"No one likes"**: Ibid.

193   **Journalist Nick Kotz**: Kotz 96–97.

194   **A few days**: Hiram Eastland, author interview, March 21, 2014.

194   **As the efforts**: Peter Edelman Oral History Interview, RFK, #8, March 13, 1974, John F. Kennedy Oral History Collection, John F. Kennedy Library, 43–44.

195   **"This is terrible"**: Robert M. Coles, author interview, October 14, 2014.

Chapter 10. "I'd Feel Better if I Were Doing What I Think Ought to Be Done"

197   **It was exactly**: Tom Wicker, "Kennedy to Make 3 Primary Races; Attacks Johnson," *The New York Times,* March 17, 1968.

197   **In his remarks**: "Kennedy's Statement and Excerpts from News Conference," March 17, 1968, 68.

198   **Kennedy's former aide**: John Seigenthaler, author interview, February 23, 2013.

198   **"If you talk"**: Ibid.

198   **"So when I"**: Ibid.

198   **"The point of"**: Ibid.

198   **Although Seigenthaler presented**: Ibid.

199   **Robert Kennedy's brother**: Edward M. Kennedy, *True Compass: A Memoir.*

199   **Years later, the**: Chip Mabry, author interview, March 6, 2014.

199   **"My brother's trip"**: *Delta Magazine,* 2003.

200   **When Robert Kennedy**: Adam Walinsky, author interview, June 10, 2015; Edward Schmitt, *President of the Other America,* 183.

200   **Although Kennedy**: Schmitt, 185, 190.

200   **However, Kennedy was**: Peter Edelman, author interview, June 9, 2008.

200   **Riots in other**: Arthur Schlesinger Jr., *Robert Kennedy and His Times,* 832.

201   **Kennedy had**: Schmitt, 187, 191–92.

201   **However, despite Kennedy's**: Ibid., 187–90.

201   **"In spite of"**: Ibid., 191.

201   **"By the fall"**: Ibid.

202   **All that fall**: Schlesinger, 861, 875; Tye, 400.

202   **However, Kennedy fretted**: Ibid., 861.

202   **As Kennedy hesitated**: Ibid., 868–69.

202   **America's involvement in**: Ibid., 871

203   **As 1968 opened**: Schmitt, 196; Schlesinger, 879.

203   **Kennedy was incensed**: Schmitt, 200; Schlesinger, 878.

203   **Decades later, his**: Ethel Kennedy, *Ethel,* HBO documentary, 2012.

203   **Although the Department**: Schmitt, 193, 200–201.

203   **For weeks Kennedy**: Schlesinger, 884. Edelman, author interview, November 27, 2017.
       Tye, 401.

204   **"the kind of"**: Schmitt, 200.

Chapter 11. Bring the Poor People to Washington

206   **"It is a well-known"**: Lt. Governor Charles L. Sullivan, "Reaction to Robert Kennedy
       Shooting," *WLBT* Newsfilm Collection—MP1980.1, Reel D145 LCN 281, June 5,
       1968.

206   **"I believe it"**: Ibid.

207   **Another, younger, legislator**: Ibid.

207   **"Where does it"**: Ibid.

207   **"God, they kill"**: Jack Newfield, *Robert Kennedy: A Memoir,* 344

207   **"My brother need"**: Edward M. Kennedy, *Eulogy for Robert F. Kennedy*, St. Patrick's
       Cathedral, June 8, 1968.

207   **When the train**: Tom Wicker, "President Joins Kennedy in Tribute at Graveside," *The
       New York Times,* June 9, 1968.

207   **Fourteen-year-old**: Robert F. Kennedy Jr., author interview, April 21, 2014. The fol-
       lowing descriptions are from news accounts and the author's interview with Rob-
       ert Kennedy Jr.

208   **"They all came"**: Robert F Kennedy Jr., author interview, April 21, 2014.

208   **"It was one"**: Marian Wright Edelman, author interview, July 12, 2017.

208   **"Kennedy was very"**: Peter Edelman. *Searching for America's Heart*, 54.

208   **During one of**: Taylor Branch, *At Canaan's Edge: America in the King Years, 1965–68*,
       641; interview with Marian Wright Edelman, conducted by Blackside Inc. on
       December 21, 1988.

209   **Bring the poor people**: Branch, *At Canaan's Edge*, 641; interview with Marian Wright
       Edelman, conducted by Blackside Inc. on December 21, 1988.

209   **When Wright arrived**: Branch, 640; interview with Marian Wright Edelman, con-
       ducted by Blackside, Inc. on December 21, 1988.

209   **"He treated me"**: Interview with Marian Wright Edelman, conducted by Blackside,
       Inc. on December 21, 1988.

209   **However, after the**: Kotz, 168.

209   **As discussed earlier**: Schmitt,182.

210   **"the deepest concern"**: Jacob Javits, Eulogy for Senator Robert F. Kennedy, United
       States Senate, July 30, 1968, as reprinted in Pierre Salinger, Edwin Guthman,
       Frank Mankiewicz, and John Seigenthaler, *An Honorable Profession: A Tribute to
       Robert F. Kennedy*, 110–13.

210   **"left Senator Kennedy"**: Ibid., 112.

210   **In his statement**: James O. Eastland Collection, Archives and Special Collections,
       J. D. Williams Library, University of Mississippi, box 6, file 1, subseries 18, file 10.

210 **"I have been"**: Ibid. J. D.

210 **But it was**: Kotz, 184–85.

211 **Ironically, the hungry**: Kotz, 80.

211 **Whitten had remained on**: Kenneth Schlossberg, "Funny Money Is Serious," *The New York Times Magazine*, September 28, 1975, 234.

211 **Kennedy's 1967 trip**: Previous biographers and RFK aide Peter Edelman have credited Kennedy with suggesting the idea for the *Hunger in America* documentary to CBS. However, historian Edward R. Schmitt reports in his book that producer Don Hewitt and Philip Scheffler, an associate producer, "denied this convincingly" to him in 2001.

211 **However, on May**: Jamie L. Whitten Collection, Archives and Special Collections, J. D. Williams Library, University of Mississippi, Series 1, Subseries: Excerpts, box 2, folder 2 May 1968, "Enjoining Adverse and Untrue Publicity from Being Distributed by News Media."

211 **Whitten continued to**: Ibid.

211 **A year later**: Nick Kotz, "The Politics of Hunger and the 'Permanent Secretary of Agriculture,'" *The Philadelphia Inquirer*, October 26, 1969, 127.

211 **"The FBI agents"**: Ibid., 109–11.

212 **"Perhaps more than"**: Josephine Martin, *Managing Child Nutrition Programs: Leadership for Excellence,* Jones and Bartlett Learning, 1999, 63.

212 **"During that time"**: Peter K. Eisinger, *Toward an End to Hunger in America*, Brookings Institute Press, 1998, 80.

212 **In early May**: "A Chronology of Federal Nutrition Programs." Unpublished report. Children's Defense Fund, July 2017.

212 **Advocates for the**: Ibid

212 **Although a week**: Ibid.

213 **However, it was**: Interview with Marian Wright Edelman, conducted by Blackside, Inc. on December 21, 1988. United States Department of Agriculture, Food and Nutrition Service, "A Short History of SNAP," https://www.fns.usda.gov/snap/short-history-snap.

213 **"that's no good"**: Douglas Martin, "Mildred Loving, Who Battled Ban on Mixed-Race Marriage, Dies at 68," *New York Times*, May 6, 2008.

213 **The bride wore**: The descriptions in this section are a synthesis taken from several sources: Nan Robertson, "Aides to Robert Kennedy and Dr. King Are Married in a Virginia Ceremony," *New York Times*, July 15, 1968 and photo; Adam Walinsky, author interview, August 1, 2016; Marian Wright Edelman, *Lanterns*, photo insert, 111.

214 **As the campaign**: Marian Wright Edelman, *Lanterns*, 111.

214 **In the stillness**: Nan Robertson. "Aides to Robert Kennedy and Dr. King Are Married in a Virginia Ceremony," *New York Times*, July 15, 1968 and photo.

214 **Marian and Peter Edelman**: Krissah Thompson, "Marian Wright Edelman Marks 40 years of Advocacy at Children's Defense Fund," *The Washington Post*, September 29, 2013. Style section, https://www.washingtonpost.com/lifestyle/style/

marian-wright-edelman-marks-40-years-of-advocacy-at-childrens-defense
-fund/2013/09/29/f0abc816–279b-11e3-b3e9-d97fb087acd6_story.html.

215   **"I remember watching"**: Interview with Marian Wright Edelman, conducted by
       Blackside, Inc. on December 21, 1988.

215   **"You get up"**: Marian Wright Edelman, author interview, July 12, 2017.

215   **"We still have"**: Ibid.

216   **Like many who**: Peter Edelman. *Searching for America's Heart*, 3.

Chapter 12. "It Let Us Know that There Was Somebody Who Cared"

217   **In 2013, 90,000**: Food Resource and Action Center, http://frac.org/wp-content/
       uploads/2010/07/ms.pdf. Nick Kotz, *Let Them Eat Promises,* 213.

217   **In June**: United States Department of Agriculture, Food and Nutrition Service,
       "Supplemental Nutrition Assistance Program: Number of Persons Participat-
       ing," http://www.fns.usda.gov/sites/default/files/pd/29SNAPcurrPP.pdf, accessed
       March 27, 2017.

218   **However, despite**: Tyler Mac Innis, "Mississippi Has the Worst Hunger Rate
       in the Country" *ReThinkms.org,* http://www.rethinkms.org/2014/02/05/
       people-hungry-mississippi-else-hard-food-assistance/.

218   **It must also**: United States Department of Health and Human Services, Administra-
       tion for Children and Families, "Temporary Assistance for Needy Families, Octo-
       ber 2016," https://www.acf.hhs.gov/sites/default/files/ofa/2017_monthly_tan.pdf

219   **"What Robert Kennedy"**: Peter Edelman, author interview, July 28, 2017.

219   **Other changes have**: The most recent figures available for this statistic are
       from 2006. The Joint Center for Political and Economic Studies published
       a yearly report through 2002, according to an article from *polititact.com,*
       http://www.politifact.com/georgia/statements/2014/oct/27/nathan-deal/
       deal-overstates-georgia-tops-black-elected-officia/.

219   **"the long-range"**: Robert E. Thompson and Hortense Myers, *Robert F. Kennedy:*
       |The Brother Within, 142.

219   **"Jim Eastland"**: James Hilty, *Robert Kennedy: Brother Protector,* 313.

220   **"Basic manufacturing"**: Hiram Eastland, author interview, March 21, 2014.

220   **However, the land**: United States Department of Agriculture, National Agricultural
       Statistics Service, "Mississippi Prospective Plantings Report," released March 31,
       2016, https://www.nass.usda.gov/Statistics_by_State/Mississippi/Publications/
       Crop_Releases/Prospective_Plantings/2016/msplant16.pdf.

220   **"Twenty-five thousand"**: Sven Beckert, *Empire of Cotton,* 429.

220   **Despite**: Jerry Mitchell, "Infant Mortality Falls Faster in Mississippi than the U.S."
       The Clarion-Ledger, November 28, 2015, http://www.clarionledger.com/story/
       news/2015/11/28/infant-mortality-falls-faster-mississippi-than-us/76338008/.

220   **Even today, fifty**: "Map the Meal Gap 2015 Documents Hunger in Every County and
       Congressional District," *Feeding America,* http://www.feedingamerica.org/hunger

-in-america/news-and-updates/press-room/press-releases/map-the-meal-gap
-2015.html,

221   **In the Mississippi**: "Obesity County Factsheets—Bolivar, Coahoma, and Washington,
      Mississippi, *National Institute for Children's Healthcare Quality,* http://obesity.
      nichq.org/resources/obesity-factsheets, accessed on March 29, 2017.

221   **However, in contrast**: A. Gamble, D. Waddell, M. A. Ford, J. P. Bentley, C. D. Wood-
      yard, J. S. Hallam, "Obesity and Health Risk of Children in the Mississippi Delta,"
      The Journal of School Health, October 2012.

221   **Food insecurity plays**: K.W. Dammann, C. Smith, "Factors Affecting Low Income
      Women's Food Choices and the Perceived Impact of Dietary Intake and Socio-
      economic Status on Their Health and Weight," *Journal of Nutrition, Education
      and Behavior* 41, no. 4 (2009): 242–53; M. Bruening, R. MacLehose, K. Loth, M.
      Story, and D. Neumark-Sztainer, "Feeding a Family in a Recession: Food Inse-
      curity among Minnesota Parents," *American Journal of Public Health* 102, no. 3
      (2012): 520–26; B. J. Lohman, S. Stewart, C. Gundersen, and others, "Adolescent
      Overweight and Obesity: Links to Food Insecurity and Individual, Maternal, and
      Family Stressors," *Journal of Adolescent Health* 45 no. 3 (2009): 230–37.

222   **According to one study**: Sarah Treuhaft, Allison Karpyn, "The Grocery Gap: Who
      Had Access to Healthy Food and Why It Matters," *The Food Trust.org,* 2010, 8,
      http://thefoodtrust.org/uploads/media_items/grocerygap.original.pdf.

222   **For Catherine Wilson**: The information about Freedom Village in this chapter is drawn
      from interviews with Thelma Barnes, Ora D. Wilson, Catherine Wilson, and Rufus
      Donald. It also includes details on the settlement and its demise from historian
      Mark Newman's *Divine Agitators: The Delta Ministry and Civil Rights in Mississippi.*

222   **For a few years**: Catherine Wilson, author interview, November 5, 2015.

222   **The former displaced**: Ibid., "Freedom Village May Not Survive Latest Economic
      Downturn." Associated Press, October 15, 2008.

222   **However, no significant**: Ibid.

223   **"It seemed like"**: Catherine Wilson, author interview, November 5, 2015.

224   **"We're still trying"**: Ibid.

224   **Twice, life took**: The information in this and the following paragraphs are drawn
      from interviews by the author with Charlie Dillard on January 31, 2014, and
      November 5, 2015.

225   **But, like many**: http://www.city-data.com/city/Winstonville-Mississippi.html,
      accessed December 7, 2016.

225   **For Annie White**: Unless otherwise indicated, the information in this and the follow-
      ing paragraphs is drawn from author interviews with Edna White Brisby, Lorenzo
      White, Michael White, and David White.

226   **"Meeting Robert Kennedy"**: Lorenzo White, author interview, May 6, 2015.

226   **Two years after**: Nick Kotz, *Let Them Eat Promises,* 215.

228   **"We stuck together"**: David White, author interview, August 7, 2016.

228   **Like so many**: http://reports.mde.k12.ms.us/pdf/a/2016/Grad%20Dropout%20
      Rates%20-%202016%20Report%20(002).pdf.

228   **"It aches every"**: David White, author interview, August 7, 2016.
228   **"We still talk"**: Ibid.
229   **"Now we have"**: Edna White Brisby, author interview, March 29, 2014.
229   **Brenda Luckett didn't**: Unless otherwise noted, the information in this and the fol-
         lowing paragraphs is drawn from interviews with Brenda Luckett on August 29,
         2016.
229   **"To me, it"**: Ibid.
230   **"The students—we"**: Ibid.
230   **There were some problems**: Ibid.; Françoise N. Hamlin, *Crossroads at Clarksdale:*
         The Black Freedom Struggle in the Mississippi Delta after World War II, 190.
231   **"We felt like"**: Brenda Luckett, author interview, August 29, 2016.

Chapter 13. "We Don't Speak of Statistics, Numbers. We Speak of Human Beings"

233   **Even though the**: RFK1963. "RFK Part 2 Last Speech Ambassador Hotel." Filmed
         [June 4–5, 1968]. YouTube video, 09:56. Posted [September 5, 2006], https://www
         .youtube.com/watch?v=ae7H0aWFWNY.
233   **Author Larry Tye**: Larry Tye, *Bobby Kennedy: The Making of a Liberal Icon*, 350.
233   **"The odyssey he"**: Ibid, 352–53.
234   **"Robert Kennedy was"**: Peter Edelman, *Searching for America's Heart*, 7.
234   **"in national policy"**: Ibid.
234   **"To put it"**: Salinger, Guthman, Mankiewicz, and Seigenthaler, *An Honorable Profes-*
         sion: A Tribute to Robert F. Kennedy, 110.
234   **"Politics, he remembered"**: Coles, *Lives of Moral Leadership*, 20.
235   **"If political cooperation"**: Edward R. Schmitt, *President of the Other America*, 223.
235   **Kennedy's former aides**: Adam Walinsky, author interview, June 10, 2015. Peter Edel-
         man, author interview, July 2008.
236   **Kennedy would also**: U.S. Senate. Committee on Labor and Public Welfare. Subcom-
         mittee on Employment. *Examination of the War on Poverty: Hearings before the*
         United States Senate Committee on Labor and Public Welfare, Subcommittee on
         Employment, Manpower, and Poverty, Ninetieth Congress, first session. Hearing,
         April 10, 1967. Washington: U.S. Government Printing Office. 1967, 558; Missis-
         sippi Department of Archives and History, Mississippi Medicaid Commission,
         Second Annual Report, November 1, 1971, 5–6, http://www.mdah.ms.gov/arrec/
         digital_archives/governmentrecords/files/mdm/mdm-ar/1971.pdf.
236   **In 2014, Mississippi's**: Sarah Varney, "Mississippi Burned," *Politico.com*, November/
         December 2014, http://www.politico.com/magazine/story/2014/10/mississippi
         -burned-obamacare-112181.
236   **Businessman Clarke Reed**: Clarke Reed, author interview, April 9, 2014.
237   **"Every morning"**: Coles, *Farewell to the South*, 100–101.
237   **"When asked for a comment"**: Adam Ganuchaeau, "Mississippi Can't Get off
         the Bottom," *Mississippi Today*, September 15, 2016, http://mississippitoday
         .org/2016/09/15/mississippi-cant-get-off-the-bottom/.

237 **"It is interesting"**: Ibid.

238 **Puzzling some political**: Halberstam, *The Unfinished Odyssey of Robert Kennedy*, 129.

239 **However, even though**: Adam Walinsky, author interview, June 10, 2015.

239 **Kennedy saw a**: Ibid.

239 **"feed the children"**: Address by Senator Robert F. Kennedy, University of Notre Dame, April 4, 1968, Robert F. Kennedy Senate Papers, Speeches and Press Releases, Subject Files: Poverty, box 3.

239 **"How are we"**: Joel Connelly, "Kennedy Kicks Off Indiana Campaign with Stephan Center Speech." *The Observer*, April 5, 1968.

239 **"These men and women"**: The quotes here are taken from the transcript of the speech Kennedy gave at Robert F. Kennedy, Speech, Ball State University, Muncie, Indiana, April 4, 1968. Ball State University Archives, http://libx.bsu.edu/cdm/singleitem/collection/RFKen/id/22.

239 **"Here in America"**: Ibid.

240 **"If we cannot"**: Thurston Clarke, *The Last Campaign: Robert F. Kennedy and 82 days that Inspired America*, 85–86.

BIBLIOGRAPHY

Books

Annis, J. Lee. *Big Jim Eastland: The Godfather of Mississippi*. Jackson: University Press of Mississippi, 2016.

Austin, Sharon D. Wright. *The Transformation of Plantation Politics: Black Politics, Concentrated Poverty, and Social Capital in the Mississippi Delta*. Albany: State University of New York Press, 2012.

Barry, John M. *Rising Tide: The Great Mississippi Flood of 1927 and How It Changed America*, New York: Simon and Schuster, 1997.

Bass, Jack, and Walter De Vries. *The Transformation of Southern Politics*. Athens: University of Georgia Press, 1995.

Beckert, Sven. *Empire of Cotton: A Global History*. New York: Vintage, 2015.

Branch, Taylor. *At Canaan's Edge: America in the King Years, 1965–68*. New York: Simon and Schuster, 2007.

———. *Parting the Waters: America in the King Years, 1954–63*. New York: Touchstone: Simon and Schuster, 1988.

Blackwell, Unita, and JoAnne Prichard Morris. *Barefootin': Life Lessons from the Road to Freedom*. New York: Crown, 2006.

Bryant, Nicholas Andrew. *The Bystander: John F. Kennedy and the Struggle for Black Equality*. New York: Basic Books, 2006.

Clarke, Thurston. *The Last Campaign: Robert F. Kennedy and 82 Days that Inspired America*. New York: Henry Holt, 2008.

Cobb, James C. *The Most Southern Place on Earth: The Mississippi Delta and the Roots of Regional Identity*. New York: Oxford University Press, 1994.

Coles, Robert. *Farewell to the South*. Boston: Little Brown and Company, 1972.

Cohen, Michael A. *American Maelstrom: The 1968 Election and the Politics of Division*. New York: Oxford University Press, 2016.

———. *Lives of Moral Leadership: Men and Women Who Have Made a Difference*. New York: Random House, 2000.

Dallek, R., 2003. *An Unfinished Life: John F. Kennedy, 1917–1963*. Boston: Little, Brown.

Dattel, Gene. *Cotton and Race in the Making of America: The Human Costs of Economic Power*. Chicago: Government Institutes, 2009.

Dittmer, John. *Local People: The Struggle for Civil Rights in Mississippi*. Vol. 82. Urbana: University of Illinois Press, 1994.

Eagles, Charles W. *The Price of Defiance: James Meredith and the Integration of Ole Miss*. Chapel Hill: University of North Carolina Press, 2009.

Edelman, Marian Wright. *Lanterns: A Memoir of Mentors*. New York: Harper Perennial, 2000.

Edelman, Peter. *Searching for America's Heart: RFK and the Renewal of Hope*. Boston: Houghton Mifflin Harcourt, 2001.

———. *So Rich, So Poor: Why It's So Hard to End Poverty in America*. New York: The New Press, 2012.

Eisinger, Peter K. *Toward an End to Hunger in America*. Washington, D.C.: Brookings Institute Press, 1998.

Evers, Charles, and Andrew Szanton. *Have No Fear: The Charles Evers Story*. New York: J. Wiley and Sons, 1996.

Evers-Williams, Myrlie. *Watch Me Fly: What I Learned on the Way to Becoming the Woman I Was Meant to Be*. Boston: Little Brown, 1999.

Goduti, Phillip A. *Robert F. Kennedy and the Shaping of Civil Rights, 1960–1964*. Jefferson, N.C.: McFarland, 2012.

Greenberg, Polly. *The Devil Has Slippery Shoes: A Biased Biography of the Child Development Group in Mississippi*. New York: Macmillan. 1969.

Gregory, James N. "The Second Great Migration." in *African American Urban History Since World War II*, ed. Kenneth L. Kusmer and Joe Trotter. Chicago: University of Chicago Press, 2009.

Halberstam, David. *The Fifties*. New York: Ballantine Books, 1994.

———. *The Unfinished Odyssey of Robert Kennedy*. New York: Random House, 1969.

Hamlin, Françoise N. *Crossroads at Clarksdale: The Black Freedom Struggle in the Mississippi Delta after World War II*. Chapel Hill: University of North Carolina Press, 2012.

Henry, Aaron, and Constance Curry. *Aaron Henry: The Fire Ever Burning*. Jackson: University Press of Mississippi, 2000.

Hilton, Bruce. *The Delta Ministry*. New York: Macmillan, 1969.

Hilty, James. *Robert Kennedy: Brother Protector*. Philadelphia: Temple University Press, 2000.

Howell, Leon. *Freedom City: The Substance of Things Hoped For*. Richmond: John Knox, 1969.

Kennedy, Edward M. *Eulogy for Robert F. Kennedy*. St. Patrick's Cathedral, June 8, 1968.

———. *True Compass: A Memoir*. Twelve, 2009.

Kennedy, Robert F. *The Enemy Within*. Vol. 800. New York: Harper, 1960.

———. *To Seek a Newer World*. Vol. 3844. Garden City, N.Y.: Doubleday, 1967.

Kennedy, Robert F., Edwin O. Guthman, and Jeffrey Shulman. *Robert Kennedy, in His Own Words: The Unpublished Recollections of the Kennedy Years*. Toronto; New York: Bantam, 1988.

King, Martin Luther. 1994. Letter from the Birmingham jail. San Francisco: Harper San Francisco.

Kotz, Nick. *Let Them Eat Promises: The Politics of Hunger in America*. Englewood Cliffs, N.J.: Prentice Hall, 1969.

Lemann, Nicholas. *The Promised Land: The Great Black Migration and How It Changed America*. New York: Vintage, 2011.

Marsh, Charles. *The Beloved Community: How Faith Shapes Social Justice from the Civil Rights Movement to Today*. New York: Basic Books 2008.

Martin, Josephine *Managing Child Nutrition Programs: Leadership for Excellence*. Burlington, Mass.: Jones and Bartlett Learning, 1999.

Meredith, James, and William Doyle. *A Mission from God: A Memoir and Challenge for America*. New York: Simon and Schuster, 2012.

Morrison, Minion K. C. *Aaron Henry of Mississippi: Inside Agitator*. Fayetteville: University of Arkansas Press, 2015.

Nasaw, David. *The Patriarch: The Remarkable Life and Turbulent Times of Joseph P. Kennedy*. New York: Penguin, 2012.

Newfield, Jack. *Robert Kennedy: A Memoir*. New York: Dutton, 1969.

Newman, Mark. *Divine Agitators: The Delta Ministry and Civil Rights in Mississippi*. Athens: University of Georgia Press, 2004.

O'Brien, Michael. *John F. Kennedy: A Biography*. New York: Macmillan, 2006.

Raines, Howell. *My Soul Is Rested*. New York: Penguin, 1983.

Rogers, Warren. *When I Think of Bobby: A Personal Memoir of the Kennedy Years*. New York: HarperCollins, 1993.

Salinger, Pierre, Edwin Guthman, Frank Mankiewicz, and John Seigenthaler. *An Honorable Profession: A Tribute to Robert F. Kennedy*. Garden City, N.Y.: Doubleday, 1968.

Sanders, Crystal R. *A Chance for Change: Head Start and Mississippi's Black Freedom Struggle*. Chapel Hill: University of North Carolina, 2016.

Schlesinger Jr., Arthur Meier, *Robert Kennedy: His Times*. New York: Houghton Mifflin 1978.

Schmitt, Edward R. *President of the Other America: Robert Kennedy and the Politics of Poverty*. Cambridge; London: University of Massachusetts Press, 2010.

Schorr, Daniel. *Staying Tuned*. New York: New York: Simon and Schuster, 2001.

Sealander, Judith. *The Failed Century of the Child: Governing America's Young in the Twentieth Century*. Cambridge: Cambridge University Press, 2003.

Shesol, Jeff. *Mutual Contempt: Lyndon Johnson, Robert Kennedy, and the Feud That Defined a Decade*. New York: W. W. Norton, 1998.

Sokol, Jason. *There Goes My Everything: White Southerners in the Age of Civil Rights, 1945–1975*. New York: Vintage, 2008.

Stein, Jean, and George Plimpton. *American Journey: The Times of Robert Kennedy*. New York: Houghton Mifflin Harcourt, 1970.

Townsend, Kathleen Kennedy. *Failing America's Faithful: How Today's Churches Are Mixing God with Politics and Losing Their Way*. Boston: Hachette, 2007.

Wilkie, Curtis. *The Fall of the House of Zeus: The Rise and Ruin of America's Most Powerful Trial Lawyer*. New York: Crown, 2010.

———. *Dixie: A Personal Odyssey through Events That Shaped the Modern South*. Simon and Schuster, 2002.

Willis, John C. *Forgotten Time: The Yazoo-Mississippi Delta after the Civil War*. Charlottesville; London: University Press of Virginia, 2000.
Woodruff, Nan. *American Congo: The African American Freedom Struggle in the Delta,* Cambridge; London: Harvard University Press, 2003.
Wyatt-Brown, Bertram. *Southern Honor: Ethics and Behavior in the Old South*. New York: Oxford University Press, 1982.

Newspapers

The Bolivar Commercial (Cleveland, Mississippi)
The Clarion Ledger (Jackson, Mississippi)
Clarksdale Press-Register (Clarksdale, Mississippi)
The Daily Mississippian (University, Mississippi)
The Delta Democrat-Times (Greenville, Mississippi)
The Des Moines Register (Des Moines, Iowa)
The Jackson Daily News (Jackson, Mississippi)
The Los Angeles Times (Los Angeles, California)
New Orleans Times-Picayune (New Orleans, Louisiana)
The New York Times (New York, New York)
The Northeast Mississippi Daily Journal (Tupelo, Mississippi)
The Purple and White (Millsaps College, Jackson, Mississippi)
The Washington Post (Washington, DC)

Films and Audiotapes

American Experience: JFK. 2013. WGBH Educational Foundation. Susan Bellows.
Ethel. 2012. DVD. New York: HBO Rory Kennedy.
Eyes on the Prize: America in the Civil Rights Years
Robert Kennedy. 1968.

Manuscript Collections

John F. Kennedy Library, Boston

Peter Edelman Papers
Robert Kennedy Papers, Senate; Presidential Campaign
Adam Walinsky Papers

Mississippi State University

Patricia Derian papers, Special Collections Department, Mississippi State University
Libraries.

The University of Mississippi

James O. Eastland Collection, Archives and Special Collections, J. D. Williams Library
George M. Street Collection (MUM00349). Archives & Special Collections, J. D. Williams
Library
Jamie L. Whitten Collection, Archives and Special Collections, J. D. Williams Library

Government Documents

Freedom of Communications: Final Report of the Committee on Commerce, United States Senate. Part III: The Joint Appearances of Senator John F. Kennedy and Vice President Richard M. Nixon and Other 1960 Campaign Presentations. 87th Congress, 1st Session, Senate Report No. 994, Part 3. Washington: U.S. Government Printing Office, 1961.
U.S. Department of Agriculture, National Agricultural Statistics Service. "Mississippi Prospective Plantings Report," Released March 31, 2016.https://www.nass.usda.gov/Statis
tics_by_State/Mississippi/Publications/Crop_Releases/Prospective_Plantings/2016/
msplant16.pdf.
U.S. Senate. Committee on Agriculture and Forestry. Subcommittee on Agricultural
Research and General Legislation. Food Stamp Appropriations Authorization, Ninetieth
Congress, first session. Hearing, April 25, 1967. Washington: U.S. Government Printing
Office. 1967.
U.S. Senate. Committee on Labor and Public Welfare. Subcommittee on Employment.
Examination of the War on Poverty: hearings before the United States Senate Committee
on Labor and Public Welfare, Subcommittee on Employment, Manpower, and Poverty,
Ninetieth Congress, first session. Hearings, March 15, April 10, and July 11 and 12, 1967.
Washington: U.S. Government Printing Office. 1967.

Transcripts

John F. Kennedy Library, Boston

Oral histories
Oscar Carr, Peter Edelman, Adam Walinsky, David Hackett, John Seigenthaler

Eyes on the Prize Documentary Transcripts

Oral histories
Marian Wright Edelman, Amzie Moore, Hodding Carter III

America's War on Poverty Documentary Transcripts

Oral histories
Hodding Carter III

Mississippi Oral History Program, University of Southern Mississippi

Oral histories
Andrew Carr, Amzie Moore

Open Doors Collection, Archives and Special Collections,
J. D. Williams Library, the University of Mississippi

Oral histories
Joshua Morse

Personal Interviews

Thelma Barnes
Betty Jo Brent Boyd
Dr. Joseph Brenner
Edna White Brisby
Amanda Burden
Andrew Carr
Hodding Carter III
Dr. Robert Coles
Constance Curry
Charlie Dillard
Shirley Dillard
Rufus Donald
William Dunlap
Pat Dunne
Hiram Eastland
Marian Wright Edelman
Peter Edelman
Charles Evers
Vivian Davis Giles

Winifred Green
Ron Greer
Constance Slaughter Harvey
Becky Hendrick
Herman Johnson
Ethel S. Kennedy
Robert Kennedy Jr.
Nick Kotz
George Lapides
Brenda Luckett
Chip Mabry
Melody Miller
Wilson F. "Bill" Minor
Charlotte Slaughter Moman
Sammie Rash
Clarke Reed
Bill Rose
Lisbeth Schorr
John Seigenthaler
Nevin Sledge
Frances Smith
Reuben Smith
Kathleen Kennedy Townsend
Curtis Wilkie
Catherine Wilson
Ora D. Wilson
Betty White
David White
Lorenzo White
Michael White
Willie White
William Winter
Adam Walinsky

Journal Articles

Brauer, Carl M. "Kennedy, Johnson, and the War on Poverty." *The Journal of American History* 69, no. 1 (June 1982): 98–119.

DeShazo, Richard, Wilson F. Bill Minor, Robert Smith, and Leigh Baldwin Skipworth. "An Unwilling Partnership with the Great Society Part I: Head Start and the Beginning of Change in the White Medical Community." *The American Journal of the Medical Sciences* 352, no. 1 (2016): 109–19.

White, Paul W. "The History and Development of the Mississippi Delta Economy." *Business Perspectives*, University of Memphis 20, no. 1 (summer/fall, June 22, 2009).

Presidential Records

Johnson, Lyndon. Remarks at the Welhausen Elementary School, Cotulla, Texas. November 7, 1966.
Johnson, Lyndon. State of the Union. Washington, D.C., January 8, 1964.
Johnson, Lyndon. Remarks at the Welhausen Elementary School, Cotulla, Texas. November 7, 1966.
Kennedy, John F. Inaugural Address. Washington, D.C., January 20, 1967.

Magazine Articles

McEachran, Angus, "Hardship and Heartbreak in Freedom City," *The National Observer*, December 26, 1966.
Mabry, Chip, *Delta Magazine*, Cleveland, Mississippi. April 2003.

Online Resources

Civil Rights in Mississippi Digital Archive, University of Southern Mississippi. http://digilib.usm.edu/crmda.php.
Eyes on the Prize Interview transcripts. Washington University Special Collections. http://digital.wustl.edu/eyesontheprize/.
Ganuchaeau, Adam. "Mississippi Can't Get off the Bottom." *Mississippi Today*, September 15, 2016. http://mississippitoday.org/2016/09/15/mississippi-cant-get-off-the-bottom/.
Harvard University Athletics, "Chester M. Pierce Made History on the Field and in the Classroom." http://gocrimson.com/sports/fball/2010–11/releases/101007_Chester_Pierce_NCAA.
Kennedy, Kerry. "Interview with Kerry Kennedy." *The Boston Globe,* September 7, 2008. http://archive.boston.com/news/local/massachusetts/articles/2008/09/07/interview_with_kerry_kennedy/?page=full.
Kennedy, Robert. Primary Campaign Address. Ball State University, Muncie, Indiana, April 4, 1968. http://libx.bsu.edu/cdm/singleitem/collection/RFKen/id/22.
King, Martin Luther, Jr. "I Have a Dream." Speech, Washington, D.C., August 28, 1963. American Rhetoric. http://www.americanrhetoric.com/speeches/mlkihaveadream.htm.
The Lyndon B. Johnson Presidential Library, "LBJ Biography." http://www.lbjlib.utexas.edu/johnson/archives.hom/biographys.hom/lbj_bio.asp.
Marian Wright Edelman. *Interview for Makers: The Largest Video Collection of Women's Stories.* http://www.makers.com/marian-wright-edelman. Accessed March 10, 2016.

Mississippi State Sovereignty Commission Records, Mississippi Department of Archives and History. http://www.mdah.ms.gov/arrec/digital_archives/sovcom/.

RFK1963. "RFK Part 2 Last Speech Ambassador Hotel." Filmed [June 4–5, 1968]. YouTube video, 09:56. Posted [September 5, 2006]. https://www.youtube.com/watch?v=ae7 HoaWFWNY.

Thought Co. "Marian Wright Edelman, Founder, Children's Defense Fund." http://womensh istory.about.com/od/marianwrightedelman/p/m_w_edelman.htm.

U. S. Census Bureau, Data Vizualization Gallery, "The Great Migration shown through changes in African-Americans share of population in major US cities, 1910–1940 and 1940–1970." https://en.wikipedia.org/wiki/Great_Migration_(African_American)#/ media/File:GreatMigration1910to1970-UrbanPopulation.png. Accessed March 14, 2017.

Varney, Sarah, "Mississippi Burned: How the Poorest, Sickest State Got Left Behind by Obamacare." Politico.com, http://www.politico.com/magazine/story/2014/10/ mississippi-burned-obamacare-112181.

ABOUT THE PHOTOGRAPHERS

Jim Lucas began taking photos for the local evening paper, *The Jackson Daily News,* while in high school. As a young professional photojournalist, he was freelancing for UPI, *Time* and *Life* magazines in 1967 when he covered Robert Kennedy at the Senate Hearings on Poverty and Kennedy's historic trip to the Mississippi Delta. From 1964 to 1968, as a college student, Lucas documented local marches, pickets, planning meetings, and bombings in Mississippi. Drafted in 1968, he began a career in film while in the army in Southeast Asia. His film career included news, sports, documentary, and Hollywood feature films. Lucas died in an automobile accident in 1980. Jane Hearn, who was married to Lucas, archives and curates the collection of his life work.

After serving as a combat photographer during World War II, **Dan Guravich**, a native of Canada, earned a PhD in agronomy and moved to Greenville, Mississippi, in 1949 to work as an agricultural geneticist. Three years later, he left that job to become a freelance photographer. During his forty-plus-year photojournalism career, he was best known for his favorite subjects—polar bears—a love he discovered as the official photographer aboard the *SS Manhattan* for Humble's maiden Northwest Passage voyage in 1969. His work appeared in *Life, National Geographic, Science Digest, Smithsonian Magazine,* and other popular journals. He produced more than twenty books, including five on polar bears, before his death in 1997.

Troy Catchings was a beginning photographer in 1967 and worked for more than twenty-five years for Coahoma Opportunities in Clarksdale, Mississippi, rising to serve as executive director before he retired in 1999. Since then, he has served as part-time photo editor for the *Clarksdale Press-Register.*

Maude Schuyler Clay was born in Greenwood, Mississippi. After attending the University of Mississippi and the Memphis Academy of Arts, she assisted the photographer William Eggleston. The University Press of Mississippi published her monograph *Delta Land* in 1999. She was the photography editor of the literary magazine *The Oxford American* from 1998 through 2002. Her work is in the collections of the Museum of Modern Art; the Museum of Fine Arts, Houston; the High Museum of Art; and the National Museum for Women in the Arts; and others. Her latest book is *Mississippi History*.

Alysia Burton Steele is assistant professor in the Meek School of Journalism and New Media at the University of Mississippi, where she teaches photojournalism, podcasting, multimedia production, beginning writing, and the senior capstone class. She is author of the book *Delta Jewels: In Search of My Grandmother's Wisdom*.

Mississippi native **Will Jacks** is a photographer, curator, storyteller, and educator of culture and relationships in the Mississippi Delta and the lower Mississippi River region.

INDEX